THE SPANISH ARMADA

Also available in this series

CONDITIONS OF SALE

British Battles Series

THE
SPANISH ARMADA

MICHAEL LEWIS

UNABRIDGED

PAN BOOKS LTD : LONDON

First published 1960 by B. T. Batsford Ltd.
This edition published 1966 by Pan Books Ltd.,
33 Tothill Street, London, S.W.1

ISBN 0 330 20163 8

2nd Printing 1970
3rd Printing 1972

Printed in Great Britain by Richard Clay (The Chaucer Press), Ltd.,
Bungay, Suffolk

PREFACE

To NINETEENTH-CENTURY Englishmen, the Armada Story was just another David-and-Goliath affair: an attractive, but quite uncritical view, and around 1900 realist scholars tore it to shreds. Goliath's showy armour, it seems, was tinsel, his massy sword pasteboard, while David, in his sling, had a veritable Excalibur. Moreover, David was now nearly as tall as Goliath, and much fitter. This view, obviously the truer of the two, was accepted in its turn.

Some twenty years ago, almost by accident, I stumbled on certain new material which made me suspect the rightness of this 1900 view in the matter of weapons. I determined, therefore, to re-examine the older evidence in the light of my new discoveries. The resulting investigation, published (1942–3) in eight numbers of the *Mariner's Mirror*, the quarterly of the Society for Nautical Research, amply confirmed my suspicions. Unquestionably Goliath's armour was less vulnerable, his sword heavier and much sharper, than had been supposed; while David's sling had revealed unexpected weaknesses in action. Further, my findings not only appreciably modified the accepted view: they also seemed to explain certain aspects of the fight which had always puzzled me; and subsequent writers (I think without exception) have done me the honour, consciously or unconsciously, of accepting my interpretations.

Although this work is naturally based upon my 'new look', I have not repeated my arguments in full for three good reasons. First, they would, by themselves, fill a book as long as this one. Second, they are being reprinted anyway, in full and in book form, under the title of *Armada Guns* (Allen & Unwin). Third, and most important, I am attempting in this work something much more than a mere survey of technicalities like ships, guns and tactics. These figure here, but only as incidental to the understanding of a wider and more human theme, a conspectus of the whole composite campaign and battle: the things, yes; but above all the people –

the directors, the officers and the men on both sides who won, and lost, the Armada Fight.

My grateful thanks are due to two friends in particular: George Naish of the National Maritime Museum, who has lent me much valuable contemporary material from his own collection; and, as usual, Richard Ollard who, once again, has put his time and great critical ability very freely at my disposal.

ACKNOWLEDGEMENT

THE AUTHOR and publishers wish to thank the following for permission to reproduce the illustrations included in this book:

The President of the Excma Deputacion Provincial de Vizcaya, Bilbao; Biblioteca Nacional, Madrid; the Bodleian Library, Oxford; the City Museum and Art Gallery, Plymouth; the Duchess of Medina Sidonia; Musée de Peinture Ancienne, Brussels; Museo Naval, Madrid; Museo del Prado; the Director and Trustees of the National Maritime Museum; the Science Museum.

CONTENTS

ILLUSTRATIONS IN PHOTOGRAVURE

LINE DRAWINGS

Part One:

DRAMATIS PERSONAE

1

THE PRINCIPALS

PHILIP AND ELIZABETH

WHO WAS THIS King Philip II who sent his Armada against us in 1588, and what manner of man was he?

In that year every Englishman, provided he were forty years old or more, would remember him well: a quiet, gauche young man, rather colourless but intensely unpopular, whom they had known, and hated, thirty years ago. They were unlikely to have forgotten him because, then, he was the titular King of England, though his power as such was hedged about by many restrictions, imposed upon him by a hostile and suspicious parliament when he married our first Queen Regnant. But he was also the autocratic ruler of Spain, of much of Italy, of the Low Countries and – save for Brazil – of all the Americas known and unknown; and therefore, in the view of the majority of mankind, the most potent sovereign on earth. By 1588 he had grown, or at least looked, stronger yet, having meanwhile become King of Portugal too, and controller not only of all the Americas but also of all those parts of the East in which Europeans had established their interests. By now, too, he was accepted as the temporal champion of one side in the great religious controversy which was rending Western Europe, and, as such, the avowed enemy of that Queen to whom the other side looked – his sister-in-law, Elizabeth of England.

Friend or foe, then, he was a formidable man: but, fortunately for England, not a great one. His most obvious weakness, perhaps, was that he could not decentralize. With more to engage his attention than a dozen men could manage properly, he gradually allowed himself to become enmeshed in a web of his own devising. Sitting lonely in his palace of the Escorial, he worked, day in day out, with spider-like assiduity reading endless reports and, with his own hand, scribbling annotations and directives on every subject, however momentous, however trivial: striving, in fact, to administer, virtually single-handed, an empire upon which the sun never set. That web became ever more complex and opaque, until it threatened to obscure the whole view from the Escorial windows. No other spider can ever have woven more intricate patterns. His system of espionage, for example, was so involved that no one yet has ever completely unravelled it – possibly, before the end, not even himself.

Let one instance suffice. In 1588 Don Antonio, the recently displaced King of Portugal, had in his pay two 'faithful' agents – double traitors both. One, Escobar, was constantly reporting to Philip in cypher, or milk or lemon-juice, on everyone at Antonio's *fainéant* court, from Antonio himself down to the meanest hanger-on. Among others, he dealt minutely with the suspicious behaviour of one Andrada who (though neither ever discovered it) was dealing equally faithfully with Escobar! The result, certainly, was that Philip received plenty of information, but most of it so disreputably and deviously acquired as to be at once untrustworthy and contradictory. In the event, in fact, Philip was seldom well-informed about the plans and movements of his enemies.

Yet, within his own limits and in his own eyes, he was a good man: certainly in his own rather narrow way a religious one, who prided himself upon the purity of his faith, earnestly striving to live up to his hereditary title of Most Catholic Majesty: one who held it his first duty to stamp out, utterly and for ever, those rank heresies from Germany and Geneva, from the Low Countries and England, which men called Protestantism. He had been serving that great cause in a smaller way when, as Mary I's husband, he had approved the burning of English heretics; and he was doing it in a much bigger way when, as an elderly man, he dispatched his Armada in 1588. Indeed he believed, and more than half the civilized world agreed with him, that this urge to convert the heretic was his major strength. It made Almighty God his ally, especially after he had succeeded in enlisting on his side a somewhat sceptical Pope. Because of this his great expedition, when it came, had all the trappings of a full-scale crusade, bearing Holy Cross in red (for war) upon the white (for purity) of its standards; not only countenanced, but solemnly blessed by his Italian Holiness, and pledged to destroy the abominable woman who had so wickedly usurped the English throne. The religious aspect, therefore, was carefully stressed throughout. Every soldier, every seaman was, by Philip's orders, shriven before he embarked and, implicitly, assured of felicity hereafter should he unfortunately encounter a heretical roundshot. Further, everyone was exhorted to refrain from blasphemy, swearing and excess of drink, lest he should sully the sanctity of the enterprise. No women were allowed, but several hundred priests, friars and officers of the Inquisition embarked, partly to administer spiritual comfort on the voyage, partly to convert a conquered England. Even the days' watchwords were chosen to remind the men of their holy purpose. Sunday's was *Jesus*; Monday's, *Holy Ghost*; Tuesday's, *Most Holy Trinity*; Wednesday's, *Santiago*; Thursday's, *The Angels*; Friday's, *All Saints*; Saturday's, *Our Lady*.

In so emphasizing the religious side, however, Philip was not merely gratifying his own and his people's piety. He hoped for dividends of another kind. For all his spies, he did not know (no one knew, not even the English) how many of the Queen's own subjects would respond to such an appeal. All that either side knew was that there were many of the Old Faith in England. Where they differed was in their estimate of what these native Catholics would do when faced with a straight choice between their Faith and their Queen. Philip, naturally sanguine, and primed by agents who tended, after their kind, to tell their paymaster what he wanted to hear, really seems to have thought that an enormous number would declare for him. Elizabeth, on the other hand, hoped that very few would. But it was only a hope; and she took the precaution, before the Armada arrived, of rounding up all the more prominent Catholics, and interning them in Wisbeach Castle; though characteristically enough, she did not tell them why she did so. She merely announced that she was locking them up for their own good, lest, if the Spaniards landed, their infuriated fellow countrymen might be tempted to do them a hurt.

The Anglo-Spanish War, then, was a war of religion. But it

was political and dynastic too; it was national; and it was economic. Leaving the economic aspect for the moment, let us examine the other three. When the time came, and after a certain vacillation, Philip claimed the throne of England for himself, by right of birth; or at least asserted his right to dispose of it to a nominee of his own. His political motive for this was that he wanted to prevent England from joining forces with the one European rival whom he had cause to fear – his Most Christian Majesty of France. Herein (from our point of view) lay the national element of the war. Had he succeeded, England would certainly have become a satellite in the Iberian orbit, an appanage of Spain, with little (if any) prospect of a national English future.

His claim to our throne was, theoretically, far from fantastic. It was based upon two things. One was his own dynastic claim, as a direct descendant of one of those famous seven sons of Edward III, who figure among the ancestors of every subsequent English sovereign. This was the positive half of his claim, and perhaps it would not cut much ice by itself. But there was another half, more negative but potentially much more formidable: that the actual, the *de facto*, occupant of the throne had no right at all to sit upon it, being, in the eyes of God, a bastard. This too would perhaps not have greatly signified, since those who had set her there, presumably, thought otherwise. But what made Philip's case so strong was the fact that most of the western world agreed emphatically with him. And so (if he read things aright) did God, whose mouthpiece, the Pope, had declared that, at the moment of Elizabeth's birth, her mother (Ann Boleyn) was Henry VIII's mistress, not his wife. Moreover, that old reprobate had admitted as much on his deathbed by declaring Elizabeth illegitimate. And so she had remained, in English law too, until the very moment of her succession. Then, naturally, the law had been altered and the taint removed. But that was the law of man: no one could change the Law of God. So, once more, all hinged upon a guess. When the time came, how many Englishmen would take this Catholic view or, taking it, allow it to sway their allegiance?

But Philip had yet another claim. If Elizabeth had no right there, who had? There were several possible candidates, but the best-fancied (especially by the Catholics) was Mary, Queen of Scots. No explanation of why the Armada was launched against England can afford to ignore this romantic lady, if only because, by 1588, she had willed her claim whole to Philip. How real that claim was, how much more solid than such mere dynastic claims as Philip's own, is shown by the fact that every British sovereign after Elizabeth is descended from Mary Queen of Scots.

Once, long ago, Philip had thought of marrying her himself. That was when he was still King Consort of England. As poor Mary Tudor neared her end, still desperately hoping to give Philip a Catholic heir who would solve all her religious troubles and his political ones, he, as he too gave up hope, turned his eyes towards the north. Here, across England's border, the other and much younger Mary had just succeeded to the throne of an altogether independent Scotland. After all, if one Mary failed him, why not take the other? True, a son by her would not so surely secure England for Spain; but he would secure Scotland, and inherit his mother's strong reversionary claim to England too. Here, however, Philip's hopes were quickly frustrated. Before English Mary freed him by her death, Scottish Mary, a fifteen-year-old girl residing at the French court, was hurriedly married off to the Dauphin of France; and Scotland looked to have passed into the orbit of his principal enemy. For the time being he relinquished all thought of her.

Even this unexpected development, however, had one important result, most favourable as it turned out for England, but, ultimately, fatal to Philip. Still bent, after the custom of his family, on the famous Habsburg policy of 'conquest by marriage', he turned his thoughts to his sister-in-law Elizabeth. This enigmatical red-haired girl, though (he thought) atrociously brought up by heretics, and tainted in blood as the bastard of heretical parents, was still young enough, if gently handled and protected, to be led back to Mother Church. If this could be done, why not marry her himself and, through her, achieve his end of acquiring England? So, in his wife's last days, he protected Elizabeth from the persecution of her sister, who saw in her succession the ruin of all she had lived for: and he made no attempt to exclude Elizabeth from the throne.

In the event, he never made a bigger mistake in his life. The lonely young woman, hitherto in constant danger of her life (she had once already passed through the Traitor's Gate at the Tower and remained there for over a year), now became Queen Elizabeth of England. And what a Queen! Though appearances at the start may have seemed all against her, she never looked back, nor seriously faltered. A more complex character, perhaps, never mystified historians, and this is no place for studying the fascinating contradictions of that many-sided personality. But the master-key to her astonishing success is not hard to find. She began at once to seek the love of her people: all of them; from the highest to the lowest. That devotion she gained at once, and she never lost it. Rather, it grew and grew until, long before the end, she had become much more than simply their 'gracious Princess'. She was the core, the symbol, the embodiment of a new England. Did she deserve it? That may be arguable, but it is immaterial: it does not alter the fact. The England that she ruled for forty-five years became, and still remains in our hearts and understandings, Elizabethan England: and that great formative period in our national life is still the Age of Elizabeth.

It was this lady, newly come to her inheritance, and not yet the imperious Virgin Queen that she became, whom Philip thought of wedding. Why not? Spain and England had been allies for many years, and it suited neither party just then to sever the connection. But she had no intention of being so entangled. She fenced with him without quarrelling, as only Elizabeth could, and he soon gave up the idea, though for a time he cherished schemes of marrying her off to some creature of his own. But she would not have that either – Philip and all his tribe were too unpopular with her loving subjects – and, soon, events elsewhere put such thoughts out of his head. Mary Stuart, though she remained a Catholic, and even became

Queen Consort of France, soon lost her feeble little husband, and returned to a Scotland which, in her absence, had become a fortress of the Reformation under the hand of the relentless John Knox. Here she found herself a Queen in little more than name. But now she became interesting to Philip again because, with her French connections weakened, she still had her strong claim upon England. Thereupon Philip transferred his hopes and schemings from Elizabeth to the Scottish Queen.

Nothing came of it, however, but tragedy. Mary played her many good cards badly. The story of how she lost her northern throne needs no retelling, nor how, in despair, she crossed the Solway, a fugitive, and sought the protection of her 'dear cousin' Elizabeth. That lady accepted her, insomuch as she did not return her to her rebellious subjects. But the arrangement was embarrassing to both guest and hostess, because the guest proved a very troublesome one, entering into endless intrigues with both foreigners and Catholic malcontents at home, to dethrone, and even to assassinate, the hostess. This went on for nearly nineteen years until at last, forced to it by the outcry of her English subjects, Elizabeth consented to her execution. Through all this period Philip had kept intermittent touch with the captive, and his reward for the dubious benefits which he thus conferred upon her was that, before her execution, she made over to him her rights to the throne of England.

We know now that this did not help him, because, by this time, almost all Englishmen were under Elizabeth's spell. Yet in the history of Anglo-Spanish relations, the transference of those claims to Philip, and still more the long-delayed execution of the Queen of Scots, were real turning-points. Until that moment Philip, not even yet committed to invade England, still toyed with the idea of securing it by Habsburg methods and not by open war. Elizabeth was still unmarried, and well over child-bearing age. A good Catholic successor in London might still do his business for him, and that successor might still be Mary. But not after that last grim scene in Fotheringay Castle in February 1587: not even though Mary had a son. For that son, though King of Scotland, had been brought up a Protestant, and had never known his mother's influence. There was no future for Philip in James VI of Scotland, even if he became (as he did) James I of England. So, all hopes of peaceful alternatives removed, the Spanish King, not without serious misgivings, decided upon the conquest of England by force.

He had plenty of provocation: and this brings us to the last cause underlying the breakdown of Anglo-Spanish friendship. Basically, it has but little to do with the problems of conflicting religions, policies and dynasties hitherto discussed. It was economic rivalry, primarily, which produced an ever-widening antagonism between the two peoples.

As soon as the explorers and conquistadors of Spain began to discover the outlines, and exploit the resources, of the New World, their rulers, behaving according to the lights of their age, claimed exclusive possession of the territories discovered and the materials found: and not only these, but also the exclusive right to trade there, even to go there. And when Portugal explored and exploited the East in a similar way, she staked exactly the same claims. As early as 1494 the lucky pioneers had decided that it would be suicidal to quarrel with one another. They had therefore agreed on the broad principle of making the West the preserve of Spain and the East that of Portugal; and they persuaded an obliging Pope to lend to the arrangement the sanction of his unique authority. Hence Pope Alexander's famous Line of Demarcation, followed by the Treaty of Tordesillas, which divided the Spanish West from the Portuguese East, leaving nothing for anyone else.

This was all very well so long as Spain and Portugal were the only interested parties. But, after a time, other competitors appeared – seamen from the Low Countries and the maritime provinces of France, and, a little later, the English. The intervention of Frenchmen did not lead to any great new war because the Spanish and French governments were at daggers drawn anyway, and the new rivalries became only one more cause of hostility. As for the Low Countries, which Philip had inherited from his father Charles V, he regarded their people as his own subjects whom, if they gave trouble, he must chastise. So, here too, the Flemish and Dutch seamen did not appear to Philip as sovereign rivals, but only as ordinary rebels. But when the English appeared, they were, ostensibly, friends; and it was as friendly rivals that, at first, they strove to establish themselves. This, broadly speaking, was the position at the moment of Elizabeth's accession; for though the English merchants and sea adventurers had already begun exploring, trading and establishing trade-routes, they had been content to operate, mostly, in areas not much used by the original monopolists, and so to avoid head-on collisions with them.

This, however, could not last. Already there was developing in England a new spirit of enterprise, and a rising class of merchants determined to give it free rein. Yet, at first, so formidable looked the might of Spain, so prudent was Elizabeth in not challenging it until she was sure of her own strength, that the English traders, for all their impatience, refrained from charging bald-headed into the coveted preserves of Spain. Instead, they sought to edge in little by little, protesting their long-standing friendship with the Spanish people. This interlude, lasting roughly from 1558 to 1569, may be called the period of 'uneasy friendship': and the protagonist of it was the eldest of our Armada heroes.

2

THE ENGLISH LEADERS

JOHN HAWKINS

JOHN HAWKINS came of enterprising merchant stock in Plymouth: and, because enterprising, successful. He was no rugged, uneducated seaman, but of the second generation of prosperity, his father – 'Old William' – having created a flourishing business. His brother – 'Young William' – was perhaps more like the father, his reputation and his work remaining local: he was in fact Mayor of Plymouth in Armada year. But John was a bigger man altogether whose reputation was nation-wide, and who had, probably, as much to do with the Armada's defeat as any other Englishman. He first came to the fore during the 'uneasy friendship' period. He it was who, in quite a big way, began to test Philip's reaction to friendly trade with Spanish America, citing old Flemish agreements between Philip's father and Elizabeth's, and making no attempt at concealment. There followed the three famous slave-voyages of the 1560s. (This we should not take as any reflection upon Hawkins's character. In his day 'black ivory' was as legitimate a commodity as any other; two whole centuries later there were still respectable merchants of Bristol and Liverpool who held that a little slavery did the poor niggers good.) Yet, after two fairly successful ventures, Hawkins failed in the third, and failed disastrously, because Philip took exception to his activities. Perhaps, indeed, Hawkins should have chosen some other commodity for his experiment. As it happened, the import of slaves into the Spanish colonies was not only a Spanish monopoly; it was the King's own monopoly, and here was a foreign interloper deliberately underselling him! Making a good profit too – usually easy for monopoly breakers, because monopoly prices are almost always above free-market levels. On hearing of the third enterprise, therefore, Philip simply sent a fleet to demolish it. He only half succeeded, even though his admiral resorted to an act of treachery: but he did quite enough to prove to Hawkins, or any other Englishman contemplating a similar move, that there was no future at all for friendly trade in the Spanish zone.

After this, Hawkins, who was nothing if not respectable, fell out of the active running. But his greatest work was only now to begin. In a happy moment, Elizabeth appointed him Treasurer of the Navy, the leading partner in that odd quartet called the Principal Officers of the Navy, or, shortly, the Navy Board: that body of (relatively) whole-time experts who were charged with the upkeep of the Queen's ships. It was a thankless task under Elizabeth, for money was always in short supply: and Hawkins soon made it more thankless still. He discovered dishonesty and pilfering at every level, and he determined to tackle it. In those days, with no proper system of auditing, this was very difficult. But he found a way. He suggested shouldering the entire responsibility of upkeep, making 'bargains' (or contracts) with the Government to do the whole job for a fixed annual sum. This was brave, for he was courting venomous attacks from frustrated peculators, and even from comparatively honest colleagues brought up in the lax old ways. Sure enough, he sustained accusations in plenty, so fierce and so circumstantial that some of the mud stuck, to be finally removed only in recent times. Yet cleared he is, and abundantly vindicated as a very honest man in a day when honesty of this kind was all too rare. But he had another justification, and for this he has not had to wait 300 years. The ships which he tended in his bargains were the key-ships which, in 1588, fought the Armada. And everyone, from the Commander-in-Chief downwards, including even some of his most persistent critics, had to admit that their state of readiness was in every respect excellent. Two testimonials, quite unsolicited, survive from the pen of the principal user, the Lord Admiral himself:

For Mr Hawkyns' bargain, he is presently to repair to the Court where he shall best be able to answer in his own de-

> fence. But this much I will say to your Lordship [Burghley]. I have been aboard of every ship that goeth out with me, and in every place where any may creep, and I do thank God that they be in the estate they be in: and there is never a one of them that knows what a leak means.

and again:

> I protest before God and as my soul shall answer for it that I think there were never in any place in the world worthier ships than these are.

Moreover, during the years covered by the bargains he saved the Queen something like £4,000 per annum – a very considerable sum in those days. His latest and best additions to the Navy Royal, the *Vanguard* and the *Rainbow*, cost little if any more than that.

England owes him one more debt, perhaps the greatest of all. During his Treasurership a most important step was being taken in ship-construction, and it is reasonably certain that it was Hawkins who took it. The 'great ships' which he found when he took over were still, largely, sea fortresses rather than manoeuvrable weapons of war. They were sluggish movers, clumsy to steer, very high in freeboard and cumbered with flimsy 'castles' in bow and stern. The new, and smaller, ones which were built under his eye were of the new 'galleon' type; longer in relation to their breadth, lower in freeboard, less 'castled', especially in the bows, and given, for the first time, one continuous gun-deck. Among the earlier of them, and often regarded as their prototype, was the unfortunate (but immortal) *Revenge*. The names usually given to the ships shown opposite are the *White Bear* and the *Ark Royal*. This identification may well be wrong, but this much is certain: the top one is of the old build, the bottom one of the new; and at least there can be little doubt which is going to be the better sea boat. By 1588, even the old types had been considerably improved by Hawkins, and were used effectively against the Armada. The new ones were incomparably the best warships afloat.

A 'pre-Hawkins' ship, probably the White Bear

A 'post-Hawkins' ship, probably the Ark Royal
Both from engravings by C. J. Visscher

His share, then, in defeating the enemy can scarcely be exaggerated. Just as Lords Barham and St Vincent forged the weapon which Nelson so brilliantly wielded, so Hawkins fashioned the fleet which confounded Philip. In 1588, of course, he went to sea in one of his own charges, the *Victory*, and played a leading part in both council and fight. During a quiet interlude of the action he was knighted, and no man ever more richly deserved the honour.

Philip's crude way of settling his argument with Hawkins killed the uneasy Anglo-Spanish friendship. But it settled nothing. The English intended to enter the closed trade-monopoly; they did not even recognize it. If they could not enter with Philip's consent, they would enter without it. Ultimately, no doubt, this spelt open war: but not immediately, because both principals still hoped to avoid it, for reasons already given. So, through some sixteen years, from 1569 to 1585, there stretched a confused period of 'veiled hostility' – today, probably, we should call it 'cold war'. As incident followed incident, especially at sea, the hostility grew, the veil became ever more diaphanous. Only the principals kept up the pretence of amiability, and that was often hollow in the extreme. Hawkins, at the Navy Board, took no direct part in all this, though he too was quietly preparing for war. The new and highly charged atmosphere demanded a rather different, and a tougher, protagonist: and it found an outstanding one – our second Armada hero.

FRANCIS DRAKE

Francis Drake, though related to the Hawkinses, was not, like them, born into the 'purple of commerce'. He had to start at the bottom. His father, Edmund, had been a sailor once, but when Francis was born was a yeoman-farmer of Tavistock. He was a hot Protestant, and, when the Catholics of the West rose in 1549, he was forced to leave Devon and find shelter in a hulk at the new royal port of Gillingham in the Medway, with the duty of prayer-reader to the keepers of the ships laid up there. So young Francis went to sea at a very early age, first as apprentice in a collier plying between Tyne and Thames, and then as its owner. For a while he served the Hawkinses – he was with John on his disastrous third voyage – but then struck out on his own. He soon prospered, for he possessed in the highest degree a genius for taking calculated risks. He was a born leader of resolute men, always knowing precisely what he and they could do: a unique exponent of surprise, a master opportunist, always daring but scarcely ever rash. To our modern eyes he seems a queer mixture of piety and un-scrupulosity. He could not exist today, being, above all his contemporaries, a child of his age and of the peculiar condi-tions engendered by 'veiled hostility'. He has been called by all sorts of names, from 'pirate' and 'hypocrite' (because he so often saw the hand of God in affairs whose morality may appear to us, to say the least, dubious), through all possible gradations, to 'Saviour of his country', 'Creator of naval war-fare', 'Father of English strategy'; and (by the Spaniards) simply '*El Draque*': the Dragon, the Devil himself.

The odd thing is that there is a case of sorts for all these views, save only the charge of hypocrisy. This cannot be allowed. The more his astonishing career is examined, the more plain becomes the sincerity of his puritan outlook; the more evident it is that he did believe profoundly, not only in the existence of God, but also in His very special directing care not so much of Francis as of Elizabeth and of England. As for the piracy charge, we must take care not to land ourselves in the ludicrous position of having to dismiss one of our most brilliant and devoted patriots as a common criminal. It is indeed fruitless to judge any man by the standards of a day not his own. It is as unprofitable to dismiss Drake as a pirate as it is to despise Hawkins as a slaver. It is more sensible to inquire what his contemporaries thought. The Spaniards, naturally, called him by opprobrious names. But this means little. Are we seriously influenced by what the Nazis called Winston Churchill? Certainly Elizabethan Englishmen did not consider him piratical, though they were not all so polite to him as we are apt to be. He had his enemies, fierce ones, even at home. But the pirate has his legal definition: he is *hostis sui generis* – the enemy (on the sea) of his own kind, of all humanity. Now Drake was never this: he invariably confined his hostility to one particular breed of humanity, the Spaniard, who also happened, throughout Drake's whole career, to be, in intent if not in fact, the enemy of England.

If not a pirate, then, what was he? The fairest answer is that, in his earlier years he was a 'privateer', and, in his later ones, a Naval Officer, though (to use twentieth-century language) rather RNR than RN. The privateer, up to the moment of his extinction a bare century ago, was a belligerent who waged 'private' war, i.e. fought his country's enemies, with the consent and encouragement of his government, but with his own weapons. This in effect is what Drake was doing throughout his earlier years. His nearest approaches to anything less creditable belong to the phase of 'uneasy friendship', when, as it were, he sometimes anticipated history, acting as though 'uneasy friendsip' had already given place to 'veiled hostility'. Then he might have got himself into trouble at home, though he was quite shrewd enough to know that, at heart, Authority thought very much as he did – that the one was bound to degenerate into the other.

As it happened, it was the private belligerent of Drake's type which at the moment exactly suited Elizabeth's requirements. Indeed, the key-actor in this 'cold war' was the private Englishman who was content, even eager, to face the common enemy at a time when Queen and Government were not prepared to show their hands, for reasons both political and economic. Elizabeth neither wished nor could afford open war. But neither could she afford to stand aside and do nothing. The man for her purpose was the patriotic, hard-bitten English seaman who would fight her delaying action for her; and the really ideal one was the man who was not afraid to take risks, blame and even punishment, should it be her short-term policy to disclaim him. Certainly this was asking much from any subject, but it was precisely this that she did ask, and precisely this that she received from such men as Drake. But Elizabeth, herself no altruist, did not expect pure altruism from others. There must be a *quid pro quo* for loyal and patriotic servants who took such obvious risks on her behalf: a financial reward, for it seldom suited her to pay them in any modern sense. Here, then, came in the profit motive, running strong, but always running parallel with the patriotic motive. Men like Drake must be paid, but Philip, not Elizabeth, must supply the wherewithal.

Most of Drake's earlier voyages, and many others like them, thus took on this double complexion of patriotism and profit which is the key to the whole Elizabethan period. Each expedition looks like an ordinary business venture, of the 'joint-stock' variety then becoming fashionable. On their economic side, indeed, this is just what they were, complete with partners, directors, shareholders and dividends. But they had their political side too, and, as the veil grew ever thinner, their military side as well. Elizabeth and her ministers often had a financial interest in them, open or secret as it suited their purpose at the moment. In fact, the method suited everybody: for when a venture succeeded, the syndicate drew its dividend while the Queen achieved her political end, at no cost to herself, and sometimes at a considerable profit. In fact, she could afford no other weapon. Thus it came about that when 'hot war' at length developed, this strange process also developed into what can only be called 'waging war by joint stock company'. It lasted throughout hostilities, wherein every considerable expedition, with one notable exception, was at least disguised as a joint stock company.

That one exception is a most important one – none other than the subject of this book. The anti-Armada fleet was not a joint stock company, but was assembled by the far older, and hitherto normal, method of an 'embargo' – a stay on all shipping and all seamen: a nation-wide effort organized by the Government. That this campaign was an exception is no accident. It could hardly have been otherwise. In all other expeditions there was at least a chance of immediate economic profit. Galleons might be taken, treasure captured, towns plundered or ransomed. But, here, the sole object was destruction, wherein lies no conceivable dividend: and a business venture with *no* prospect of profit is a contradiction in terms.

This great episode, however, was still in the womb of time when Drake was rising to the top: so, even, was 'hot war' itself. Meanwhile, he was making his fortune: but, in the long view, he was making England's too.

The school that was educating him was as hard as it was unusual: and Drake was its most promising pupil, growing yearly in stature during the 'veiled hostility', and when it was over, ready to step on to the larger and more responsible stage of open war. He had long been a prime seaman, but San Juan de Ulua, Nombre de Dios, his inimitable Voyage of Circumnavigation, San Domingo, Cartagena and a score of smaller exploits made him an outstanding sea fighter too, ripe to become (what he was in fact by 1585) the leading exponent in England of sea warfare. The year of his birth is doubtful, but he was in his prime (perhaps forty-three) in Armada year: a shortish, thick-set man, with a fresh complexion tanned by the weather, a trim little beard and very bright, intelligent eyes. He was Vice-Admiral of the main fleet and, for all practical purposes, Chief of Staff to the Commander-in-Chief. Why he was not himself Commander-in-Chief we shall see shortly, when we introduce the man who was. But first let us look at some of the other 'sea dogs' of the Drake type.

OTHER SEAMEN OFFICERS

Martin Frobisher's background was not unlike Drake's though he was no Devonian, but a Yorkshireman whose family came originally from Denbigh. He was of gentle birth but, orphaned at an early age, he was apprenticed to the sea, which he never left thereafter. But the sea, in the mid-sixteenth century, was a tough place, and Frobisher undoubtedly grew up a very tough man, brave, hardy and expert in his job, but with a fierce, unruly spirit which he was unable, and sometimes unwilling, to curb. In his earlier voyages there is more than one hint of piracy, though the details are too shadowy for us to determine whether they were more real than Drake's. Perhaps they were, a little; yet not such as to put him in bad odour with the London merchants, nor with those influential noblemen who were often their financial partners. It was in fact a combination of these groups, under the patronage of the Queen herself, which fitted out an expedition to explore the North-West Passage in 1575. Its object was to win through to the fabulous markets of China and Japan by a route far removed from all Spanish settlements. Frobisher, by then nearly forty years old, and already considered one of the most experienced of sea captains, was appointed to command it.

There followed the three voyages of exploration for which Frobisher is now chiefly remembered. All but the first failed as geographical ventures, though the fault was not his. Someone on his first voyage unfortunately brought on board a substance called 'black earth' (probably black pyrites) which an Italian assayer pronounced to contain gold. Thereafter the lure of quick returns drove out the urge for long-term discoveries, and the last two voyages yielded but little of either, since no gold was ever extracted. The expeditions hit Frobisher in pocket, though not in reputation; for, soon after, he obtained employment in the Queen's ships and, among other voyages, accompanied Drake to the West Indies in 1585. Completely restored to favour, he was highly regarded in the anti-Armada fleet, where he was given command of the *Triumph*, the greatest of the royal ships, and in the unofficial hierarchy of the main fleet ranked fourth. He had almost as much sea experience as Drake, though a good deal less fighting experience. He was emphatically no 'Drake's man': rather, his open enemy and his loudest critic. He was slightly wounded six years later, leading a land assault at Crozet near Brest, and died, it is said, a victim to bad surgery.

Many of the next flight of leaders were men of the Drake school, trained under his eye. The principal exception was Edward Fenton, second-in-command to Frobisher in two of his discovery voyages. He strikes one, indeed, as being an inferior edition of Frobisher, without his drive or flair for seamanship, though he had had plenty of experience and was to have more. Like Frobisher, too, he was openly hostile to Drake. Among those who supported Drake must be named Robert Crosse, a dyed-in-the-wool seaman who had often served with him, the last time being in the preceding year at Cadiz: and he was Drake's Rear-Admiral in his Western Squadron in Armada year. In that fight he played a considerable part, but the high-light of his career was his capture of the Spanish treasure-ship *Madre de Dios* in 1592. This fabulous carrack was the largest ship then afloat, having seven decks, a burthen of near (if not quite) 2,000 tons and a cargo still worth at least three million pounds in modern money after being half-pillaged. He was so pro-Drake that he would not serve under Frobisher. The last of the Drake men who call for notice were the sea family of Fenners: five of them – Thomas, Edward, George and two Williams, father and son. The most distinguished was Thomas, who had been with Drake in many of his exploits, his Chief of Staff in the 1585 descent on the Indies, and the Vice-Admiral of his Western Squadron now. His status in 1588 was sufficient to secure him a place on the Lord Admiral's inner council.

The Drake–Frobisher antipathy was the bitterest, but by no means the only, rift in the English fleet.* One of the English commanders, Elizabeth's own old servant William Borough, having recently been tried by court-martial and sentenced to death by Sir Francis, could hardly be expected to love him. Again, Hawkins had his detractors in the fleet, especially among his Navy Board colleagues. It would seem on the face of it that the cause of England must suffer from such feuds. But there is no evidence that it did, and there were two reasons for it. The first was the patent danger of the occasion. Defeat spelt national extinction; and not one of them intended either England or Elizabeth or himself to be extinguished; so all feuds were shelved. Even so, however, they were a strong-willed set, strong individualists too, and apt to be restive in harness. What was needed was someone – not one of them-selves – with the character and authority to make them into a

---

* After the worst of the danger was over, Frobisher was, publicly, calling Drake 'a cowardly knave or traitor – I rest doubtful, but the one I will swear'. Or again: 'He hath used certain speeches of me which I will make him eat again, or I will make him spend the best blood in his belly.' Nor was Drake the man to take abuse lying down.

team, and to lead them. He was there: he is our third English Armada hero.

CHARLES, LORD HOWARD OF EFFINGHAM

Men wonder, even to this day, why, having such a personality, such a genius as Drake at her disposal, the Queen did not appoint him out of hand as Commander-in-Chief of all her sea forces in one undivided command. That question is already half answered. Insulated from all contemporary problems of conflicting personalities, Drake doubtless had it in him to conduct the campaign to a triumphant conclusion. Alike as strategist, tactician and fighter, he was supreme. But such a vacuum did not exist. Sir Francis, great man as he was, was only *primus inter pares*. His very elevation would have inflamed hatreds and jealousies already dangerous enough; and that, as we are now to see, not only in the breasts of fellow adventurers like Frobisher, but also in the minds of another class of society altogether: men who, as patriotic as he, and bred to the art of war (even though not of sea war), were as anxious as he to lay their swords at the Queen's feet. These we must now consider as a group; and easily first among them was Charles, Second Lord Howard of Effingham.

There were then, and for long afterwards, only two social groups from which the higher command at sea could be drawn. Elizabethan England was still a highly class-conscious country, so near the Middle Ages that leadership was still the prerogative, as in feudal times, of the nobility and greater landowners. These men were the natural supporters of the Throne; were indeed in the position which they occupied mainly because they, or their ancestors, *had* successfully supported it, in the council chamber or on the field. By birth and upbringing they were 'armigerous' (which originally merely meant that they were entitled to bear arms, and were skilled in their use). They were seldom, it is true, trained *sea* fighters, but that mattered the less because, until quite recently, land fighting and sea fighting had not taken the very different paths which they have since followed. Normally, then, the

Crown required their services on land, but, when a sea cause arose, they were expected (and they desired) to transfer those services to the other element. There could be no question of just leaving them out because, land or sea, they had been accustomed to assume, as of right, the vital task of leadership: they had 'the habit of command', indeed, almost the monopoly of it. This was now shared, but still only to some extent, by that other group of fighting officers, whom we have been discussing so far; the men from humbler (or at least poorer) homes more or less bred to the sea; men who had risen by their own exertions, first to command afloat in their own private enterprises, but now, in times of national emergency, to transfer their self-taught powers of leadership and their great sea experience to command in war – the Drakes, Frobishers, Hawkinses, Fentons, Crosses, and Fenners.

In the England of Elizabeth, these two classes were the more important because there existed few if any professional sea officers – what we now call Royal Navy officers: men who gave all, or most of, their lives to the sea-services of the State. One or two, perhaps, *might* be so described: Sir William Wynter, for instance, who had been the Queen's Master of Naval Ordnance and Surveyor of the Ships for many years, during all which time he received his salary from her. William Borough was perhaps another. But they were few, and not particularly distinguished. For practical purposes it is true to affirm that the RN Officer was non-existent. This meant, of course, that all the higher command had to be drawn from either the nobility and gentry or the seamen. Both sorts were true patriots. But every class complex, hallowed by tradition, dies hard and is dangerous when unnecessarily ignored. There was evidently a risk in asking men who were our hereditary leaders, in war no less than in society, to serve under one who was, by comparison, a parvenu in both respects. This is certainly a reason, if a subsidiary one, why they were not asked to serve under Drake. Moreover, this time, it was not necessary, because there existed in the ranks of the nobles a man whose qualifications for the post shone clear for all to see.

Lord Charles Howard's position in England and his status

in the Navy were unique. He was very highly born, a relative not only of the premier peer of England, the Duke of Norfolk, but even of the Queen herself, for Ann Boleyn was his first cousin. This helped, but it was not his principal qualification; nor was it the cause of his selection. He was to all intents and purposes chosen to command the anti-Armada fleet, not in 1588 but in 1585, when he was sworn as Lord Admiral. This high dignitary, whose functions have long since been dispersed among many holders, was, like the Lord Chancellor or the Lord Treasurer, one of the great Officers of State; and his province was 'all Sea Causes' – as comprehensive a charge as can well be imagined. Though he had various subordinates to help him, all sea affairs were his immediate responsibility; and in all their aspects – the administrative, the judicial, the executive. In modern terms he was, in his one person, an important Cabinet Minister, First Lord of the Admiralty, First Sea Lord and Chief of the Naval Staff, Second, Third and Fourth Sea Lords, Commander-in-Chief of the whole fleet always, and of the main fleet in wartime: and we shall not have given a true picture of his real position until we have also stressed that he enjoyed the combined prestige of all these eminent men. In Howard's particular case, indeed, we might go even further in assessing his personal prestige. His family was so closely linked with the Lord Admiral's office that his tenure of it was quasi-hereditary. His father, two uncles and a great-grandfather had held it before him. Wearing so all-embracing a mantle of authority, he automatically took charge of England's sea effort in 1588.

In his own day this caused no surprise, as it has since to people unfamiliar with the contemporary scene. Drake, who in the earlier months of the year held local command of the small fleet based upon Plymouth, was made his Second-in-Command and (as we should say) Chief of Staff when the great man moved west with the main force. There were not wanting, it is true, a few of his contemporaries who wondered how the arrangements would work, for Drake was a man of distinctly fiery temperament, and much more accustomed to command than to obey. But they need not have been nervous. Drake, of seaman origin, never had the remotest chance of supreme command, and, knowing it, did not expect it. Instead, he was transparently delighted with his vice-flag, an almost unprecedented honour for one who had begun so humbly: and his relations with his superior were of the happiest throughout. Each perfectly understood the part allotted to him, and each was admirably suited to it. The one had the fire, the expertise, the true strategist's eye, the gift of inspired leadership. The other, perhaps, had none of these gifts in any outstanding degree. Though he had once before commanded at sea (in 1570), he had seen no fighting there; and he had very little experience of ships and the handling of them. Nor had he the dynamism of his Second. But – and this is the important thing – he knew it: and that gave him one attribute of true greatness, a rare one, which calls to mind the much-loved American who was Supreme Commander in the West in World War II. He had natural dignity, charm and, above all, tact. He could handle difficult people, appreciate and encourage greatness in others. He had firmness too, and fairness of mind, and he was neither vain nor obstinate. He made mistakes, but was not afraid of admitting them: if he held wrong views (and he sometimes did) he was not above listening to others and changing his mind. He loved the navy over which he ruled, both ships and men. He loved to mete out praise when it was deserved, and he never failed to censure what might have been better. Thus, because he trusted people, and showed that he did so, he was in his turn trusted and loved by those who served him. He had a difficult team to handle, but he handled it magnificently. Hear him removing from Walsingham's mind any lingering fear of how Drake would behave as an underling:

> Sir, I must not omit to let you know how lovingly and kindly Sir Francis Drake beareth himself; and also how dutifully to her Majesty's service and unto me, being in the place I am in; which I pray you he may receive thanks for by some private letter from you.

This was typical of Howard. He was generous, and wise too. This arrangement, so sensible and so successful, is surely a classic example of the way in which Britain has so often faced and overcome her historical crises. She is apt – we love proclaiming it – to 'muddle through'; but, at the central crisis, she is also apt to cut through Gordian knots of protocol and patronage, of politics, precedence and pelf, with the sharp sword of plain horse-sense. We must have the right man for the job. Who is he? 'Technically', say those who know, 'Drake is the best man to direct operations: but there are insuperable objections to him as C-in-C.' 'Very well,' says Common Sense. 'Then divorce direction from Command for once. Howard is the best commander? Then let him command. Drake the best director? Then let him direct.' This was done, and this is why men watched a little anxiously to see whether the director would take kindly to being commanded by the commander, and whether the commander would be big enough to allow himself to be directed by the director. Both, being big men, cheerfully obliged, and England had the best of both worlds. This is among the earlier examples of British horse-sense in action. It is very far from being the last.

Howard's interest did not stop at the leaders, however: it spread to the humblest seaman. On them and their welfare he lavished his time, his health and, towards the end, his not very considerable patrimony. We shall meet him again when the danger is over, persisting, to the verge of angering his royal mistress, in his uphill fight against the Government's poverty. In fine, no one who reads his many surviving letters can fail to see in him a fine Christian gentleman, a leader wise and talented, respected and loved. There were recriminations, both from above and below, but none touched Howard. There grew up a story, long after his death, that he was a Catholic. This, though it would in some ways redound to his credit as an Englishman, has no contemporary foundation whatever, and may safely be dismissed as a later invention. The moving picture of Howard and Drake, kneeling side by side at Plymouth to take the Sacrament on Whitsunday, should convince the sceptic if nothing else can.

Yet the Lord Admiral's reputation was sadly diminished before his death, because, for all his great service to England, both before and after 1588, he made a mistake. His office was a life-appointment, and he clung to it much too long. He was Lord Admiral for thirty-four years – thirty-one of them after 1588, though even then he was fifty-two. Well before the end unscrupulous underlings were taking advantage of his failing powers. At last, in 1619, he was bought out by the Duke of Buckingham: but he lived for five more years, to die, by far the last of the English Armada heroes, at the age of eighty-eight.

OTHER NOBLE AND GENTLE OFFICERS

There were, of course, many other representatives of the nobility and gentry: and of them no less than six, all in high command, were related to Howard by birth or marriage. This sounds like – and was – plain nepotism. But for centuries, both past and to come, such was the norm. One of the least-challenged rights of a man appointed to a post of responsibility was to provide for his relatives and protégés out of the patronage which went with the appointment. Thus Lord Henry Seymour (son of Protector Somerset), who commanded the fleet guarding the Straits, was his sister's brother-in-law. Lords Sheffield and Thomas Howard, his nephew and cousin respectively, served on his inner council.

This body, already mentioned more than once, was his advisory staff, vital to the proper conduct of the campaign in view of the Admiral's known weakness in technical knowledge. He chose its members himself. Of the seven selected, four were seamen – Drake, Hawkins, Frobisher and Thomas Fenner: two – Sheffield and Thomas Howard – were noble: the last, Sir Roger Williams, was our leading professional soldier. The balance was both sound and subtle. The fighting seamen commanded a majority, but not necessarily a majority at the council table, where Howard presided himself with an eighth – and casting – vote. In the event, seamen and non-seamen never formed cliques against one another, for the Lord Admiral soon became an enthusiastic convert to Drake's strategic views; and that gave the pair of them a hard-core majority which could not be worse than five to three: for Fenner was essentially a Drake man, while the two nobles were Howard's men. All this merely confirms the view expressed above that the true director of the whole campaign was the man best qualified to direct it – Sir Francis Drake.

Though they fought bravely in 1588, most of the 'gentle' officers left the fleet when the campaign was over, and returned no more. To this rule, however, there was one rather notable exception. Lord Thomas Howard, the Duke of Norfolk's second son, undoubtedly owed much to nepotism. When appointed to the council, he was only twenty-six, and had never been to sea before. He was not given a ship at first: but he soon acquired one – and a knighthood – for gallantry in the fight. Thereafter, unlike his fellows, he continued afloat, to become an experienced commander and a competent seaman: he was, for instance, Grenville's commanding officer 'at Flores in the Azores' in 1591. Six years later he left the sea and, entering politics, contrived to play a spectacular part in an affair if possible better known to Englishmen even than the Armada and the last fight of the *Revenge*. He it was who, on the afternoon of November 4th, 1605, came upon one Guy Fawkes standing over certain suspicious barrels in a lumber-room beneath the House of Lords, and gave the alarm. Later he became Lord Chancellor of England.

Two other famous Elizabethans, it may be noticed, are so far absent from this gallery of heroes – Sir Richard Grenville and Sir Walter Raleigh. Both were already national figures, and both played distinguished parts in Armada year, though not afloat. Grenville, known as a soldier rather than as a sailor, held the very responsible post of organizing and commanding the land defences of Cornwall, most exposed of English counties. As a shipowner in quite a big way, too, he sent a fully victualled squadron to the fleet. Three of its ships were his own property: one was commanded by his cousin, another by his son. Sir Walter Raleigh also enjoyed a soldier's rather than a sailor's reputation. He was responsible for the land defences of Devon. He too provided ships. One – the *Roebuck* – we shall meet again, and, much more often, another: for

Howard's fleet flagship, called indifferently the *Ark Royal* or, simply, the *Ark*, had been, till 1587, the *Ark Raleigh*. Then he handed it over to the Queen, who did not pay him for it though, long afterwards, £5,000 was struck off a debt which he owed her. One other most important duty he had already per-performed. He was the life and soul of the special Commission appointed to review the defences of the whole of England and to co-ordinate all local plans.

3

THE SPANISH LEADERS

THE ARMADA HEROES

THE SOCIAL PATTERN of Philip's Spain was a good deal more aristocratic than that of Elizabeth's England. The wall which separated the noble from the commoner was a good deal higher, thicker and less passable. Every son of a noble was noble, and never fell to commoner's status: moreover, it was rare for a nobleman (or his son or grandson) to marry outside his caste. Hence the existence of a highly exclusive, closely fenced-in 'Don' class; and, at a rather lower level, yet still essentially gentle, a 'Hidalgo' class. In England, even before the Tudors, it was far otherwise. The caste wall was there, but there were many more gates in it, and the traffic through them – both ways – was much brisker. It was no easy passage, but the services of commoners were rewarded with peerages or grants of land, sparingly yet fairly regularly; while a peer's younger sons or grandsons, not being noble *per se*, soon lost their noble status or their tenure of land, unless they could regain them by their own exertions.

By Elizabeth's time, the relative social structures had moved even farther apart. The Spanish system was virtually unchanged, but in England the Tudor monarchs had deliberately decreased the political power of their nobility and, as a counter-weight, had raised up a new class from below them – a true Middle Class. The most useful and successful they had ennobled; others, though not so honoured, had prospered economically and, by acquiring land in considerable quantity, had moved socially towards the nobility, and formed a wider land-owning aristocracy. It was becoming rather easier, in fact, for men to ascend a class or two in a generation or two; either by patent of nobility or, more often, merely by making money and investing it in land. Conversely, too, it became commoner for younger sons and their families to go down the social scale, even to losing their gentility altogether.

Spain and England thus faced very different problems in officering their fleets. Spain was never short of an officer-class, because the land teemed with nobility – not indeed titled, landed or wealthy nobility, though there were quite enough of these to fill the really top commands: but with all those sons of younger sons through the generations who, though they may have owned no acre of land, and inherited little but a sword, a coat of arms and a tradition, still retained their title to nobility, and were still born and bred to command. They were roughly, in fact, young Howards, Cumberlands and Grenvilles. A few, but (as in England) a very few, might almost be called RN, like Wynter and Borough. But none, or practically none, were seamen like Hawkins, Drake or Frobisher, the products of the English Crown's alliance with Commerce. Here indeed is the cardinal difference between the Spanish and the English officers: here was Spain's great desideratum. She had hardly any of the people who had learnt (rather than inherited) the art of leadership, and who at the same time were real professional sailors: she had hereditary war leaders in plenty (good ones too and at all levels) but singularly few sea leaders, at any level.

How noble or gentle the ordinary Spanish officer was, and yet not necessarily either landed or wealthy, can be gleaned from surviving lists of prisoners. Many of them bear high-sounding names: often those of the great leaders, though they were probably but poor and distant cousins. In one pathetic list made in Ireland, there are no less than thirteen Dons; Don Luis de Cordova, Don Alonzo de Argotta, Don Antonio de Ulloa, Don Diego de Cordova, Don Diego de Santillana and so on. But only one, the first-named, could find enough money to make his ransom or his keep worthwhile to his captors; and the remaining dozen, being a charge upon their jailers, were incontinently slaughtered after the brutal usage of the day.

Spain's fighting leaders, who alone can concern us here, were a magnificent body of men, noble, all of them, in birth and character alike: great leaders of men, the military pick of a profoundly military caste, trained to arms from its youth and with plenty of practice. They had the abiding qualities of their race – personality, colour, superb courage, unbending pride. But, and it is a fatal 'but', they were most of them amateur seamen, not professionals; they did not really know what a workable, fightable ship was; nor how to make it so; and, worse, they had no underlings to tell them these things. Yet, with such staggering disadvantages, they put up a magnificent show of sheer courage and endurance, borne up by the pride of their tradition and the morale of a score of victories – on land. The English won, but they never broke the spirit of that great band of Spanish squadron leaders – Juan Martinez de Recalde, Miguel de Oquendo, Pedro de Valdez, Hugo de Moncada, Alonso de Leyva, Martin de Bertendona.

The Armada's second-in-command was Recalde, Knight of Santiago and a native of Bilbao. Deservedly he enjoyed the greatest reputation in seamanship; and indeed he was something of an exception, for he had much experience, not only in sea fighting but also in navigation and sailing. He had been commanding fleets for some sixteen years. He had gained a great reputation as second-in-command of the expedition of 1582, which had won from Don Antonio the battle of St Michaels and the whole of the Azores, events which were to have dangerous repercussions in Spain. On the beaten side, which consisted largely of French privateers, there chanced to be a small contingent of English privateers, who, having no motives other than pay and plunder, had (like most of their French consorts) misbehaved themselves in action. From this circumstance, entirely untypical of English seamen, the Spaniards had drawn unwarrantable conclusions, supposing – wishfully – that the English would put up no better show when it came to defending their own homes. It is unwise to underestimate the enemy; and, though the subsequent exploits of men like Drake had convinced Philip that a sea invasion of England would be no triumphal progress, he still thought fit to harp on St Michaels as a sample of the opposition his Armada might expect. Not that Recalde was so deceived. He probably knew his enemies better than any other Spaniard.

He knew their coasts better too, having made an extensive reconnaissance of them; and much of the coast of Ireland, being the officer who had landed that luckless expedition which had been massacred at Smerwick in 1580. For good measure, he had been Superintendent of the Royal Dockyards, and so knew something of the care-and-maintenance side; and he had commanded the Indian Plate fleets, and so knew something of sailing in company and in convoy. Throughout the fighting of 1588 he was invariably given the post where the greatest danger threatened, and so had more than his fair share of the battle. His ships, his weapons, his men, his superiors might fail him: but he never failed them: a lionhearted, competent, trustworthy old man, unquestionably the most valuable officer they had.

Don Miguel de Oquendo of San Sebastian ('the Glory of the Fleet', they called him) was, in reputation as a sea commander, little if at all behind Recalde; but otherwise of a very different character. He had a great name for flamboyance and élan, and was brave to the verge of rashness: a much more typical Spaniard. He was the kind of whom tales are told round campfires and in sailors' messes. He was in the thick of it at St Michaels, taking on single-handed, they said, the flagship, the vice-flagship and three other French ships; and, in the Armada expedition, he 'handled his ship like a light horseman'. But – alas for the gallant Oquendo – 'light horse' is no simile for any Armada ship ('heavy elephant' would be a truer); and, though he gained immortal honour from his countrymen, though always in the tightest corner, and the very last to give the English best, his gallantry availed him nothing. It is said that his pride could not support the ignominies inflicted upon it by the vacillations and half measures of his chief, and by what seemed to him the gratuitous insults of a hated enemy whom he could not chastise; and that he returned to Spain sick, as much in mind as in body, and without the will to live. Anyway, he died on October 2nd, within a week or two of his return: and Recalde, less fiery by nature and more balanced in mind, was also dead before that same month was out.

The next in repute and sea experience was Don Pedro de Valdez, also a knight of Santiago. His place in the team lay somewhere between Recalde's and Oquendo's: less experienced and solid than Recalde, less dashing than Oquendo, yet probably more dependable and certainly more thoughtful. He too had experience of high command in the Indies. He had been Admiral of the Galician Squadron at the conquest of Portugal, and was considered a good navigator and seaman; also, rightly, a man of great character and initiative. Indeed, his initiative had once got him into trouble. During the Terceira campaign he had attempted a landing without leave and, being repulsed, was imprisoned on his return. He knew his Englishmen better than most. He had been gravely wounded in action with them off Ferrol, and had no illusions as to their softness. In the years immediately preceding 1588 he had been working his passage back to favour; and indeed the advice which he gave to Philip at this time was probably the best that that monarch ever received. He was constantly urging his master to strengthen the Armada's artillery since, his experience told him, it was upon this weapon that the enemy would principally rely. Apparently he convinced Philip, though rather too late to be useful. In the meantime, however, he was practising what he preached, and trying hard to increase the gun-power of his own ship and squadron. He figured prominently at the beginning of the fight, but soon sank out of sight, into the relative peace of an English prison. Four and a half years were to elapse before he saw Spain again, and then only by finding a princely ransom of £3,550.

Don Hugo de Moncada was a different type of man, more like Oquendo, perhaps, in his pride, though inferior in his performance, and the least attractive of them all. Of very high birth, he had served long in Flanders, and, when afloat, had always been with the rowed craft, not with sailing ships. This explains why, in 1588, he was commanding the small squadron of those oar-cum-sail hybrids, the galleasses which loom so large in the Spanish accounts. He was, as we shall see, killed in action, the only one of the squadron commanders to meet that fate. This alone brings posthumous glory: *pro patria mori*.

But, shorn of this incentive, we may be more severe, and conclude that his pride was altogether excessive, making him unpardonably touchy, too apt to take offence and to question orders, even those of his commander-in-chief. The impression he leaves is of a difficult, prickly man, yet no less valiant than the rest.

By contrast, Don Alonso de Leyva was the most attractive of them all: young, handsome, gay, and of course bred to war, though not specifically to sea war. He was of the brotherhood of the English Sidney and the French Bayard, 'chevalier sans peur et sans reproche'; the idol of court and country alike, withal a man of real talent and enterprise. For such reasons Philip had secretly appointed him to lead the expedition should anything happen to the Commander-in-Chief, and all the great families of Spain with sons and nephews eager to win their spurs vied with each other to get them sent to England under his eye. Hardly a noble house but was represented in his following. Here were the elements of pure tragedy, which we shall have to narrate in due course. He himself perished, universally mourned. Philip himself, we are told, felt his loss more keenly than that of all the rest.

The only one of the six to return to Spain with the survivors and to be alive when October ended was Don Bertendona, a native of Bilbao. He was of the second generation in sea command, for his father had been the officer entrusted to bring Philip to England for his marriage with Mary. His is a more shadowy figure than the others, and perhaps less colourful, though he had been considered important enough to guard the sea approaches to Spain and Portugal when the main forces went to the Azores in 1583. Now he commanded the Levant Squadron, and fought with some skill and more courage in all the up-Channel fights. But, unlike the others, he had a future as well as a past. He was to meet the English again. The first time was at Corunna in 1589 when, opposing Drake in the *Revenge*, he was forced to burn his own ship to avoid certain capture. Deeply mortified, he vowed vengeance – and redeemed his vow. Fate ordained that he should meet the *Revenge* again, though not Drake; and, in a way, he had the

last word. It was he who, in the immortal fight of 1591 between 'the one and the fifty-three', first grappled Grenville's
flagship, clinging on with desperate pertinacity, though with
vast losses, until the *Revenge* was reduced to immobility. She
shook him off at last, but, as all know, her crew surrendered
in spite of her dying commander; and such credit as accrued
to the Spaniards for this most pyrrhic victory went, by right,
to Bertendona.

THE HIGH COMMAND

Such were the real Spanish heroes. Yet, strangely enough, not
one of them had any say at all in the Armada's preparation,
management, higher strategy or policy. For the men who held
these responsibilities we must look elsewhere; and this very
necessity shows beyond the shadow of a doubt that there was
no one on the enemy's side in the least resembling Hawkins
or Drake. Two men, under Philip – always under the dead
hand of the Recluse of the Escorial – directed everything.
They were Don Diego Flores de Valdez, Chief of Staff to the
Commander-in-Chief and sailing with him in his flagship *San
Martin*, and the Commander-in-Chief himself.

Fate, and Philip, decided that Flores de Valdez should be the
real commander of the expedition, and history has fastened
much of the stigma for its failure upon him. In his own day, his
country and his king made him the only scapegoat: he alone,
among all that gallery of unsuccessful colleagues, was signalled
out for disgrace and imprisonment. Yet two things may be
urged in his defence. First, under existing conditions, some
other Spaniard might have achieved a less unredeemed failure;
but it is more than doubtful whether any Spaniard, living,
departed or yet unborn, could have commanded success.
Second, Flores did not appoint himself, nor did he appoint his
Commander-in-Chief. The man who could make two such
monumental blunders as these cannot possibly be acquitted of
blame for what happened. That man, of course, was Philip, the
sole and unchallenged fount of all appointments.

The very choice of Don Diego seems to reveal the King as a

fundamentally stupid man, lacking either in psychological awareness or in elementary knowledge of the facts, if not in both. He should certainly have known that the man selected for the all-important post was not *persona grata* with any of his underlings. On the contrary, they all hated and despised him. The reasons for this are not all clear: it was partly, no doubt, a matter of clashing personalities. Yet this does not excuse Philip: it is just such up-to-date information which he should have made a point of possessing. What we do know of the Chief of Staff is that he was of a highly jealous, touchy and quarrelsome disposition, and a good hater himself. Such weaknesses alone should have been enough to keep him out. But what makes the choice even stranger is this: his past record was far from good. He had been sent to fortify the Straits of Magellan against any repetition of Drake's Voyage of Circumnavigation. He had not only failed completely: he had shamelessly deserted a brave underling, the much-loved Sarmiento; and for this no Spanish seaman ever forgave him. He had, it is true, considerable technical qualifications – twenty years' command of trans-Atlantic fleets, and a reputation as a hydrographer and naval architect – but these could never outweigh his universal unpopularity. Nor is this the summit of the King's folly. Having made a bad appointment, he deliberately stepped up that appointment's importance, giving explicit orders to his Commander-in-Chief that he was to follow his Chief of Staff's advice on every matter of fleet movement, on every question of tactics and strategy. This seems more stupid still – until we have made the acquaintance of the said Commander-in-Chief, and plumbed the depths of *his* unsuitability. Then at least we shall realize that he had to have a wet-nurse of some kind, even though Flores was the wrong one. In fact, Philip's choice of a Commander-in-Chief was his crowning blunder.

The person signalled out for this unenviable and unsought distinction was, to give him his full style, Don Alonso Perez de Gusman el Bueno, twelfth Señor and fifth Marques de San-lucar de Barramada, ninth Conde de Niebla and seventh Duque de Medina Sidonia; or, more concisely, Medina

Sidonia – the 'Good'. And good there is every reason to believe he was – a quiet, friendly sort of person, colourless, highly and sincerely religious, blameless of ambition; free, almost, from pride, that besetting Castilian sin; asking nothing more of life than to live in peace among his orange groves at San Lucar. He had of course been bred to arms, but he never attempted to conceal the fact that arms were the last things he cared about. Indeed, his military record was not even negative. He had failed egregiously at Cadiz when Drake visited it in 1587, and he was to fail there again, quite as badly, when Howard and Essex returned in 1596. He was devoted to his King and Country, but that was almost the only personal qualification he had. What secured him the post, of course, was his social qualification, the social accident that made him a grandee of Spain, and a very elevated one at that.

We must not malign him, however. If, through no fault of his own, he was essentially a little man, his noble and – in both senses – his gentle background largely saved him from real dishonour. He rose to the occasion, in so far as there was anything in him capable of rising. During the hell he went through he invariably conducted himself with what dignity he possessed: which, however, is but faint praise. He had none of the attributes of a popular leader: he could not inspire men to fight and die for him. But his personal bravery in action was exemplary. When he panicked, as he often did, he showed it in his indecision at the council board, not *coram populo* on the quarter-deck. After the fighting was over he broke down completely, morally and physically too; and on reaching port he left his flagship immediately, too sick in body and spirit to wind up affairs. Indeed, the pathetic part of it is that no one seems to have expected him to do anything else. When he could travel, he went straight home to San Lucar, to a wife *not* lacking in Castilian pride; and, Heaven help him, he doubtless paid for his littleness there. But it was the only price he had to pay. His countrymen simply dismissed him with rather pitying silence, and neither then nor since have they been unduly harsh to him. Indeed, who could be, having read the remarkable letter in which he sought to escape the burden when first he learned that it was being fastened upon him? It is very long, and all in the same vein. Here are but a few extracts from it:

> I humbly thank his Majesty for having thought of me for so great a task, and I wish I possessed the talents and strength necessary for it. But, Sir, I have not health for the sea, for I know by the small experience that I have had afloat that I soon become seasick. . . . The force is so great, and the undertaking so important, that it would not be right for a person like myself, possessing no experience of seafaring or of war, to take charge of it. . . . I possess neither aptitude, ability, health or fortune. . . . For me to take charge of the Armada afresh, without the slightest knowledge of it, of the persons who are taking part in it, of the objects in view, of the intelligence from England . . . would be simply groping in the dark, even if I had experience, seeing that I should have suddenly and without preparation to enter a new career. So, Sir, you will see that my reasons for declining are so strong and convincing in his Majesty's own interests, that I cannot attempt a task of which I have no doubt I should give a bad account . . . for I do not understand it, know nothing about it, have no health for the sea, and no money to spend upon it.

If, after this, the King was fool enough to force his faithful but wretched subject to undertake a task which was obviously beyond him, who is to blame? Not, assuredly, the little man who knew how small he was and made no bones about admitting it.

Yet he did make one contribution which his detractors have forgotten, which was yet, probably, the only one the humble little man really could make: he contributed nearly 9,000,000 maravedis in cash.

THE MARQUIS OF SANTA CRUZ

Clearly, then, Philip had chosen very ill – one man whom no one *would* follow because he was so hated, and another whom no one *could* follow because he did not lead. Whom, then, should he have chosen? Recalde, the steady near-professional? Pedro de Valdez, the talented near-amateur? Certainly, as Chief of Staff, either would have been infinitely preferable to Diego. But the Commandership-in-Chief was not so simple a choice, for, here, Philip was limited in much the same way as Elizabeth, only (Spain being so much more aristocratic) even more so. His selection had to possess very high social rank, for men like Moncada, and even Oquendo, would have been but sorry underlings to one who was not at least their social equal: unless, that is, the candidate's claim to the distinction was universally admitted. It was just here that Fate dealt a cruel blow to Spain. For such a man existed, right up to February 1588. Till then the Command was in no doubt at all: it was automatic, fore-ordained. The officer in question was Don Alvaro de Bazan – if not a Duke at least a Marquis – the famous Marquis of Santa Cruz, whose name must on no account be omitted here. For Santa Cruz, in a way all his own, *was* the Spanish Navy. He had for long occupied, in Spanish eyes, very much the position of Drake, Howard and Hawkins all rolled into one. He was the man who had built the fleet, administered it, commanded it and won its battles for it for so many years that he had become an institution. To his credit he already had two great naval victories – the greatest of the century as the Spaniards thought and, in one case, perhaps rightly. He was the man who had defeated the French (and English) at St Michaels, thereby clinching Philip's conquest of Portugal. The Spaniards, as we saw, exaggerated the magnitude of this naval achievement; but of the other great jewel in their champion's crown their judgement was sounder. In 1571 their fleet had won the tremendous battle of Lepanto, an epoch-making engagement in several ways. It had broken the naval power of the Turks in the Mediterranean, handing control to the Spaniards. It also marked the last important galley action in the history of the world. On that great day, Santa Cruz had not been in supreme command. Yet he had won the battle of Lepanto just as surely as a subordinate Nelson was to win that of Cape St Vincent two centuries later. Santa Cruz commanded the reserve, and it was his deft and timely move of that force which converted a colleague's error into a Turkish rout.

This does not mean, of course, that his presence in charge of the Armada Fleet would have changed the course of history: for conditions were quite different. Whereas at Lepanto such sailing-ships as were present had positive orders to take no part in the main fight, in the actions of 1588 no vessel propelled solely by oars was even present. Yet it does almost certainly mean that many of the more elementary mistakes of the Spaniards would have been avoided; the ships would have been in better posture to sail and fight, the men in better heart. Besides, in terms of collective courage, the loss of a skilled and trusted leader is shattering to those who miss him, especially when, in the big man's room, there appears the self-confessed little one. To replace a Santa Cruz by a Sidonia must have been devastating to morale. It is almost as though Jellicoe had died on the eve of Jutland and been replaced, not by Beatty or Keyes or Goodenough, but by Clarence, Ninth Earl of Emsworth.

If there is anything in physiognomy, a comparison of the portraits reproduced opposite page 97 is surely revealing.

Santa Cruz was, however, much more than a battle winner. He was the father of the whole Spanish Navy, and of its war effort: he was to Philip's Spain what von Tirpitz was to Wilhelm II's Germany. Moreover, the whole Armada idea was his special child. He more than any other had persuaded his master to attempt it. In 1585 he had drawn out the first blueprint of it, and, when it proved too grandiose, had produced others of more reasonable dimensions; and he had laboured long and hard at translating his ideas into solid ships, equipment and men. His task was immense. He had to overcome at the same time the *mañana* complex of his countrymen and the devilish machinations of *El Draque*, that wizard who watched in his magic mirror what his enemies were up to, and who thwarted them accordingly. Once convinced, too, Philip turned into a menace only less trying than Drake. The Armada was, originally, to sail in 1587. This Drake prevented by his classic descent on Cadiz, his occupation of Cape St Vincent and half a dozen other maddening expedients. But Philip refused to be influenced by mere facts. Daily, almost hourly, his messengers poured in upon the weary, ageing admiral, praying him, cajoling him, commanding him to achieve the impossible and start without delay. All through the winter of 1587–8, the great man stuck it out, working himself to the bone. But there is a limit to human endurance – after all, he was sixty-three years old. In the dark days of February he suddenly gave in, took to his bed, turned his face to the wall and – was succeeded by Sidonia!

Upon his death, it is clear now, the Armada's last hope also flickered and died.

Part Two:

'THE ENTERPRISE OF ENGLAND'

4

THE COMING OF WAR

THE COLD WAR ENDS

SINCE FORMAL WAR was never declared between Spain and England, the date when veiled hostility passed into open war is somewhat academic; but consensus of opinion places the moment in 1585. It was slow in coming because, in their own way, Philip and Elizabeth were both prudent, frugal souls who hated unnecessary risk and, still more perhaps, unnecessary expense. If, without giving up any of his basic ideas, Philip could secure a reasonably acquiescent England, he would be more than content. So would Elizabeth, if she could secure her life from assassins, her throne from rivals, and her people from the domination of Spain and the Pope – with, perhaps, her subjects enjoying their fair shares of the West Indies trade. But it was not to be. Philip's main aims were all based upon principles and convictions which he was incapable of compromising. Elizabeth could not compromise in the last resort, save at the price of personal and national suicide. So what followed was probably inevitable, and must be related here with such brevity as its complexities admit.

The chief tension areas were the Low Countries and the British Isles. In the Netherlands the trouble began in 1576, when Philip's brilliant half-brother, Don John of Austria, was sent to subdue their rebellion from Spanish rule. His ambition, but ill-concealed, was to marry Mary Queen of Scots, expel Elizabeth, seize England by force and rule it himself. Elizabeth could but try to thwart his plans; but as indirectly as possible, since she did not want to precipitate matters. So she gave the Netherlands a substantial loan, to help their resistance, and subsidised the Count Palatine to invade what was legally Philip's territory in their defence. Also, just to show that she held a trump or two, she let Drake loose in the Spanish trade zone. She did not explain her reasons to Philip, of course; indeed, after Drake had inflicted untold damage in his Voyage of Circumnavigation, she declared that she had known nothing whatever about it beforehand, and was immensely cross with the villain for what he had done. Naturally, this did not deceive Philip, who accused her angrily of sending Drake. Both were partly right. Elizabeth had not 'sent' Drake; but she had allowed, even helped, him to go, and some at least of his captures – loot to Philip – had unaccountably found their way into her pocket. Besides, he might well ask, why did she punish her villain when he returned by publicly knighting him?

Meanwhile Philip was attacking Elizabeth, indirectly also, but much nearer home. In England, he and the Pope, who naturally backed him here, let loose the devoted priests of the newly founded Society of Jesus to fan the zeal of the English Catholics and induce them to rise against their heretic Queen. The attempt failed. Strong Recusancy Laws were passed which, among other things, raised the fine for non-attendance at church – the Church of England – from one shilling to twenty pounds a month, a crippling mulct which none but the extreme zealot would endure. In Ireland too the trouble-makers were at work; with more success at first, because the bulk of the people were Catholics. In 1579 the Earl of Desmond rebelled, and next year, with the moral countenance of the Pope and more material help from Spain, defeated Elizabeth's Lord Deputy at Glenmalure. Thus encouraged, Philip landed a small force of Spaniards and Italians. Such a blow at England's back door could only be met in one way. Elizabeth sent over a considerable force which hemmed in the invaders at Smerwick, captured them, and killed the lot. This sounds brutal; and it was. Yet contemporary usage condoned it. For who were these invaders – officially? Not, at the moment, the armed forces of the King of Spain; Philip had to disown them, unless he was prepared to begin the war at once. So, in law, the wretched men were nothing but a band of stateless adventurers who had landed to aid and abet unlawful rebellion. After this the Irish revolt fizzled out.

Elsewhere, however, the Spanish cause was prospering. The

Duke of Parma, a subtle man and a great sailor, was now sent to the Netherlands. He succeeded in crushing the resistance of the southern provinces, and turned upon the gallant seven of the north. He was aided by open murder, barely avoided in England, successful in Holland. In December 1583 only the vigilance of her ministers saved Elizabeth from Throgmorton's plot to assassinate her and put Mary Stuart on the throne: and Mendoza, the Spanish Ambassador, caught red-handed as an accessory, was expelled the country. A few months later, William the Silent, the core of anti-Spanish, anti-Catholic resistance, was shot dead – at the sixth attempt! A surge of anger swept the English people, who loudly demanded the head of the dangerous Mary. Elizabeth refused; but she saw that she could not let the Seven Provinces go without a struggle, and sent out troops under the Earl of Leicester to help them. This was near the bone indeed. England's armed forces, under Elizabeth's known favourite, were aiding rebels against Spain in what was a Spanish possession; at least, so the Spaniards said. Elizabeth could only reply that she was not attacking Philip, still less invading Spain, only helping her allies!

For the moment Philip accepted that too, lame as it was. He also had not quite made up his mind. He did, however, stage a reprisal, and a rather mean one. Grain was short in Spain in 1585, and he invited some English merchants to send over a fleet of corn-ships, giving at the same time a most specific safe-conduct. But as they arrived at Bilbao he took steps to seize the lot, corn, ships and men. His success was almost complete, but not quite. One Foster, Master of the *Primrose of London*, had his suspicions when several boatloads of ostensible merchant seamen, sweetly smiling and dangling luscious bunches of cherries in their hands, were seen approaching. 'All their bosoms,' however, (as Hakluyt quaintly puts it) 'were stuffed with paper' – odd wear for merchant seamen. When therefore they tumbled on board and proved to be ill-disguised soldiers, the English were not taken altogether by surprise, but fought back so stoutly that, after a brisk scuffle, the twenty-eight 'Primroses' flung the ninety-seven Spaniards overboard. Then, instantly making sail, they escaped, the only ones who did, and brought the news to England. They also brought another exhibit of an unusual nature, as a witness to their veracity and Philip's treachery – the Corregidor (or Sheriff) of all Biscaya himself, whom, far out to sea, they found clinging to the ship's side and fished out.

This flagrant act of ill-faith infuriated the English. Their wrath exploded. With one voice they demanded retaliation. Elizabeth was even then hesitating whether to unleash Drake again, and this decided her. A bare month later he was off, first to Vigo Bay, where he coolly completed his watering and victualling at Spain's expense; then to the West, where he captured and burned Santiago and Porto Praya in the Cape Verde Islands; captured and gutted San Domingo, chief city of the Spanish islands; captured, sacked and ransomed Carthagena, capital of the Spanish Main, and utterly obliterated the new Spanish settlement at St Augustine in Florida. Was *this* war, or was it, still, diplomacy? It was war, and no mistake. The guise of the expedition, it is true, was still that of a joint stock company. But the Queen's open contribution, in men and ships, made pretence impossible. The commanding officer, as everyone knew, was not on his own, but working directly for his sovereign: no longer a privateer, but an officer of the Queen's Navy Royal. Besides, for good measure, he carried with him a formal army, complete with General, which landed and fought regular land-battles. No privateer, still less pirate, ever did that. But was it more of an act of war than, say, Leicester's campaign in the Netherlands, or the affair at Smerwick? It was; for no one, whoever he might be, could allege that Leicester was landing in Spain, nor that the Spaniards had landed in England. But the towns which Drake devastated *were* Spain, and valued jewels in her crown at that – San Domingo, for instance, was in size, wealth and magnificence the third city of the whole Empire. To understand the impact of its loss upon the ordinary Spaniard, one must imagine the feelings of the English man-in-the-street had he learned that a Spanish fleet (having victualled at Plymouth) had sailed up the Bristol Channel and sacked Bristol. No one could explain it away: even Elizabeth did not try.

THE ENTERPRISE TAKES SHAPE

Philip had long been toying with the idea of direct invasion. San Domingo and Carthagena went far towards deciding him. He now saw that he would never reduce his own subjects in the Netherlands until he had settled his account with Elizabeth; and that he could no longer do this by seducing her Englishmen, or by murdering her and replacing her by Mary – had not these heretical islanders positively enacted that, if any fatal accident befell their monstrous Queen, the life of anyone pretending to the Crown should be forfeited? But Drake's descent upon the Indies had now taught him something more, and more immediately dangerous. England was threatening Spain's existence by severing her life-lines with the West, whence came almost all her revenues. So, still strangely reluctant, almost as though he could half probe into the future, he began to listen seriously to his war-party, headed (for naval purposes) by Santa Cruz. This was in 1586, even before Drake returned with so much Spanish wealth. And before many months were out, the matter was clinched once and for all by the news from Fotheringay in February 1587. Caught in her conspiracies once too often by the brilliant detective work of Francis Walsingham, Mary had become such a menace in the eyes of all good Englishmen that Elizabeth had been forced to give way at last, and sanction her execution. Now neither marriage nor murder could help Philip. Nothing was left but a final trial of strength.

Though far-seeing Spaniards had been urging this upon Philip ever since 1569, the real inception of the Armada dates only from 1583. After Santa Cruz had won the Azores from Don Antonio, he proposed to his master that his fleet should be kept together to form the nucleus of 'the Enterprise of England'. At that time, Philip was already interested, but not convinced. So, being a careful man who liked to know the cost down to the last maravedi, he told his Admiral to produce an estimate of requirements. This Santa Cruz did; but the result had a distinctly damping effect on the prudent King. It demanded not only the combined maritime strength of Spain and

of the newly acquired Portugal, but an extensive building programme as well. Philip hung back, but did not say no, indeed
allowed much of the extra building and refitting to proceed.

Santa Cruz's Estimate of March, 1586, survives, and to read
it, even now, takes one's breath away. He demanded 556 ships
and a mighty army of 94,222 men. Indeed, in addition to his
556 ships sailing on their own keels, he wanted 20 *fregatas*, 20
faluas and 200 flat-bottomed boats, all to be carried in the
larger ships, bringing the total of floatable craft up to 796.
This vast number included 196 of what might be called 'front-
line', or even, nowadays, 'capital' ships – vessels of sufficient
tonnage and armament to play an active part in any fighting
which might occur. Of these, 150 were large sailing-ships,
40 were oared galleys, and six hybrid sail-cum-oar galleasses.
Of the 196, however, only 71 were the property of the Crown
of Spain: namely, 15 Portuguese Royal galleons, 10 Spanish
galleons (both groups sailing-ships), the 40 galleys and the six
galleasses.

There are signs of megalomania in these proposals, so much
so that, possibly, Santa Cruz meant more by them than he
cared to admit. Ostensibly, he was saying, 'Only give me what I
ask and I will conquer England.' But perhaps what he really
meant was, 'I have been into this matter closely, and reluctantly conclude that it is impossible without an expenditure
of resources which is clearly beyond your means.' An examination of but one sub-heading of his requirements – victualling –
seems to confirm this suspicion.

To find food and drink for nearly one hundred thousand
mouths over a voyage of unknown duration, but certainly not
less than half a year, and into waters where replenishments
would be exceedingly difficult, was probably quite beyond the
powers of any sixteenth-century commissariat. The Admiral's
list of wants has an almost fairytale quality – to name but a
few items: biscuit, 373,337 cwt; bacon, 22,800 cwt; cheese,
21,500 cwt; tunny-fish, 23,200 barrels; salt beef, 16,040 cwt;
pease, beans and rice, 66,000 bushels; strings of garlic, 50,000;
vinegar (to make it all eatable), 11,200 gallons; water, 20,000
pipes; wine, 46,800 pipes. A pipe was a large cask holding

110 gallons, or two hogsheads. It would thus seem that over five million gallons were demanded. The water-requirement was a good deal more modest; but, as it is listed among the provisions for horses and mules, it may be deduced that the men were not expected to drink it. Even so, the average wine ration works out at nearly 55 gallons per mouth. This seems a great deal more generous than in fact it was. The victualling was reckoned on a basis of eight months, so that a man would have rather less than a quart a day. This too sounds handsome enough until it is recalled that the time-honoured ration of the English seaman was one gallon of beer a day – four times as much!

To find the total cost, one must add the equipment of all the ships, the hire of most of them, the wages of nearly 100,000 officers and men, the hospital stores, the artillery (1,280 pieces) with all the shot and powder it required, and a host of other items (for the Admiral was determined that nothing should be lacking). He gives the answer, without apparently counting the actual value of the ships and all their appurtenances. Doubtless it was to this figure that the King directed his first glance. It was 1,526,425,498 maravedis.

The various items were to come from all parts of Philip's wide-flung European possessions: from all the provinces of Spain, from Portugal, from Naples, from Sicily, from Majorca and Minorca, from Genoa, from Milan, from Germany, from the Levant. But even so the load on each area was back-breaking. Whether the Marquis ever really hoped to obtain all this must remain a secret. In fact he never looked like getting it. Philip, a realist, recognized the impossibility at once. But he did not give up the idea; rather, he remodelled the scheme on cheaper lines. He already had in the Low Countries a first-class, well-found army, and this he decided to make the spear-head of his invasion. Instead of transporting from Spain an army, whole and fully equipped, he would leave the brunt to Parma and his veterans, and dispatch from Spain only a fleet strong enough to defeat the English and secure the crossing for Parma. The army which sailed with it was to be an integral part of the fleet, to help it to victory, and then to act as a rein-forcement and reserve. It was not to be the actual invasion army. In this way he brought the project into the realm of practicability. He gained enormously by easing the strain on that part of the undertaking least able to bear it, the maritime part.

Yet he was to pay heavily for it: indeed, to lose his best, if not his only, chance of ultimate success. Neither he nor his advisers, apparently, were seamen enough to realize the difficulty inherent in getting a sea-borne force (especially a sail-driven one) to turn up at exactly the right time and place. More than two centuries later Napoleon was to be guilty of a similar oversight, with similar results. The difficulty lies in co-ordinating two forces, the one land-borne the other sea-borne, so that the latter arrives at the rendezvous exactly when the former is ready for it: not before and not after. In this case Parma had a relatively easy journey to make – only down to the Flemish invasion ports. But Sidonia's task was infinitely harder – to sail over hundreds of miles of water dominated by a vigilant and determined enemy, to sweep that enemy aside so that he could not interfere with the junction and the subsequent ferrying operations, and still to be at the rendezvous on time. It was in fact impossible. The original project, on the other hand, had not suffered from this weakness. If the whole expeditionary force as visualized by Santa Cruz (and commanded by him) had sailed as one unit to the shore of England, perhaps it would not have succeeded, but at least it would have had an infinitely better chance. Its commander could have attempted his landings at his own time, in his own way and, within limits, at the place of his own choosing. He would never have had to dawdle about in waters made dangerous by both nature and the enemy, where no strategic or tactical surprise was open to him; for, as things were, the English could not fail to spot Parma's embarkation ports (and so Sidonia's rendezvous); while Parma's point of entry into England must lie within rowing-distance of his ports of embarkation – i.e. in the southeast corner of England.

The Admiral's Estimate, then, was in the course of the next two years drastically cut down, and drastically changed in form. The nature of that change must be grasped: it is vital to a true understanding of what followed. Here, then, is set down, for straight comparison, the Proposal of March, 1586, alongside the Actuality of May 30th, 1588, when, after birth-throes which all but produced it stillborn (and which did kill its devoted parent), the 'Most Happy' Armada at last cleared the Tagus.

SHIPS

Classes	1586 No.	1586 Tons	1588 No.	1588 Tons
(i) Galleons and Great Ships	150	77,250	65	45,522
(ii) *Urcas* (hulks or store-ships)	40	8,000	25	10,271
(iii) Small ships (*pataches, zabras,* etc.)	320	25,000	32	2,075
(iv) Galleasses (oar-cum-sail)	6	—	4	—
(v) Galleys (oared)	40	—	4	—
TOTAL	556	110,250	130	57,868

MEN

Classes	1586	1588
(i) Sailor	16,612	8,050
(ii) Rower	9,800	2,088
(iii) Soldier	58,920	18,973
(iv) Others (volunteers and non-combatants)	8,890	1,545
TOTAL	94,222	30,656

ARTILLERY

	1586	1588
Guns for ships	1,150	2,431
For land-service	130	—
TOTAL	1,280	2,431

(For a break-up of these into classes, see pp. 77–87)

The food and drink supplied in 1588 look much more manageable on paper. But there are two reasons for this. First, there were less than one-third of the mouths to feed and throats to lubricate. Second, the 1588 fleet was victualled for six months only, not eight. Taking these factors into account, we find the two scales of solid rations so equal that it is not worthwhile to record further details. It is, however, worth noticing that the drink ration was materially revised. The allowance of wine remained proportionately unchanged, but evidently water was now introduced for human consumption. *Pro rata* there was more than twice as much carried in 1588, though the number of beasts to be satisfied was considerably reduced, Parma now providing most of them. Had Philip realized, perhaps, that his men's work was going to be thirstier than he originally thought? Had he, however, concluded that the extra spirit required for it should stem rather from religious zeal than from alcohol?

These comparisons reveal much. First, they show how much less grandiose the reality was than the blue-print. The ships which finally started were, numerically, less than a quarter of those projected, and that without counting the small 'carried' craft, now of course to be furnished by Parma. Only 73, as against 196, could by any stretch of the imagination be called 'front-line'.* The total tonnage was only half its former size, and the human cargo had shrunk to less than a third. Philip's basic change of plan is best exemplified in the relative figures of the soldiers, reduced to less than a third because Parma was now providing the expeditionary force.

Clearly here is a smaller affair: quantitatively much smaller. But, qualitatively, the story is significantly different. In several respects, some of them most important ones, the striking-power of 1588 is much superior to that of 1586. Consider first the galleons and Great Ships. In 1586 the average tonnage of this group was just over 500; in 1588 it was 700, a formidable average for those days (though, as we shall see, not quite so formidable as it looks). Then there are the store-ships, more than doubled in size from 200 to over 400 tons. But the greatest accession of strength in the later fleet was what was omitted from it. The galleys, sinking from 40 to four, had all but disappeared.

* i.e. Classes i, iv and v.

5

THE CHANGING FACE OF WAR AT SEA

THIS FACT REGISTERS a major change in man's conception of how to wage war at sea. The whole art of naval war was just then in the melting-pot, and any account of the Armada Fight which fails to notice the change cannot hope to succeed. Two different revolutions were in progress – in ships, and in weapons.

SHIPS

Hitherto, for many centuries up to – and including – 1571, the year of Lepanto, the fighting navy of Spain, like that of any other Mediterranean power, had consisted practically exclusively of galleys, those time-hallowed warships propelled in battle by heavy oars or sweeps. Such craft had clashed with their rivals in the great inland sea for at least 2,000 years, with Salamis and Aegospotami at one end of their long history and Lepanto at the other. During nearly all that time, moreover, they had been the only warships.

It is no accident that the Latin word for warship is *navis longa* – the long ship, or the galley. Sailing ships existed of course: St Paul had been shipwrecked in one some fifteen centuries before Lepanto. But they were for trade, not war. They were known by various names – 'great' ships, because of their bulk above water; 'tall' ships because of their high masts; 'round' ships to mark their salient difference from the long, low, lean galleys. (It is no accident, either, that the Greek for merchantman is στρογγύλη ναῦς – a literal translation of round ship.) Even in 1586 it was only as it were yesterday that the sailing-ship had come to be considered in Spain as a war-ship at all. What chiefly caused this long-delayed, and still uncompleted, change of view were the activities of the French, Dutch and English corsairs and privateers outside the Mediterranean. For when Spain found that she must deal with them, she soon learnt that her galleys, serviceable enough in the quieter Mediterranean, could not stand up to the long rollers and the fierce sou'-westerlies of the Atlantic. So almost the first of Spain's sailing-ships were the new galleons of the Indian Guard, built in 1581 to protect her trade homeward-bound from the West Indies and the Main; and at almost the same time came her second and greater accession of sailing-warship strength, when, in conquering Portugal, she took possession of the Portuguese Royal Fleet. These were fine galleons, truly ocean-going because Portugal, unlike Spain, was a purely Atlantic power. So, of course, were the new sea powers of the North, even now growing up. Foremost among them was England; and England had never had much use for galleys: in 1588, in fact, she had only one, which she wisely kept out of harm's way in the Thames.

We can now appreciate the shape of the fleet proposed by Santa Cruz in 1586. He was an elderly man, perhaps inevitably a little conservative. He had been brought up in the 'galley' school, and the greatest day of his life had been the one when he manoeuvred his galley-reserve into a winning position at Lepanto. Naturally, then, the main galley fleet of Spain looms large in his blue-print. The 40 galleys and the six galleasses (to be discussed presently) were in fact to be the backbone of the whole effort – a mistake, but a natural one. Though prepared to supplement the Royal Fleet with other units, both he and Philip regarded it as the core of their sea power, just as Elizabeth and the English regarded her Navy Royal as the core of theirs; and, to the Spaniards, the galleys were the core of their official navy.

Between 1586 and 1588, then, something must have happened to make Philip so change his mind that, when his Armada sailed, only four galleys went with it. Something had indeed happened, and it was most revealing, even to Philip who was inclined to be conservative himself. He was, first, warned by several of his most trusted officers that the galleys would make but a poor showing in the English Channel and against English sailing-ships, even if they survived the hazards of the Bay of Biscay on the way. Then, in April 1587, came news which rudely confirmed this advice. Drake, sent out to disrupt the Armada preparations, entered Cadiz harbour – with sailing-ships only, and only two 'Queen's ships' at that. He was attacked by 12 of Philip's royal galleys, in confined waters and under the most favourable galley-conditions imaginable. He punished them with almost insolent ease. The reason is quite clear now: the galley was designed, primarily, to ram other galleys. It had no broadside of guns; it could never fire more than five guns at once, and of these only one was of a size to hurt a ship. The *Elizabeth Bonaventure*, Drake's flagship, was far too massive for a much lighter craft to ram, and she carried at least 35 battery-guns, of which some 28 could be deadly to a galley. Philip is sometimes depicted as an obstinate man who would never learn from his opponents. Nothing could be more unfair. He learnt his lesson at once, and made a revolutionary decision. He would not send his main galley fleet at all.

This was brave. Only consider the shock to his preconceived notions, the upset to his plans. For what Drake had taught him at Cadiz was that, for his assault on England, some four-fifths of his established battle fleet was obsolete! But his new decision was rash. At this point, no doubt, he should have called the whole thing off, and so his more responsible councillors advised him. But he was not that kind of man. He would learn from his foes: he would not listen to his friends. On this point his mind was closed. If his conventional fleet could not go he must organize an unconventional one to replace it. A small fraction of the original navy – the sailing part – would have to be the spearhead of the new effort. This consisted of the 10 effective Portuguese royal galleons. There were also, it is true, 10 galleons of the Indian Guard, and four Great Ships of the *Flota* of New Spain: but their duties of protecting the Plate fleets and the Atlantic Trade were so obviously important that, up till now, he had not meant to use them against England. But now he did so, combining them into a Castilian Squadron, 14 strong, which he allotted to Diego Florez de Valdez. But even this supreme risk only gave him (with the Portuguese contingent) 24 sailing *war*ships (i.e. ships built exclusively for fighting), and this was obviously not nearly enough. Then and there he set about collecting as many and as large merchantmen as he could find, converting them, as well as he could in the time available, into fighting ships. The list on p. 65 shows the measure of his success. He assembled 65 galleons and Great Ships, of which 24 were his own hard-core warships (the galleons), and 41 the improvisations – big merchant *naos* and *naves* which, for our purposes, we may regard as synonymous terms and collect under the heading of 'Great Ships'. All these were in fact temporary warships, with lofty castles in bow and stern and suitable artillery. He had hitherto intended to send some ships of this kind, but as auxiliaries to reinforce his regular fleet. Now, however, they were to play the much more important part of front-line ships; even of flagships, for he was wise enough to keep the galleons together in his two crack squadrons of Portugal and Castile. To these he added four Neapolitan galleasses and four galleys (but Portuguese ones, not Spanish at all), making, altogether, 73 fighting units. In one way his decision was justified before the Armada reached the Channel, because the galleys failed to get there. One of the Great Ships failed too. The remainder, which make the full tally of the 125 ships that arrived, were 32 light craft of the oar-cum-sail type, each carrying a few small guns, and the 25 *urcas* or hulks, non-effective store-ships. So in fact the fighting strength of the Armada which fought the battles was 68: 24 royal, 40 auxiliary and the four Neapolitan galleasses.

This last-named category must next engage our attention: for they represent an important stage in the ship revolution then in progress. The Spaniards were not completely surprised by the galley's poor showing at Cadiz. They knew they had potential weaknesses as well as great strengths: and that the Great Ships, so favoured by their enemies, had strengths as well as weaknesses. Already, in fact, they were seeking a compromise between galley and galleon, and, in 1588, the galleass was the point in that compromise reached by Spain, though not by England.

The basic problem, common to both Spaniards and English, was this: the Long Ship's great advantage lay in its oar-conferred mobility. It was the only known type which had 'free movement', the power to proceed in any direction its owner liked. It was highly manoeuvrable, therefore, and an excellent tactical weapon in battle against its own kind. Until recently, too, it had possessed another advantage over the sailing-ship. In its heavy iron-shod ram it had possessed the only known weapon that could sink an enemy ship. By contrast, the Great, Tall or Round Ship was elephantine. Its course was at the mercy of the wind. It was a poor mover and a clumsy manoeuvrer. Often it could not reach its enemy, and even when it did, could not hurt him much, though of course its crew could hurt his. Yet, it had always possessed potentialities denied to the Long Ship. It was much more heavily built, deeper in draught, higher of free-board. It had to be, to withstand the stress set up by masts and sails, whereas the Long Ship had to be light enough to be pulled by oars; which, in their turn, had to be worked from near water level for obvious mechanical reasons. These things gave the Round Ship two advantages, both strategical – seaworthiness and sea endurance. It could stay out in weather which sent the galley scuttling for port, because of its strength and high freeboard; and its great belly contained holds and storage spaces such as the long, lean, shallow galley could not emulate. It could therefore remain at sea much longer. It was, of course, for such reasons that the Spaniards had kept both types of ship, using each for the purpose for which it seemed best suited – the Long Ship for war, the Round Ship for trade.

It was the English, however, who upset this conventional division of labour. They had never favoured the Long Ship, mainly because its frail build was ill-suited to the 'ocean' conditions prevailing around their island. They had always confined themselves to the Round Ship, for both peace and war, and so, having discovered, quite early, its limitations as a warship, had been the first to try and remedy them. By Elizabeth's time they had succeeded, in several different ways. First, they had improved its sailing capacity, by lengthening it, so making it less 'round'; by giving it a larger and better sail-plan; and, primarily by the introduction of the bow-line, enabling it to sail a good deal nearer to the wind. It still had nothing like free movement – the sailing-ship never had (nor has) that – but its movement was becoming much freer than before.

Their second great innovation was to give it a weapon that could sink other ships: not the ram, which was useless in so heavy and unwieldy a vessel, but the heavy gun, introduced into his ships by Elizabeth's father, Henry VIII. He it was, also, who first packed his great guns into the hulls of his ships, so spacing them that they fired along the ship's length and at right angles to the line of her advance. In short, he invented the broadside, a feature which the galley could never possess, since its sides were always bespoken for the oars. This was the turning-point in the strife of oar versus sail. Till then their respective merits had been nicely balanced. But, now that the great gun had proved itself capable of dealing out destruction to all rivals, the pendulum inevitably swung towards its carrier, the large sailing-ship. The fight at Cadiz in 1587 greatly accelerated the swing. Even a dozen galleys, each armed with but one battery gun, could make no sort of headway against a single broadside of at least 16 guns fired simultaneously. By Armada year, in fact, the English were pinning all their faith on their two inventions, which now amounted to a new form of sea warfare altogether: broadsides of potentially ship-killing guns mounted in much-improved sailing-ships. For such advantages, of course, some price had been exacted: and that was free movement. None but the very smallest of our ships was oar-propelled.

The coming of the great gun posed the same problem to the Spaniards. But, with their different past, they favoured a different solution. The free movement of galley warfare was dear to them. Its technique was so cut-and-dried, hallowed by centuries of experience. They were experts in it, and naturally tended to cling to it. Moreover they disliked the gun, and the kind of warfare it engendered. Indeed the aristocratic military caste professed to despise it. It was, they said, 'an ignoble arm'. So, and for precisely similar reasons, the French knights, some centuries earlier, had inveighed against the

English longbow. Both longbow and gun hurt the pride of the privileged, by allowing base blood to humble blue blood from afar, well outside the range of 'noble' weapons like lance or mace or gleaming blade. Yet those responsible for Spanish policy were not so purblind as to veto the gun, ungentlemanly as it was. Instead, like the English, they introduced it into their ships, but not nearly so enthusiastically, nor to the exclusion of free movement.

The galleass represented the stage reached in their compromise by Armada-time. It was half galley, half Great Ship, and it would, they hoped, combine the advantages of both. It was more heavily built, deeper in draught and, in proportion to its length, wider than a galley; therefore it could carry more and bigger guns and more stores. But it was not so heavy, so deep or so wide as a Great Ship. It more than made up for this, however (or so they hoped), by having dual propulsion, oar and sail. Its main armament, a heavy one, was a broadside mounted on a full gundeck extending over the heads of the rowers who (for mechanical reasons) still had to pull their great sweeps from a position as near sea-level as possible. Indeed, in its tactical and strategic aspects, the Armada fight was a trial of rival systems, with all interested in sea warfare for audience. How would the Spanish compromise, which sought to retain both hitting-power and free movement, fare against the latest English models, which had sacrificed free movement altogether, in exchange for better sailing? Wise after the event, we know the answer. The galleass was a failure, though not a disgraceful one. It was a poor sea boat, at least in extra-Mediterranean waters. Its sailing was indifferent (as probably even the Spaniards expected); yet it was too cumbersome to give it the full free movement of the galley. In squally weather, too, it was found that the heavy guns, placed so high above the waterline, put the vessel's centre of gravity too high and made it dangerously crank. We shall see Philip's four galleasses trying very hard to vindicate themselves, but only floundering about and getting nowhere. This is all too often the lot of those who seek the best of two worlds: they find that they have achieved the worst of both.

On the other hand, the English experiment was much more successful, and, though no one recognized it then, much more revolutionary. For the future lay with sail, whose empire was now beginning, to last unchallenged until dethroned by steam. The experiment changed the whole face of war too, and that at once. The ship itself was taking on a new role in naval warfare. We have seen (p. 24) how, under the careful eye of Hawkins, the *Revenges* began to appear: ships which were no longer mere floating castles, mere platforms for artillery, but weapons in their own right, swift, flexible and deadly. Indeed, the battle was to prove that we were now one good lap ahead of Spain. Our older, bigger (and pre-Hawkins) ships were still all too like immobile fortresses, but even they were more mobile than the best sailing-ship Spain could offer. Even her galleasses, her last word in mobility, were no better than our second-best, if as good. To say that our best could make circles round any ship in the Armada would be not only metaphorically but also literally true.

The English fleet, in its origins and general composition, was essentially of the same pattern as that of Spain, though, of course, it had this advantage – its hard core did not have to be sacrificed at the eleventh hour. First and last, 197 ship-names appear in surviving lists; but, as with the enemy, their fighting values varied from much to nothing at all. A number of them, even, had assembled and dispersed before the Armada appeared; others (like the Spanish *urcas*, though neither so numerous nor so large) were merely store-ships. But, again as with Spain, the nucleus was the Sovereign's Navy Royal. This contained 34 ships (one of them the galley in the Thames), about one-sixth, that is, of the total array. But, still like their rivals, they were not all big ships: only 21 of them could lay any real claim to being first-line, and even these varied enormously in tonnage and hitting-power. Large or small, however, this little force was essentially the opposite number of the Portuguese and Castilian squadrons, the first-line strength of Spain. These, we recall, consisted of 20 galleons and four large ships from New Spain. So, numerically, these hard-cores were strangely equal. But England had nothing to set against the galleasses.

What now about the relative size of the rival's royal ships? A surprise may be in store for those brought up on the nineteenth-century view of the great fight. Imprinted on their minds, perhaps, is Tennyson's awe-inspiring picture of 'huge sea-castles heaving upon the weather bow'; and they still see

... the great San Philip *that, of fifteen hundred tons*
And upshadowing high above us with her yawning tiers of guns,
Took the breath from our sails, and we stayed.

This, it is true, was not in 1588; but it was only three years later. It was also an exceptional case. The *San Felipe* of the famous Last Fight was the biggest of Philip's 'Twelve Apostles', all post-Armada ships; and she *was* of 1,500 tons – Spanish measure. The *Revenge*, on the other hand, was what contemporary Englishmen called 'of the middling sort', and displaced at most 500 tons (English), perhaps less. But where relative size is concerned, two factors must be remembered. First, the Spanish ships *looked* big, the English relatively small. The Spaniards had (as Sir Walter Raleigh puts it) more 'majesty'. They stood much higher out of the water, since they retained the high forecastles now discarded by the English. But this retention was a weakness. They were the worse sailers for it, much less amenable to the helm than their English rivals which were 'all built very low at the head, but very high at the stern', thereby greatly increasing their seaworthiness. Second, the rivals' methods of tonnage-measurement were markedly different. The Spanish calculation gave considerably higher figures than ours; perhaps 25 per cent, or even more. This is revealed whenever any straight comparison is possible. For example, the Spanish *San Salvador* was registered in Spain as a ship of 953 tons, but when we captured her and measured her ourselves, we made her a 600-ton ship.

Distasteful though it is, then, to have to discard well-loved traditions, this venerable one of Spanish Goliaths and English Davids must go, insofar as it concerns royal ships. Even were Spanish and English tons equal, Spain had no advantage here. According to the official figures, the greatest warship in either fleet was Frobisher's *Triumph*, of 1,100 tons (English). The next was the *San Juan*, Almirante (Vice-Admiral) of the Portuguese squadron, of 1,050 (Spanish), followed by the *White Bear*, 1,000 (English) and Sidonia's flagship, the *San Martin*, also of 1,000 tons (but Spanish). Of the next dozen, six are English and six Spanish. This means equality – if the relative tons were equal. But as they were not, the conclusion must be that Elizabeth's royal ships were appreciably larger than were Philip's.

The rest of the front-line English fleet was, again like Spain's, composed of auxiliaries – temporarily warships, normally merchantmen, and privately owned. Here the old traditions are much sounder. The Spanish advantage in auxiliary tonnage was real enough, if not very important. Some of these ships were very large – five over the 1,000-ton mark, of which four were larger than any Spanish warship. The biggest of all, possibly as big as the *Triumph*, was *La Ragazona*, *capitana* of Bertendona's Levant Squadron. Howard had nothing like these. His heaviest auxiliaries were the Earl of Leicester's *Galleon Leicester* and the Levant Company's *Merchant Royal*, both 400-tonners, but both, though built primarily for trade, also fitted out for private war as well, and little inferior to royal ships of a similar tonnage. These were followed by four 300-tonners, Sir Walter Raleigh's *Roebuck*, the chief London ship, the *Hercules*, a West Country volunteer called the *Sampson* and another Levanter, the *Edward Bonaventure*. (This last was a most historic ship: it was her voyage to India, in 1591–3, which led directly to the foundation of the East India Company.) Next came five of 250 tons and 23 of 200 or thereabouts. Add to these those royal ships which were not quite formidable enough to count with the 21 front-line ones – some half dozen – and we have a group of about 40 sail capable of real hard hitting. These are the counterparts of the 40 Spanish auxiliaries already discussed, and, though they did not bear the brunt, must like them be regarded as essentially fighting ships. So, once again, numbers seem very equal. The enemy no doubt had here some considerable advantage in size, but in nothing else, for ours surpassed them in enterprise, superior skill with both sail and gun, and in their far higher mobility. On neither side is it easy to compute exact numbers since, in both fleets, there are several borderline cases which might or might not be counted as effectives. This much, however, can be safely asserted: each fleet had something between 60 and 70 fighting units, each with an *élite* of rather over a score.

The hulks deserve a word. The Spanish *urcas* both looked, and were, much larger ships than ours (most of whom, indeed, did not sail with the fleet at all). This was only natural. The Spaniards, journeying beyond reach of replenishments from home, had to carry enough stores to last the full six months: we, fighting as it were at our larder door, were not bound to take any such precautions.

In both numbers and sizes, then, the combatants were very equal: but the English had a very marked advantage in the quality, and especially the sailing quality, of their fleet. We have now to examine the power of their respective armaments.

GUNS

The coming of the ship's gun, as we have seen, was the prime cause of the revolution then in progress. The English had decided that it was the battle winner of the future, and were therefore filling their ships with artillery. The Spaniards, here too, were a good lap behind. They had not gone so far as to ignore the ignoble thing altogether. But they still clung to their old view that it was not the only, not even the principal battle winner, which was, still, the successful clash of man with man in close fight. Thus their great aim was still to lay the enemy ship aboard, grapple her and enter her with their men-at-arms, fighting it out on the enemy's deck as though the combatants were on the plains of Flanders or the beaches of Kent. The key-man was still the soldier; and that, of course is why, in both 1586 and 1588, the *tercios* of the invincible Spanish infantry so heavily outnumbered the mere seamen.

Yet, a comparison of the guns proposed for 1586 with those actually carried in 1588, shows that, once again, Spain had had second thoughts. For here – and, in all the figures, here only

– the actuality considerably exceeds the proposal; and this in spite of the fact that the number of ships to carry the guns has been so drastically reduced. At almost the eleventh hour there had evidently been a major reappraisal in Spanish planning: once more Philip was deigning to learn from the enemy.

The artillery of the 1586 proposal is weak in both quantity and size. There were a mere 1,150 guns for 556 ships. Though naturally they were not to be spaced evenly throughout the fleet, this gives an average in each ship of only two. Further, they were almost all small (by English 'ship-killing' standards very small) and many of them, again by English standards, obsolete and inefficient types. No details will be given here since, after all, these are only proposals which did not materialize. But it is incontrovertible that the armament of 1586 was too sparse, too poor and too light-shotted to hurt the hulls of the enemy at all. They could still, however, hurt his men, especially at close range, damage his masts and yards, and so slow him up: and that, really, was all that they were for.

Very different is the scale of 1588. The guns, in sheer numbers, are more than doubled, the ships to carry them are cut down to less than a quarter. Now the average per ship will be not two but nearly 19, while the best-gunned ships might carry as many as 40, and, thus armed, be quite comparable with the best English ships. The question of the size of these pieces is even more important, but this we will leave for a little, until we have seen what caused this new revolution.

There was first the experience of Cadiz in 1587. The weight and rapidity of Drake's fire were eye-openers to the Spaniards who witnessed them. They reported, one and all, to the Escorial, and many of the King's most trusted advisers joined the chorus, urging him not to launch his fleet against a power which owned many *Elizabeth Bonaventures*; it would, they said, be merely suicidal. Foremost among those who counselled prudence was Alonso de Leyva, whom Philip loved, and even occasionally listened to. But a more important advocate was Pedro de Valdez, one to whom most people listened, and who never minced words. There followed a stream of 'advices out of England', the reports of Philip's innumerable spies who communicated with him through Mendoza, now ensconced at the Paris Embassy. All sang the same tune: the English would make the whole affair a gun-duel if they could. Everyone in London knew it; there was no attempt at concealment. Philip was quickly convinced. Instantly he issued orders for guns to be collected – begged, borrowed, stolen, bought. But guns just then, especially the bigger ones, were hard to come by; and for all his efforts he did not acquire as many as he wanted. But he certainly tried, competing sometimes in the most unlikely markets. One of them, surprisingly enough, was England. The English guns, especially their larger long-range ones, were reputed the best in the world; and, by various tortuous channels, Philip acquired some (exactly how many is not known) through middlemen in Holland and traitors in England.

It was not, however, the comparatively light-shotted, long-range pieces that he coveted. He felt bound to take out insurance against the new English methods of fighting by gunfire only; but, as a Spaniard, he still believed in his innermost heart that the winning trick was to be won on the enemy's deck. So he did not diminish his army by a single man, nor alter his proportions of soldiers to sailors. But he did try, with no little success, to raise the numbers of his heavy battering pieces, which, he hoped, would smash the swift-sailing enemy ships to a standstill. Then, but only then, his troops could board and enter at will – and, by corollary, win. For the English had no troops to oppose them. His instructions to his new C.-in-C. reveal the extent of his conversion. They should fill us with admiration, for they contain a prophecy, penned two months before the Armada sailed, stating exactly how the English meant to fight. It was almost entirely right.

It must be borne in mind that the enemy's object will be to fight at long distance, in consequence of his advantage in artillery. . . . The aim of our men, on the contrary, must be to bring him to close quarters and grapple with him. For your information a statement is sent to you describing the way in which the enemy employs his artillery, in order to deliver his fire low, and sink his opponent's ships.

So we see postulated thus early, and by an enemy, the relative fire-policies of the English on the one hand and, on the other, of almost all their opponents of the next two and a half centuries; gun tactics which endured, with but few exceptions, as long as the sailing warship itself. 'Fire on the upward roll,' said the Spaniards and the French. 'Destroy sails, masts, yards, and therefore motive-power. Leave the enemy wallowing on the sea, and at your mercy.' 'Fire on the downward roll,' said the British, 'right into their hulls. Sink them if you can: but if you cannot (for wooden ships take a deal of sinking) at least set the splinters flying; smash their men, and so induce them to surrender.'

The Spaniards tried to take their King's advice and failed. The English tried to do what Philip said they would try, and, in this their first attempt, also largely failed. Why? That question we can only answer when we have completed our study of the fighting. But meanwhile we can take a first step towards it by trying to discover what sort of guns each side had. So far, we have found that England intended to rely upon guns to the exclusion of every other weapon, while Spain meant to use them to neutralize her enemy's superiority in sailing, and to immobilize his ships so that they could not avoid being boarded. How did they set about it?

First the Spaniards. What they wanted was heavy battering pieces, a very few hits from which would so shake the English that they could not escape. The sea-specimens of this class were known (to use the English names) as cannons and demi-cannons, and they fired heavy roundshot weighing anything from 60 to 30 pounds; but, being only of medium length of bore, they did not project them particularly far. There was also another type of battering piece called the cannon-perier or pedrero, a short gun throwing a shot of some 24 pounds (in the older models made of stone) to an even shorter distance. At its own range it was indeed very effective, its 'shaking' force being immense. But it was rather old-fashioned, using only a small charge of powder: and (in England though not in Spain) it was on its way out because its range was so limited. These two classes of gun – the 'cannon-type' (can-

non and demi-cannon) and the 'perier-type' (cannon perier) –
constituted the heavy or 'battering' ship-armament of the day.

It was long believed – by English writers too – that the
Armada was, to the last, very badly off for guns, especially
large ones. Even Sir John Laughton, the first Englishman to
study Naval History scientifically, could declare that 'as a
rule they [the Spanish guns] were small four-, six- or nine-
pounders: they were comparatively few, and they were badly
worked.' His last point is probably true – the things were so
ignoble that the knightly Spanish leaders seldom insisted upon
their gunners practising and becoming efficient. But the rest
of the dictum has seriously misled subsequent historians, giving an utterly erroneous impression of the Armada's gun-
power. It is based, probably, upon a confusion between the
1586 Proposal and the 1588 Actuality. The former states the
total number of guns proposed, and breaks them up into
classes. The only figure known for 1588 is the grand total of
2,431: no details survive. Laughton, it would seem, unable to
find any, assumed, quite wrongly, that there had been no
change in Spanish gun-policy between 1586 and 1588. His
verdict is, therefore, based solely on the Proposal and, as such,
it is probably fair enough. But as evidence of what the Armada
carried in 1588 it is quite useless.

It is, however, the break-up into 'weight-of-shot-fired' (and
as we shall soon see, into 'range') that is far more profitable
than a mere count of numbers. The smaller guns were very
numerous (on both sides, and not, as Laughton infers, in the
Spanish fleet only): but in the battles as they came to be
fought – at the range of our choosing – they played no serious
part whatever, and may be virtually ignored. Only the heavy
pieces, on both sides, counted at all. Here, a close study * leads
to a conclusion radically different from Laughton's. The
Armada guns which are worth counting far exceeded those
proposed for 1586, in both numbers and power, while, at the
heaviest end, they actually exceeded those of the English fleet,

* This study the author undertook many years ago. His findings
appeared, in eight numbers, in the *Mariner's Mirror*, January 1942
to October 1943, Vols. XXVIII–XXIX. (See Preface.)

overwhelmingly too. The principal figures are given below (p. 83), where it will be observed that the Spaniards carried some three times as many cannon-types as the English, and nearly eight times as many perier-types. Moreover, and for good measure, the English cannon-types were – all but one, and that a doubtful one – demi-cannons, the smallest pieces of the class: but of the Spanish cannon-types probably over half were full cannons, far the heaviest-shotted guns afloat.

So far, however, we have looked at one factor only – weight. This is important, but it is not everything. In all eras of naval warfare there is another factor more important still: and that is range. Of what avail the biggest gun ever constructed, loaded with the heaviest and deadliest projectile ever invented, if its missile falls short? The veriest popgun, if it will reach, will be more effective. But here, we must consider weight and range concurrently.

In those days, with few exceptions, the longer the gun the longer was the range. But, in those relatively small ships, there was a limit to the workable length of a gun. Thus, though it was possible to construct a really long land-gun to fire a really heavy shot, this was impracticable at sea, and especially upon a broadside. The longest (and therefore longest-ranged) gun that the English could manage on shipboard was the 14-foot whole-culverin, with a bore of only $5\frac{1}{4}$ inches and a roundshot of only about 17 pounds. This means that its length was about 32 times its bore, so that, to produce a gun of similar proportions with a $7\frac{1}{4}$-inch bore (and so a 50 shot), one would have to make it nearly 20 feet long; impossible in any contemporary ship. One could, then, concentrate upon heavy shot or long range, but not both; and what was happening, roughly, was that the Spaniards were going for weight, and the English for range. We had long since decided that that would pay us best, partly because we thought that, with our better sailing-ships, we could dictate the range, and so might, with luck, fight our battle within our range but outside the enemy's; partly because, being without an army, we must at all costs keep our distance, not only from his grappling-hooks but also from his battering pieces, which might easily rob us of our mobility.

But, as usual, there was a price to pay for our advantages; and that was the lightness of our shot compared with his. No excuse need be offered for thus emphasizing these concurrent factors of weight and range. They are the key to the whole Armada fight, without which no pattern whatever can be discerned in most of it.

THE GUNS IN THE RIVAL FLEETS IN THE ARMADA CAMPAIGN

(including 4-pounders but not smaller ones)

	Weight of shot fired	Spanish	Types	English
Gun-carrying ships		124		172
Guns per ship (average)		9		11·5
Full cannons ⎫ (medium-	50	say 90 ⎫	Cannon-types ⎫	1
Demi-cannons ⎬ range)	32	say 73 ⎬	Span. 163; ⎬	54
			Eng. 55	
Cannon-periers (short-range)	24	326 ⎰	Perier-types ⎫ Span. 326; ⎬ Eng. 43	43
Full culverins ⎫	17	165 ⎫	Culverin-types ⎫	153
Demi-culverins ⎬ (long-	9	137 ⎬	Span. 635; ⎬	344
Sakers ⎰ range)	5	144 ⎬	Eng. 1874 ⎬	662
Minions ⎭	4	189 ⎭		715
Total (over 4-pounders)		1,124		1,972
	Cannon-type	14·5%		2·8%
Percentage ⎨ Perier-type		29·0%		2·2%
	Culverin-type	56·5%		95·0%
Total weight of shot thrown	(lb.)	19,369	(lb.)	14,677
Av. weight of shot per ship	,,	156	,,	85
Av. weight of shot per gun	,,	17·2	,,	7·4

There were at least seven culverin-types recognized in England, all long, graceful pieces belonging to one family in build and proportion. The whole-culverin came first, then the demi-culverin, roughly a 9-pounder, weighing some 2,900 pounds as against the culverin's 4,000 pounds: then the saker, a 5-pounder of about 1,800 pounds; the minion, a 4-pounder of 1,000 pounds; the falcon (2¾-pounder of 900 pounds); the falconet, a 1¼-pounder of 400 pounds, and the minute robinet, a 1-pounder of 300.

The figures in the table above go down only to the minion, for reasons already given. Also, we can see what all these guns

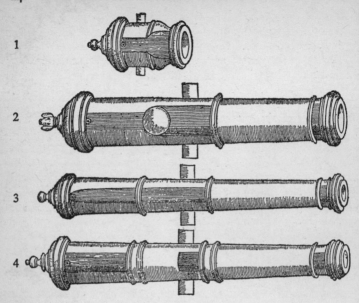

ELIZABETHAN GUNS
Cyprian Lucar's illustration, 1588 (no attempt at scale)

1. *Mortar*   2. *Cannon Perier*   3. *Bell-bore Cannon*   4. *Cannon*

looked like. The left-hand illustration is a contemporary
drawing, showing general form and shape, but little more, as
there is no attempt at proportion; and indeed the most important type, the culverin-type, is missing. On the right is a
modern reconstruction, drawn to scale from contemporary
specifications, which includes a whole-culverin. (The squat
mortar, shown in both, hardly concerns us. It was a very short-
range man-killer firing anything from roundshot to rusty nails;
and we took good care to see that it never came into its own.)

Not forgetting the Spaniards' great advantage in heavy-
shotted pieces of short and medium range, we can turn to the
relative strengths in culverin-types. What a contrast! But, even
here, the contrast does not begin with the heaviest guns of the
class. It would seem that in whole-culverins, and here alone,

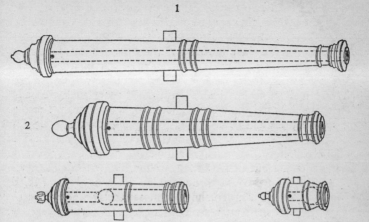

ELIZABETHAN GUNS
Modern scale-drawing, from dimensions in Lucar's text
1. *Culverin*   2. *Cannon*   3. *Cannon Perier*   4. *Mortar*

there was something like parity. We are now about in the middle of the weight-range. The Spaniards, hankering after weight, work down as far as this and then tail off sadly: but we, tending to concentrate at the light end (because it was also the long-range end) work up as far as culverins: which in fact only the larger and beamier ships could conveniently house. There is also some evidence that Philip's last-minute drive for guns was directed at acquiring as many whole-culverins as possible – especially English ones, widely regarded in 1588 as the best pieces in the world. As soon, however, as we look below the 17-pounders, the discrepancy becomes most marked. We had two and a half times as many demi-culverins as the enemy, four and a half times as many sakers and not far off four times as many minions.

The evidence available precludes arithmetical accuracy, and no claim for such is made here. In places there may be quite wide errors, especially on the Spanish side where the evidence

is scarce. But two things can be claimed. The Spanish estimates are, throughout, minimum figures: almost certainly they
should be somewhat larger. Second, whatever the errors,
they are quite insufficient to alter the wide conclusions
drawn from them here. Thus, though the Spaniards may not
have had just three times as many cannon-types as we had,
it is certain that they had a great many more than we had –
perhaps only twice as many though, more likely, four times as
many.

Clearly these figures bear out our preceding remarks. The
Spaniards have the advantage in weight, the English in range.
The total weight of iron that our foe could throw at us exceeded what we could throw at him, by, roughly, one-third.
The size of his average shot is almost exactly whole-culverin
size: ours is halfway between demi-culverin and saker size.
His average ship had a broadside nearly twice as heavy as ours,
though it carried rather fewer 4-pounds-and-upwards pieces.
On the other hand, we had nearly three times as many long-
range guns. In fact – and this is most striking proof of how we
had gone all out for length – no less than 19 out of every 20 of
our guns were long-range culverin-types.

No attempt is made here to enumerate or classify the smaller
guns. It would be neither worthwhile nor possible. We know
that rather over half the 2,431 Spanish pieces were under 4-
pounders – 54 per cent of them – but the corresponding English figure is quite unknown; indeed unknowable, because in
all probability no one ever attempted to tot up the privately
owned guns. One thing, however, seems certain: the English
percentage would be higher than the Spaniard's 54. Many of
our small ships carried nothing heavier than a falcon; many
more carried only the odd minion; while all, even the largest,
carried small culverin-types in considerable numbers. So, here
too, we see the wrongness of Laughton's implication – that the
Spanish artillery was lighter than ours. It was far heavier,
though shorter in range and smaller in number. Indeed, his
unfortunate dictum would have been more fortunate had he
been describing the guns of the *other* side. 'Four-, six- and
nine-pounders', wildly inapposite to the average shot of 17·2

pounds, becomes strangely apposite to the modest English average of 7·4!

To sum up, then. The Spaniards had provided themselves with an army to board, enter and capture our ships. But they knew how well those ships sailed, and they knew (had not their own King told them?) that they would not stand to be boarded. So they decided to bring the wherewithal to make them stand – heavy-shotted (if short-range) artillery to smash their motive power. The English, as Philip had rightly guessed, had no intention of standing, but proposed to use their great assets of sailing-power and ship-handling to keep their distance from both Spanish men-at-arms and Spanish battering-pieces. They had therefore provided themselves with long-range (if light-shotted) culverin-types to the exclusion, almost, of every other weapon.

6

THE PEOPLE

WE HAVE NOW examined the rivals' directors, planners and fighting leaders; their policies, hopes and fears; their ships and their weapons. There remains only that most important group of all – The Common People: the rank and file who, throughout man's history, are the ones who win – or lose – the battle.

Here are some basic figures for analysis. Again no mathematical accuracy can be expected from so unstatistical an age. All lists, on both sides, vary considerably. This was partly due, on our side especially, to the difficulties of the medieval pseudo-Roman notation still employed by many authorities (including the great Burghley himself). But also, in both fleets, there was a constant wastage, weekly, even daily, from desertion, disease or death. Who can say now how many people survived, even a fortnight after any particular count was taken? We can do our best to assess numbers, but for all our efforts, every figure is only an approximation.

THE PEOPLE IN THE FIGHT

	Soldiers	Sailors	Rowers	Others	Total
Spanish	18,973	8,050	2,088	1,545	30,656
English	1,540	14,385	—	—	15,925

The English figures, it will be observed, are arranged very simply under only two headings, and probably represent very closely our true manpower, because they are based on payrolls and victualling lists. Let us examine first those categories in which, apparently, we had no representatives.

The rowers (*personas de remo*) need not detain us. They were certainly not soldiers, and, as persons without civil rights – slaves, convicts or even (we alleged) some English prisoners – too subhuman to be regarded as sailors. We had none of this class. If, in a small ship, a man was called upon to pull an oar, he would certainly be a free sailor, and counted as such in the above table. Incidentally, 888 of the Spanish rowers, though they started, did not arrive, being the wretches who drove the four galleys.

The other group absent from the English list is that labelled 'others', and it is worthy of study in its own right. It is composed of four very different elements: (a) volunteers, (b) servants, (c) artillerists and (d) non-combatants.

(a) The volunteers are of two kinds: gentlemen adventurers and unattached officers. Both were essentially officer-types, the first very blue-blooded indeed. There were 122 of this superior group, and just half of them were noblemen, headed by a Prince of the Blood (Philip's own natural son, Ascoli), a Duke, two Marquesses and a Count. They were all, as their title implies, adventuring their lives, unpaid, in the cause partly of religion (had not their King and the Holy Father given the expedition the aura of a Crusade?), partly of honour, that compelling offspring of Castilian pride. But many of them, as well, had a more prosaic motive: they had ventured money in the enterprise – much worth having would be in the King's gift in a conquered England. The other volunteers, 219 in number, were there for much the same reasons, but were paid salaries. This was doubtless necessary; for, though still gentle, they were rather humbler members of Spanish society. They were attached to no specific fighting unit, but were intended, and anxious, to fight when the chance came; and indeed, once let loose on the English countryside, they could have set us an awkward problem.

Figuring among both sorts of volunteer is a sorry little band – traitors, English and Irish. There are at least four Englishmen among the adventurers, perhaps more, for their names are all spaniardized. But two are labelled *inglés* – Rafael Asal and Guillermo Brun (in happier days William Brown). Other suspicious ones are Jusepe Justen (Joseph Justin?), Juan Cler (John Clerk?) and Pedro Dere (Peter Dare?). Among the unattached officers there are no less than 19, including five knights, three with Irish names; but some of this group were certainly English. Traitor is a strong word, perhaps too harsh a one. These men, as a class, were quite unlike the English spies, whom it is difficult to exonerate. Their choice of sides had depended mostly upon the strength of their religious convictions for which they must have been prepared, at the very least, for exile. While not crowning them with glory, we should not forget that of such stuff, under other circumstances, heroes and martyrs are made.

(b) All these volunteers, being noble or gentle, were of right entitled to servants, each according to his quality. Thus Prince Ascoli had 39, Alonso de Leyva (who travelled in this capacity) 36, and so on down to people who were positively expected to make do with one. Between them they had 628 servants. Most of these would be real menials, but many of those attending personages like Ascoli and de Leyva were scions of the highest families. None of them, however, can be labelled soldier or sailor. Fifty more served the gentlemen of the Duke's household, themselves 23 strong, while another 50 attended the Inspector General and his staff. This brings the tally of servants up to 728 (not counting the servants of 'attached' – i.e. ordinary – officers, who came from the army ranks): rather unnecessary top-hamper, we may think, in terms of combatant value, but an aristocratic society has to face such disabilities.

(c) The artillery comes next, segregated from soldiers and sailors alike: evidently a self-contained unit, hedged within a sort of *cordon sanitaire* lest its ignobility should prove contagious. It included, in addition to its officers (not a Don among them!), its own physicians, surgeon, apothecary, carpenters and blacksmiths, muleteers, officers' servants and 95 gunners – 148 souls in all. Indeed, most of them were not even Spaniards. It needed an intelligent fellow to be a good gunner, and intelligent Spaniards were all too apt to ape their social betters, and to despise gunnery as an ignoble art. Thus many, if not most, of the 'Spanish' gunners were Flemings or Germans.

(d) Last come the true non-combatants. First, the hospital staff. A solitary Don commands it, and it includes five physicians, five surgeons and four priests. These latter are not the friars, who come next in the list, 180 of them; then the Inspector General, and his staff of 20, the pursers and paymasters; and last, 19 Officers of Justice.

On the English side no 'others' appear. Hangers-on were certainly not encouraged. Yet there were certainly a few 'others': there were some volunteers, for instance. Only 13 are named in the lists; but there must have been more, and they would certainly be allowed servants. There was this difference, however: in common with all other officers' servants, they would have their quarter-stations, and in action would be serving, not their masters but their guns or sails. They are already included, therefore, in the first two columns of our table. So are all the people who, in English ships, worked the guns. Unlike the artificially segregated Spanish artillery, they were fully woven into the pattern of the ship's company. There were, however, the counterparts of (d) above – the true service non-combatants – and it would seem that they are listed under neither soldier nor sailor; but, no lists survive. All we can say for certain is that there were pursers in most of the royal ships and some of the others, in reasonable but not excessive numbers. There were also a few ministers of religion, but probably very few; and a few surgeons, but not nearly so many as there should have been, badly supplied with drugs and instruments, and not noted for their skill either. In fine, it would not be surprising to find that real non-combatants did not greatly exceed the number of ships in the English fleet.

We can now turn to the principal categories common to both fleets.

SOLDIERS

Spanish

The Spanish Army, which provided nearly two-thirds of the Armada's manpower, was a body of professional soldiers, reputed the best in the world, especially in infantry. In the century now growing old, it boasted, it had never lost a pitched battle, and its morale and discipline were consequently very high. Its rank and file, probably, had few inhibitions or doubts about the task now allotted to them; and, if they had, they would be given no opportunity to express them. They were grouped, in the normal Spanish way, in five heavy infantry *tercios* or brigades, each commanded by a *maestro de campo* or colonel. There were also 32 companies of light troops, each of rather over 100 men. The *tercio* commanders were among the best in the Army, and several of them, notably Don Diego Pimentel, Don Francisco de Toledo and Don Alonso de Luzon, played stirring parts in the drama, especially when it was fading into tragedy. The Major General commanding the whole was Don Francisco de Bobadilla. All four of these distinguished soldiers had a rough passage. Two, Pimentel and de Luzon, were taken prisoner; the other two were luckier – a little. Toledo's ship was cast away on the Flemish banks, but he swam for it and escaped; Bobadilla's ship was wrecked off Ireland and most of his people lost. But he had been called to the flagship to bolster the Duke's morale. In addition to these front-line Spanish troops, there was a contingent of 2,000 Portuguese soldiers.

The *tercios* had no opportunity of displaying their prowess on their own element, but this is not to say that they spent their time afloat in idleness. Though the fact is nowhere definitely stated, some at least must have been set to help the seamen, who were in lamentably short supply. The 8,000 mariners could not, by themselves, have worked 43,400 tons of shipping* – that would mean 5·4 tons to each man. (The English ships had a man to every 2·2 tons, and there is nowhere any evidence that they were overmanned.) Those *soldados*, however, were stout fellows, mostly country-born and accustomed to march far in heavy equipment and carrying heavy pikes. Though ignorant of all the finer points of seamanship, they could hand a rope or heave a gun with the best.

So far, we have considered only the Armada Army, the reserve or the reinforcement of the real Army of Invasion – Parma's. How did that compare with Sidonia's? In two ways favourably; in one a good deal less so. It was superbly led: Parma at his best was a great soldier, and his officers knew

* i.e. tons (English): 57,868 tons (Spanish), if we allow the 25 per cent difference between the tons used.

war at first hand. Its *soldados* too were seasoned veterans, incomparably more formidable, on paper anyway, than any troops that we could set against them. Their numbers were very great – more than three times greater than those with Sidonia. On the other hand, they had not quite their quality, and nothing like their homogeneity. The composition of Parma's army illustrates to perfection how mighty a sovereign Philip was, how wide were his domains and those of his Habsburg kinsman, the Emperor. But it was not, primarily, a Spanish Army as Sidonia's was. This is revealed by the abstract of it, sent by Parma to the King just before the Armada sailed:

Infantry	Men
Spanish	8,718
Italians	5,339
Burgundians, Irish and Scottish	3,278
Walloon	17,825
High German	11,309
Low German	8,616
	55,085
Cavalry	
Light Horse, Italian and Spanish	3,650
Staff, etc.	668
Garrisons	1,180
TOTAL	60,583

For obvious reasons (the Dutch 'rebels' he was facing, the impossibility of transport for so many, etc.) he could not bring them all. But there they were, all of them a potential threat to Elizabeth: and he could afford to take risks with the rebels for a time, because, once England was conquered, they would be 'no more than Caesar's arm when Caesar's head is off'. If only he could get 40,000 or even 30,000 across bringing his invasion-force (with the Armada contingent) up to 60,000 or 50,000, who can blame him and Philip if they thought the result a foregone conclusion? Probably they were right – if. . . . It was that 'if', however, which spoilt Parma's pleasure in the affair. He never really liked it. He put on the air of being dutifully

enthusiastic and (in spite of what many Spaniards said afterwards) he never tried deliberately to thwart it. But he certainly
failed, throughout, to show one tithe of his normal talent. It
was not that he feared what would happen when he landed;
he was gravely doubtful whether he could start. Such doubts
alone showed him up as a strategist of infinitely greater pene-
tration than his master. For, as we are soon to see: he was right.
The risk was not worth the prize, great as that was.

English

To do them justice, the English did not panic at so formidable
a threat, though (again on paper) they had every reason to be
scared. For the English soldier of our list had really nothing in
common with the Spanish *soldado*. Where the Spaniard was a
professional he was an amateur: at the best a militiaman, at
worst a complete civilian. He could hardly be more, because
England had no standing army at all, in the Spanish sense of
those words. Nor had she, so far as people were concerned, any
standing navy either – no 'service men', as we should say now.
In war, on both elements, she relied almost exclusively upon
amateurs. This is no bad word, because the ordinary Elizabethan, though untrained for specialized war, was by no means
pacific in disposition, especially over what he conceived to be
his rights. Given congenial conditions, he thought that scrap-
ping was quite a good sport and, like other amateurs, was partial to it – and remarkably good at it. (Not for nothing did the
English people strike foreigners as 'the fiercest nation upon
earth'.) But our English shipborne 'soldiers' need not detain
us long, partly because they were not soldiers, and partly on
the score of numbers. Our list shows only 1,500 of them, and
they appear in 24 ships only – the largest royal ships. No
auxiliary carried any.

Since, then, the soldiers were not army men and the sailors
were not royal navy men, there was really only one important
difference between them. This was their trade or occupation
in civil life. The sailors were usually seamen anyway; the
soldiers were usually not seamen. Anything, therefore, which is
said about our soldiers applies equally to ordinary Englishmen.

The sailor's isolation in ordinary life did make some difference – he was not quite an ordinary Englishman. But when it came to joining the fighting services in 1588, the process of recruitment going forward briskly in the spring and early summer reveals no marked difference between any of them, not even between army and navy officers. The matter was largely geographical. In the inland heart of the country, most recruits would naturally be for the army: in the seaport towns they would be for the navy. But in London, even then very much the hub of England, the pattern was different. On May 17th, the spy de Vega in one of his many 'advices from England' gave an interesting picture of a citizen army (and navy) in the making:

> The 6,000 men raised in London meet for drill twice a week. They are certainly very good troops seeing that they are recruits, and are well-armed. They are commanded by merchants as are also the ships contributed by London and other ports. . . . The troops are divided into 40 companies of 150 each. . . . In London they are drawing 50 men from each parish at the cost of the City to send on board the ships; 4,000, they say, being obtained in this way. They give to each man of them a blue coat, whilst those who remain here receive red ones.

In London, evidently, there seems to be no more difference between citizen soldier and citizen sailor than the colour of the coat handed to him – an early and interesting reference to navy blue and army red. After this, it should come as no surprise to learn that the few who, for all that they wore red coats, turned up in blue surroundings, did full seamen's duties when they got there. There are no signs at all of army organization in the ships. De Vega does not explain the principle upon which the colour of a man's coat was decided. Probably most of the 'blues' were already seamen or watermen in the port of London. But some no doubt were not. Rather, perhaps, when any local shortage of hands was reported from the London contingent fitting in the river, the authorities simply ordered on board any party which happened to be available just then, even though recruited as 'reds'. Thereafter, though it is just possible that Howard used a few of his redcoats for such duties as would have fallen in later days to the marines, most if not all of these anti-Armada 'soldiers' were simply sailors.

Now, however, a word must be spared for those temporary soldiers whose duties really were military: those who turned out to serve the Queen on land. It must not be supposed that, before the great day, England as a whole placed absolute trust in her navy. No one, save perhaps some of her seamen leaders, did that – until afterwards. But the English were a robust, resilient people, newly awakened to their destiny; raw in their outlook upon life, in their passions and in their humour, and, it may be admitted, very pleased with themselves. To them 'an Englishman was a match for any three foreigners'; and they turned out at the summons of the county authorities, not indeed with ostentatious cheerfulness – rather with their own special brand of tooth-sucking which deceived no one – but yet with workmanlike determination. They were put through the pike- and the harquebus-drill, usually by officers who were one page ahead in the drill-book. They repaired their bows, tipped their arrows, and scrounged an old headpiece or breast-plate if they could come by one. But such articles were rare, and often had to be taken down from the walls of castle or cottage, where they had long hung as memorials of the last time Englishmen had been called out in the mass. In this sense the English, for all their fierceness, were the most unmilitary people in Europe. Now they were moved hither and thither and, in the end of course, never used; nor, for that matter, ever properly fed, for the improvised commissariat was as amateur as the men themselves.

The Government, on the advice of Raleigh and others, had organized the defence by counties. Sea forts, where they had not mouldered away, were hurriedly repaired and manned; beacons were installed on prominent landmarks to warn every-one of zero-hour, and orders were issued to drive all cattle inland, to deny free rations to an invader. It is even possible that, in places, quite elaborate field-works were dug, carefully sited to command likely landing-places. How many of these local fortifications were ever completed it is hard to say, but

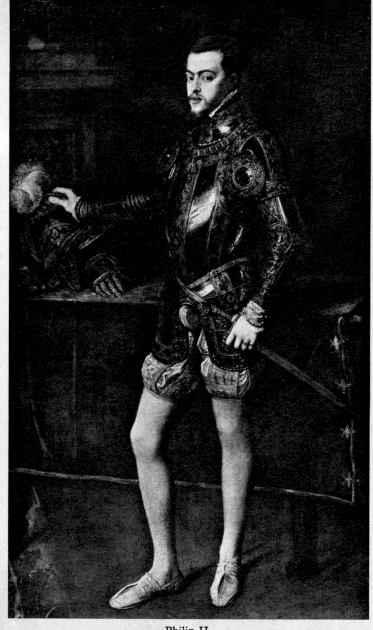

Philip II

Sir Martin Frobisher

Matthew Baker's draught of ship and sail-plan, 1586

Don Alvaro de
Bazan, Marquis
of Santa Cruz

Don Alonso Perez de
Gusman, Duke of
Medina Sidonia

they were certainly projected. A contemporary map among the Cottonian MSS shows the plan of them for the exposed counties of Devon and Cornwall which, presumably, would be among the best fortified. The works look most formidable – on the map. Round Land's End, for instance, they appear as almost continuous, and again from the west of Falmouth right up to Plymouth, while the Dodman seems to be converted into a veritable fortress. In both counties the shore bristles with pikemen and harquebusiers. The effort, if it ever came to fruition, must have demanded a fabulous number of men, and pikes, firearms and powder in quantities which, probably, never existed. What would have happened had the Spaniards tested these defences, who shall say? What would have happened had Napoleon attempted a landing? Or Hitler? None can doubt that the works would have been defended to the death. But it seems certain that – even if they really existed – such wide dispersion of such limited strength could not have delayed the Spanish army for any appreciable time, especially as no strategic reserve is anywhere shown. Yet the whole plan is interesting, if only as stressing the difference between the problem of defending England as seen by the seamen (which we are shortly to examine), and that envisaged by landsmen, including both Queen and ministers.

It is safer, perhaps, to regard these plans as recommendations and pious hopes rather than as realities. Whenever we have a glimpse of what *was* happening, a very different impression emerges. In a typical report from another key area, the County of Southampton, we learn that some 12,000 men were raised – but one could hardly say armed: 'furnished and unfurnished' is how the report to London puts it. The best-accoutred 3,000 had been sent off to the Isle of Wight – a wise move. The rest were

very rawly furnished, some whereof lacketh a headpiece, some a sword, some one thing or other that is evil, unfit or unbeseeming about him.

In addition to these static defence-forces, composed of local people who could be relied upon to defend their homes to the last, two field armies were raised: one 'to go against th'enemy', the other (smaller) for nothing but 'the defence of the Queen's person'. Elizabeth was the focus of it all. If she fell or were taken who else was left but a dribbling young foreigner from Scotland, son of the blackest traitor of them all, and who might, for all they knew, be one himself? The field army was entrusted to the Earl of Leicester, not perhaps the best choice, but the Queen thought so. It was based upon West Tilbury, on the Essex side of the Thames, and a part of it (or another army ancillary to it: it is never quite clear which) was to operate in North Kent. This was a sensible disposition because, if Parma landed south of the estuary, the Essex contingent could cross higher up, without uncovering London, and join the Kentish men; and *vice versa* if he landed in Essex. If he land both north and south, well, Heaven help us! But at least some Englishmen would be there to oppose him. In numbers, this field army seems to have fluctuated considerably. When the Armada reached the Straits, Leicester had, apparently, only 4,000 men with him, though he was expecting a further thousand from London, and was far from polite about their quality. But a day or two later reinforcements appeared from somewhere unspecified – probably the inland midlands – and he was to throw a force of 5,000 forward to Harwich when he heard that the danger was past. So her soldiers did not save England, though it was not through want of trying. It was her seamen who did that.

SEAMEN

Here England was at her strongest: stronger than Spain at every grade from Lord Admiral to the youngest boy. The officers on both sides have been discussed, but our advantage did not end there.

Spanish

The 8,050 *gente de mar* may be grouped under three broad headings. The first group, but probably the smallest, was that of ocean-going seamen: men from Corunna, Vigo, Oporto and of course Lisbon, who had often done the American run or the voyage round the Cape. Even these, however, were hardly the equals in seamanship of our best mariners. The standard Spanish 'triangular' run, using the trade winds outward-bound, and picking up the westerlies to the northward for the return trip, was the easiest of all ocean-routes, and not to be compared as a school for seamen with the hard, cold and uncertain conditions of the North Atlantic, where so many of our seamen and deep-sea fishermen had learnt their trade. Still, these few on the enemy's side must be conceded the status of 'oceangoing'; and they were the best that Spain could find for a voyage where North Atlantic weather was to be expected. The next class comprised men who were also seamen, but, comparatively, fair-weather seamen. No disparagement is intended. They were good men, even good seamen, but with experience limited to the Mediterranean, and this amounted almost to another profession from that followed by the Atlantic men. Many of them, it seems, actually disliked the ocean and its moods. They were scared by them, and that does not make for efficiency. They came from Barcelona and Cartagena on the east coast, from the Balearic Isles, from Sicily and Naples. They were probably the largest of our three groups, and certainly more useful than the last, which was composed of landsmen, entirely unacquainted with the ways of the sea.

Santa Cruz and Philip had not meant, originally, to use such people at all. Most of them were last-minute importations, taken to fill gaps caused by disease, accident and desertion, themselves the inevitable result of the long-delayed start; brought in, too, because the Government, aware of the shortage of seamen, assumed that these sturdy shoulders and hardened hands would at least be better than nothing. For such people would be simple peasants: honest, devout, and, though obviously not eager to go, prepared to listen to their priests when they played up the 'crusade' motif of the Enterprise.

Certainly we have no right to despise the *gente de mar*, any of them. Given their unavoidable shortcomings as seamen and the incredible hardships they had to endure before the end, their showing was worthy of all admiration. Often they revealed a gaucheness in handling their ships which, after all, was only to be expected. Sometimes, but not often, they gave way to panic; very occasionally we hear of the Officers of Justice performing their duties with ropes at the yardarm – and this phenomenon was not confined to the men. But, all things considered, the Spanish *gente de mar* had little to be ashamed of.

English

We, however, held all the trumps here. At risk of some slight over-simplification, we may divide the 14,385 English sailors into two, not three, classes: seamen and non-seamen. Spain's large middle category of fair-weather seamen is hardly represented on our side. Moreover the seamen class was by a very great deal the larger of the two and (giving us a still further lead) many of them were North Atlantic men, round-the-cape men, Greenland, Newfoundland or Iceland fisherfolk; or, even if they did not normally fare forth so far, there was much that was essentially North Atlantic about their own home waters. They were not, of course, 'Royal Navy' ratings – such were not destined to exist for another 265 years. But they had many of their essential qualifications. They were practically all bred to the sea from early youth, learning their trade at best in middle-sized ships and mostly in very small ones. The sea was still, in those days, the profession (nearly the only one) for those who dwelt by or near it; and, once embracing it, a man would almost certainly follow it thereafter. For the sea-going population was something of a community apart: hereditary, apt to mistrust landsmen who, in their turn, were secretly a little afraid of them because they were so different, so uncouth, so strangely aloof. Yet, though prepared to face hardships altogether uncongenial to modern sailors, though they were content to disappear for years on end, right outside the ken of family and country, they were still essentially home-loving, loyal to both Country and County – especially perhaps to the last. They were mostly merchant seamen, manning the ships of the ordinary merchants or of those less ordinary ones like

Hawkins, Drake, Frobisher and the Fenners, who associated themselves with the joint stock enterprises. But the kid glove was no part of their outfit. Between whiles many of them, if not engaged in rank piracy, were not above taking what came their way, and no questions asked: certainly not above smuggling. It would be mere waste of time to look for haloes round their shaggy heads. Most assuredly profit was a prominent strand in their 'gowns of falding'.

Yet passionate patriotism was there too. England was threatened, and perhaps more to the point, so were Plymouth, Falmouth, Southampton, Deal, Harwich, Bristol. When the 'stay' or 'embargo' was put on, towns and districts had to find their quotas, not only of ships but also of seamen. Thus the Devon quota was manned from Dartmouth, Plymouth or Bideford; the Kent quota from the Cinque Ports, Margate or Gravesend; the East Anglian from the fishing ports, and so on. Most of those already on board a ship, when it was selected for service by their local authority, would never leave it, but pass straight from their owner's service to the Queen's. Others were pressed, but we must not think of Elizabethan pressing as being quite that unpopular and brutal thing that it became later. 'The press' still had much of its original meaning of 'the prest', which was merely earnest-money, a token that a man had entered the Queen's service: very like, in fact, the King's shilling in the army. It was only later that it came to carry the more sinister implication of crude compulsion. It would doubtless be wrong to assert that no real seaman was forced to serve in 1588, but certainly most of them, scenting danger to all they loved best, were by no means reluctant, even if they did not actually volunteer. These men, with their officers, were 'the Few' who saved England.

There remain the non-seamen, and there were not many of them. They arrived on board for the same reason which brought the soldiers – and indeed, on the other side, the Spanish peasants. They were rounded up in a hurry, and mainly from the towns where they could most readily be found at short notice. Some, notably from London, the only town in which strictly urban conditions then prevailed, were doubtless wasters whom no one missed (and they, no doubt, would have to be pressed in the more modern sense of that word), but there is no evidence whatever of any landsman letting down the morale of the whole body, which throughout the entire action was obviously very high. There were too few of them anyway for their poison (if they had any) to infect the rest. Above all, however, in considering the strength of these our weakest links, we must remember that the stakes were not equal. Spain was invading England, not England Spain. Pedro and Sancho might reconcile themselves to the journey, both because they were promised Paradise if they should chance to fall, and because they had been told that *El Draque* had juicy infants served up for dinner when he captured a town. But such things were, relatively, faith and hatred at second hand. From what they were told, they did not really anticipate having to pay any penalty at all – the thing was to be a walk-over. Nor was Drake at all likely ever to come their way: to the large town or seaport, possibly, but to their own little plots and homesteads – well, hardly.

On the other hand, Jarge the yokel and Dick the hostler had been told, and firmly believed, that one whole, huge Armada ship was loaded with nothing but halters to hang them with; that every Englishman between the ages of sixteen and sixty – some said twelve and seventy – was to be turned off forthwith, his womenfolk rounded up for the use of the soldiery, his children, if of seven or under, branded on the face that all might tell thereafter the master from the slave. And those halters, those foul ravishers, those branding irons – they were on the high seas! They were actually on the way!

It was, in fact, the old story of the hound and the hare. The Spaniard was running for his supper, or thought he was; the Englishman for his life, and he knew it.

Part Three:

THE CHANNEL FIGHTS

7

THE FLEETS APPROACH

May 4th – July 19th, 1588

[In 1588 the Spaniards were using the Gregorian Calendar, or New Style (N.S.): the English the Julian Calendar, or Old Style (O.S.). The Gregorian was ten days ahead of the Julian – e.g. July 30th, Spanish (N.S.) equals July 20th, English (O.S.). Here all dates are given in the English or Old Style. It is, strictly, the wrong one, and more than a century and half later we corrected our error and adopted the Gregorian Calendar, we being by then eleven days behind it. But as most modern English works have perpetuated the original English dates, it seems less confusing to retain them here, for both sides.]

ON MAY 4TH the Armada dropped down the Tagus, and lay at Belem. Throughout that late spring and summer the weather was bad, unfriendly to both sides. It showed its teeth at once. For fourteen days the Armada awaited a wind favourable for sailing. Medina Sidonia was in daily communication with his sovereign, and his innate pessimism is instantly revealed. Everything was wrong. The ship-tackle throughout the fleet was indifferent – when not actually absent; the provisions were half putrid already, the water stank: each cask opened, whether of food or drink, was fouler than the last. Unfortunately, in the main, Sidonia was right here: for now the evils of delay, stemming from the exploits of Drake, were coming home to roost, and Philip was more to blame than anyone. Throughout the preceding winter he had so harried his servants, and not least the willing Santa Cruz, that vast efforts had been made in many directions. But not in all. Thus, by untiring efforts, the old Admiral had succeeded in getting almost everything ready by February: he had even filled all the water-casks. Then he died, and his demoniac energies were replaced by the placid régime of Sidonia. Progress stopped in the dockyards, and so did the water in the casks which the Marquis had filled. No wonder it bred dysentery in anyone foolhardy enough to drink it; no wonder the only things that multiplied in the hot holds were the germs, the weevils and the maggots.

Philip answered his new commander's tale of woe with soothing words, but on one point he was adamant: the fleet would sail on the first fair wind. That presented itself at last on May 18th, and the Armada sailed – to the south! For no sooner had the ungainly array cleared the coast than a fresh northerly wind arose, and, soon, the fleet was off Cape St Vincent, beating helplessly back and forth and losing distance at every tack. A fortnight later, however, it was once more abreast of Lisbon, and once more Sidonia was sending his daily complaints to Philip, who still received them with exemplary patience, but without relenting. At length, however, the wind obliged, coming up fair from the southwest on the last day of May; and, three days later, the fleet was off Finisterre.

The King was delighted. But there are limits. Dysentery was sweeping the ships and Sidonia, in his despair, called a council of war. Here all its members, Recalde, Oquendo and Pedro de Valdez no less than Flores de Valdez and Sidonia, agreed that some ships, now almost out of water, must enter Ferrol. His own inclinations thus substantially reinforced, Sidonia hastened to implement the council's finding. Then, abetted by the threat of a westerly gale, he scuttled for port, and was safely berthed at Corunna before the storm broke. Most of the larger ships followed; but not all, and not nearly all the smaller ones. These had adventures of their own. Some were blown into the Bay of Biscay; some actually stood on for England and in due time sighted the Isles of Scilly, where they waited for a few days, and then returned.

Meanwhile, Sidonia lay snug, rewatering, revictualling, and repairing his human wastage from up-country. Gradually the missing ships limped in, for the storm had not been so serious after all; and by June 17th only 35 were still absent. Encouraged by his recent experience of councils of war, he now called another, and tried to persuade it to back him in his plea for calling the whole thing off. But here he met determined opposition. The squadron leaders were of very different mettle. They knew their Sidonia by now and spoke out vigorously: for whatever their private views about the success of the Enterprise, they were too proud to give in without putting things to the touch. Pedro de Valdez here took a very strong lead and carried the day. But neither he nor anyone else could speed the laggards, nor repair, rewater and revictual them instantly upon their arrival. So more time was lost.

Ultimately, however, all was done, accelerated by a daily harangue from Philip. The month's rest, fresh food and water had restored the health of the men, and a part at least of their morale. Even Sidonia was, for the moment, in comparatively good heart. On July 12th a second start was made, and The Most Happy Armada left Corunna a good deal happier than it had been on entering it. There were a few minor changes in its composition, but for all practical purposes its strength in ships and men was the same as when it left Lisbon: still approximately 130 ships and 30,500 souls. But in some ways it was considerably stronger. Its provisions were now largely eatable and its water drinkable. Some of its weaker brethren were dead or discharged sick; some of its worst characters had contrived to desert, and the peasants who replaced them were, though unskilled, or least neither weak nor vicious. To add to the good cheer, a fair and pleasant breeze from the south wafted them on their way. There was no turning back now.

On Monday, July 15th, they had reached the Sleeve of the English Channel. Here, however, there was a hitch. The following wind fell to nothing, and, on the Wednesday, began blowing up from the west. The Spaniards called it a *tormenta* – a full gale. But, here as elsewhere in our story, we cannot fail to notice that many more gales are recorded by the Spaniards than by the English. This was partly because the English were better acclimatized to a strong blow, partly because, in any wind, their ships could be worked much better. Here is a case in point. The 'gale' which now dispersed the Armada for a while – with, according to themselves, 'the sea so high that all the mariners said they had never seen the like in July' – is nowhere mentioned by the English, save only for a casual remark by Hawkins that 'a little flaw took them'. This particular wind, it has been estimated, was about Force 6 on the Beaufort Scale, or at most Force 7, once considered a moderate gale but now no gale at all. Two days later the Armada was reassembled, but its number was permanently reduced by five. Whether they experienced a *tormenta* or only a fresh Atlantic breeze did not greatly matter to the galleys: they could take neither, and all four, in grave danger of swamping, ran for the French coast. One was wrecked, the other three survived, but returned no more. This loss did not appreciably weaken the fleet, but the fifth casualty was more serious. The *Santa Ana*, flagship of Recalde's Squadron of Biscay, did not rejoin. It is not clear why – probably she was an old, patched-up ship. Fortunately for Spain, however, Recalde himself had already moved into the Armada's vice-flagship, the galleon *San Juan*, so that his services were not lost. But the *Santa Ana* was out of it for good. She made Le Havre, and there we attacked her when all was over. We failed to take her, but she never reached home again.

On the very day of reassembly, at 4 pm on Friday, July 19th, a lookout at the *San Martin*'s masthead descried land ahead. It was the Lizard. Thereupon the Duke hoisted his Pope-consecrated banner at the main – Christ Crucified, with the Virgin Mother on one side of him and Mary Magdalen on the other. The Crusade had begun.

How did the English use those eleven weeks of grace, so frustrating to Philip, which stretched between the Armada's last view of Lisbon and its first glimpse of the Lizard? It is not a very edifying story. Elizabeth had not even yet made up her mind. She still wanted to avoid an all-out war, and she strongly suspected that Philip wanted the same. She was partly right, as we have seen, but what she did not realize was that Philip was rapidly reaching a point of no return. He was still willing enough to call his assault off if he could get his way without it, and, like Elizabeth, he still hoped for a compromise favourable to himself. But he could not afford to hold up his preparations, which were on a scale, and with an intent, impossible to disguise. So there came the inevitable day when, with the world watching him, his Armada had to sail. If it did not, he would lose face altogether: all his high talk of crusades, consecrated banners and black infidels would look merely silly. He might still hope that, somewhere between Lisbon and London, Elizabeth would behold his might, lose her nerve and compound for survival. But even that involved the Armada's departure: and depart it did.

Elizabeth's hopes, *mutatis mutandis*, were not very dissimilar from Philip's. But she was not nearly so publicly committed, and so clung to the possibility of a composition longer than he did – indeed, dangerously long. From the beginning of 1588 right up to the moment of the Armada's arrival she was busily engaged in negotiations; not, it is true, direct with Philip, but with his Viceroy, the astute and fair-spoken Parma. At first, some of her ministers thought that there was something in this policy. But as time wore on, and Philip's threat grew daily more concrete, more blatant, they began to think again. They felt that defence measures should at least match with negotiations. Elizabeth, it is true, did not completely neglect these precautions, though she seemed dangerously irresolute. Once she was with difficulty restrained from ordering a total demobilization and, once, she did cut down the ships' complements. Anyway, she was far more reluctant to commit herself than her advisers were, considering that the more obvious her preparations the less would be her chance of composition.

To her able and faithful sailor-servants such vacillations looked suicidal, and most of all to Drake. His ideas on how to make naval war, we can see now, were far ahead of anyone else's. He had somehow chanced upon two principles of strategy which had entirely eluded his contemporaries, and especially his Queen. The first was the proper defensive station of a fleet that would defend us from sea-borne invasion. The second – a wider concept still – was the use of the offensive in naval warfare, not only *qua* offensive but also as the best means of defence. After his day his ideas became the norm: before it they were unknown. He may fairly be hailed, then, as the Father of British naval strategy.

Space forbids any detailed examination of these great concepts; yet, since they condition the whole campaign, they cannot be ignored. Briefly, then, the whole period of suspense, from January 1588, right up to Sidonia's arrival in late July, resolved itself into a fierce tussle of wills between, on the one side, practically all the English Powers-that-were and, on the other, Francis Drake, at first almost alone. He had come to realize (as, later, everyone did) that, in an age when the wind alone gave motive-power to ships, and in an area like the Channel where the westerlies prevail, any defending fleet *must* keep to windward – that is, westward – of any potential invader: for only so could the defender be certain of coming up with the aggressor. Hitherto, the accepted sea strategy of England had been to mass her entire naval strength in the Straits of Dover, over against the invasion ports of Parma's army. This, Drake saw, was fatal because, once Sidonia sighted, say, the Lizard, the English in the Downs could only get at him after a long, tedious and uncertain beat against the prevalent winds. Before they could reach him, in fact, Sidonia might well have sailed eastwards as far, perhaps, as Beachy Head: and he might have landed his troops anywhere between, say, Falmouth and Portsmouth.

So Drake weighed in, and won – in two stages. First, in February, he was given, rather grudgingly, a small 'Western Squadron', a splinter of the main fleet based, under his command, on Plymouth. This was something: but it was not nearly enough, and Drake said so, loudly. He won again. In May Howard was ordered to join him at Plymouth with most of the remaining ships. He arrived on the 23rd, after the Armada's first start but, owing to its delay at Corunna, still in time: and now the great bulk of our naval strength lay sufficiently far west to be effective. This was the fleet which, by itself, fought all the Armada actions but the last. Let us look at it. It contained 105 ships classified as opposite.

This accounts for 19 of the Queen's ships; but she had 34. What of the other 15? They are the measure of Drake's partial failure. They stayed behind. One – the galley – never left the Thames; the rest, mainly small, remained in the Straits. No sea commander, not even Seymour, wanted this. There was some case for leaving a few small craft to watch Parma's invasion flotillas, though these could hardly be called sea-going, and, anyway, a scratch, but far from despicable, Dutch squadron was eagerly awaiting their sortie. But the rest should certainly have gone west, and especially Seymour's flagship the *Rainbow* and her twin, the *Vanguard*, Hawkins's latest and best contributions to the Navy Royal. As it was, all these ships were a dead loss until the final day's fighting.

	Class	Before May 23rd	Arrived May 23rd	Combined	
Front line	Navy Royal	5	11	16	62
	Auxiliary	16	30	46	
Small	Navy Royal	1	2	3	43
	Auxiliary	16	24	40	
TOTAL		38	67	105	105

We must turn now to Drake's second strategic discovery, even though, this time, his efforts to exploit it failed. Later, the principle of it was summed up in the words, 'The watergates of England are the ports of the enemy': that is, the frontier of England runs, not through Dover, but through Calais; and what lies between them is not neutral territory, still less French territory. It is England. Similarly, England's western frontier in a war with Spain is not the coast of Cornwall or Devon, but Corunna, Lisbon, Cadiz. The best means of naval defence is attack!

Drake had proved this by deeds before ever he put it into words. In April 1587 he had thwarted invasion by entering Cadiz harbour and smashing the shipping there: now he was panting to try again. As early as January he nearly persuaded the Queen to allow it: but she was not prepared for the audacity of it. She stopped him at the last moment, and he, in a frenzy of enthusiasm and exasperation, got his ideas down on paper, a little confusedly, when he wrote to her on March 30th. This epoch-making letter was the first recorded exposition of the policy which has been Britain's ever since – at least whenever her naval strength has permitted it. If, he tells her, Philip means to invade England, 'then doubtless his force is and will be great in Spain'. She ought, therefore 'not to fear any invasion in her own country, but to seek God's enemies and her Majesty's *wherever they may be found* . . . for that, with 50 sail of shipping, we shall do no more good upon their own coast than a great many more will do here at home'. It was indeed because Elizabeth's successors accepted this view that Louis XIV's legions never scrambled ashore on the south coast of England, but were stopped off Barfleur and La Hague; that Napoleon's *Grande Armée* never left Boulogne, but was held off Camperdown in Holland, off Brest in France and off Cape St Vincent, Ferrol and Trafalgar in Spain. Even in 1940, when the very dimensions of warfare had changed, Hitler's panzer-divisions never roamed the southern shires. They were halted on the French shore by our offensive-defensive, this time in height rather than depth, over the fair fields of Kent and Sussex. Each time we stopped the enemy invasion forces from starting: and that is everything. Those who fail to start do not arrive.

This time, however, England – the wider England of the Watergates formula – *was* invaded, because they would not let Drake have his way in time. If they had, the Spaniards would not have entered the Channel: Philip's beard would have been scorched beyond repair, probably in Corunna harbour; and 'the Defeat of the Spanish Armada' would not hold the picturesque and vital place it does in our history.

So here Drake failed: but by what a narrow margin we must now see. He never gave up hope. When the Lord Admiral arrived, he quickly brought him to his way of thinking. Yet even Howard failed to move the Queen, and the valuable weeks slipped by. At last, however, she showed signs of succumbing to the combined insistence of the trusted Howard and his brilliant second, and finally gave way; but half-heartedly and, one suspects, with unworthy mental reservations. Though he now knew that Sidonia was recuperating at Corunna, Drake was still desperate to be gone. But it was full late: and, before a start could be made, a further delay occurred, arising from an apparently different cause altogether. The fleet was not victualled for such a journey.

This introduces the English Commissariat and its astonishing inadequacy. Admittedly the circumstances were unique. Never before had we attempted to raise so large and nation-wide an array of ships and men, nor to maintain it for anything like so long a period. Everything was hand-to-mouth from the first. The ships were being victualled not, like Spain's, for six months: not usually, even, for one month; but from week to week – sometimes, literally, from day to day. Philip, obviously, had had to do better, because his men could hope for no replenishments where they were going. But Elizabeth had thought – or pretended to think – in terms of local defence only: that her ships would never be more than a few miles from their bases. Indeed it has been asserted (though never proved) that she kept the fleet in short supply in order to prevent it from participating in such adventures as Drake proposed. Be that as it may, the situation was clearly bordering on the ridiculous when Howard had to write to Burghley:

> I thought it good to put your Lordship in remembrance how necessary it is to have a better proportion of victual than for one month, considering the time and the service that is likely to fall out, and what danger it might breed if our want of victual should be at the time of service. We shall now be victualled, beginning the 20th of this April, unto the 18th of May, and the advertisement that giveth the largest time for the coming out of the Spanish forces is the midst of May, being the 15th. Then have we three days' victual. If it be fit to be so, it passeth my reason.

That Howard was no scaremonger is clear from the fact that this very thing happened, and at the very 'time of service'. By mid-July his warnings had at last shamed the Government into authorizing the Queen's Assistant Surveyor, Marmaduke Darell, to furnish victual up to August 10th – 20 days! Darell was a good man – by the generous Howard's account a very good man – and he had been anticipating the order by getting the provisions ready (to be rapped over the knuckles from London for his pains). The authorizing letter, however, did not arrive until July 21st. Luckily, a little – very little – had been put surreptitiously on board at Darell's risk. His 'disobedience' may well have saved England, for, on July 19th, Howard had been summoned to keep the one appointment he could not possibly break. The Armada was in sight: England's fate might well turn upon a single tide. Off he went that very night, near-empty holds and all.

But we anticipate. This was the crowning act of the victualling farce. Already Drake had been having his men on short rations in port, in order to collect enough for his dash Spainwards: and at no time was the spectre of famine far removed from the ships. Meanwhile poor Darell (in the hardly exaggerated words of Sir John Laughton) 'was scouring the country round, buying up what he could, more like a mess-steward with a market basket than the agent-victualler of a great fleet'. The only commodity in good supply was the beer. But there was a reason for this. It was so sour that the men could not swallow it. Yet so tightly were the purse-strings held that no one dared adopt the obvious remedy of pouring the lot overboard and procuring more. The old was therefore rebrewed along with a small addition of new; with the result that the last state of that beverage was – if possible – more undrinkable than the first.

Nothing, perhaps, illustrates so clearly the will-power and stamina of these great men than the fact that, in spite of all, they did put to sea, with victual enough to take them to Corunna – just. But that was only on July 7th: full late – it would not do to be passed by Sidonia on the wide ocean before they could reach Spain. They ran south with a fair wind till the 9th when, they reckoned, Cape Finisterre was only a few leagues below the horizon. Then the wind veered to the southwest – fair for Sidonia if coming north. Thereupon they gave it up, not only because the enemy might creep by unseen, but also because, if they beat about waiting for a wind, they would have nothing to eat! Reluctantly they returned, regaining Plymouth on July 12th.

On that same day (though they did not know it) the Most Happy Armada cleared Corunna and, sailing large on that very wind, followed them to the Sleeve of the Channel.

So, through the faults of others, Drake's great concept had failed; and, worse, placed the fleet and the fortune of England in real peril. For there the ships lay, in a port difficult to leave on a southwesterly wind, with, as like as not, the Armada only just below the windward horizon: caught in landlocked waters where they could not use their great advantage of mobility; with no army on board to repulse the huge Armada army if it boarded them; low in water, and almost without food. To such a pass had Elizabeth, her vacillations and economies brought them. The campaign could hardly have opened under auspices more discouraging to England.

8

THE FLEETS MAKE CONTACT

4.0 pm, Friday, July 19th to dawn, Sunday, July 21st

FROM THIS DANGER the English were saved by the ineptitude of the enemy, and their own vigour and resource.

Its landfall made, its banner hoisted, the Armada – lay to. He was waiting, says Sidonia, for the last of the scattered ships, and especially for Pedro de Valdez who had made a cast towards the Isles of Scilly to retrieve them. When they rejoined, he put the Armada into the formation in which he proposed to take it up-Channel. What that formation was is never made clear. The Spaniards do not tell us with any exactitude; nor do the English who, strange as it may sound, probably never knew it. The best contemporary evidence comes from the set of charts drawn by the artist Adams and engraved in 1590. These doubtless transcribe faithfully enough the information which Howard and others gave the draughtsman. They show the Armada in the form of a quarter-moon, its convex curve pointing up-Channel, its horns trailing west. Unfortunately, however, our seamen (having no air reconnaissance) never saw their adversaries at anything but sea-level, and so had no clear view of their formation in depth. From these charts Cornelis de Vroom took his designs for a set of tapestries which Howard was ordering for himself. These, in due course, found their way into the House of Lords, only to be destroyed in the fire of 1834. Nearly a century before that, however, engravings of them had been made by John Pine, and these survive. They are a good deal less map-like than the Adams charts, yet still fail to tell us the real Armada formation; and for the same reason. But a fair guess may be made.

When Sidonia sighted the Lizard, his knowledge of his enemy's whereabouts was extremely vague. He supposed that the main English fleet was far to the east, in or near the Straits, but that a detachment, probably under Drake, was at Ply-

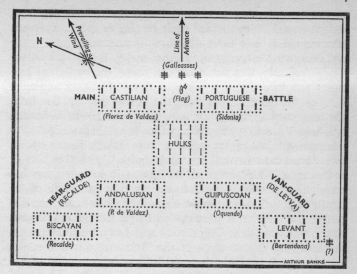

mouth, or at any rate fairly far west – a supposition once correct, but now nearly two months out of date. Drake, he thought, would either sit tight in Plymouth or lurk even farther west; then follow astern and try to take him between two fires, attacking his rear as the main fleet engaged his front. This meant that he must maintain two fronts, or rather, perhaps, a hard core leading up-Channel and another strong force bringing up the rear. The hulks and non-combatant craft were to be tucked for safety in the heart of the array, between the two fighting bodies. From the various Spanish sources we can get even nearer than this. Sidonia in his flagship *San Martin*, with both the true warship-squadrons – the galleons of Portugal (his own squadron) and the Indian Guard or galleons of Castile (Flores de Valdez's) – were to form the east-facing main battle; and (at first) three of the four galleasses were to bear them company. The four squadrons of non-royal Great Ships, each 10 strong, were to be the covering force, with the fourth galleass.

The names which the Spaniards gave to the various squadrons have led to some misunderstanding. Essentially a

military people, they used army terms throughout. On land,
on the march, they divided their forces, as indeed everyone
else then did, into three divisions – vanguard, main-battle
and rearguard, stepping out in that order. But on the battle-
field, obviously, this would not do: there, the custom of centuries ordained that the vanguard should fall back and align
itself on the main-battle's right, the post of honour. Similarly,
the rearguard advanced and took station on the main-battle's
left. It was precisely this military formation that the Spaniards
were now adopting at sea, nomenclature and all. The eastward-
facing hard core they call the 'main-battle', with the C.-in-C.
in its centre. The 'vanguard' division, still so called, has become the right wing: only, because it is to be part of the covering force, it is drawn up well astern of the main battle, and disposed *en échelon*. It is commanded by de Levya, and consists
of the 20 ships of the Guipuscoan and Levant squadrons. On
the left-wing the 20 ships of the Andalusian and Biscayan
squadrons are similarly disposed under the command of Recalde, the whole forming the 'rearguard' division. Those unfamiliar with this military nomenclature are apt to be puzzled
when they read (in Spanish sources) that the vanguard was engaged throughout in all the rearguard actions; indeed, that the
rearmost ship of all, at the extreme right-rear tip of the whole
fleet, was a vanguard ship. But the diagram on p. 117 will, it is
hoped, help to resolve the apparent paradox. Each individual
squadron of 10 ships, whether main-battle, van or rear, was
probably drawn up in two lines of five ships abreast: a notice-
able survival of galley tactics, but ill-suited to ships firing
broadsides. The placing of the galleasses in the diagram is also
a little hypothetical; but it is known that the three originally
accompanying Sidonia led the whole fleet. When he discovered
the strength of the enemy behind him he sent two of them back
to reinforce his covering squadrons. More of this later, however; for when he did this he made other changes. The posi-
tions of the smaller ships are mostly unknown, and therefore
not shown in the diagram.

If the reader will now hold the diagram up, nearly horizon-
tally and at eye-level, and then, in imagination, endow the

lines representing the squadrons with the altitudes proper to ships, he will obtain some idea of what the English saw at sea-level as they followed the Armada up-Channel. What they beheld looked like a concave quarter-moon with its horns stretching backwards towards them. They could also see, probably, that those horns were thin-through, but that, towards the centre of the concave, the depth of ships was considerably greater. And this is exactly what Adams depicts. The fighting was to prove the strength of this highly defensive formation; but it was also to reveal unforeseen weaknesses.

As day broke on Saturday, July 20th, the Armada in its new formation was sailing slowly up the coast, and within sight of it – because Sidonia reports the alarm beacons springing up on headland after headland – the first stage in that long journey which at length 'roused the burghers of Carlisle'. This must have warned them that their presence was discovered; but it did not seem to hurry them. At length, however, it struck Sidonia that some more certain knowledge of his enemy's whereabouts and strength would be useful. He therefore dispatched his own ensign-bearer Juan Gils to try to pick up information. Meanwhile he called that standby of vacillating commanders, a council of war. There are several versions of what took place in it. The most likely one makes de Leyva and Pedro de Valdez argue hotly for an immediate assault upon Plymouth, where they now thought (having seen no other trace of him) that *El Draque* himself must be lurking. Sidonia (and perhaps Flores de Valdez) argued, rather half-heartedly, against the danger of entering a defended port, the former at last playing his trump card, Philip's express order to keep straight on. How the seamen Recalde and Oquendo voted is not known. Probably they supported Pedro, who later told the King that the council's final vote was for Plymouth. Indeed, he declared, the squadron leaders left the flagship under the impression that the attack was on. But this discrepancy matters the less because, as so often happens in war, the other side had something to say about it.

Drake may not have possessed that wizard's mirror which the Spanish people attributed to him, but long experience had taught him the value of discovering, at the earliest possible moment, what was happening outside his visual range. Ever since his return a week before, therefore, his pinnaces had been out scanning the whole entrance to the Channel, and probably one of them was present, unseen, at the very moment when the Armada saw England. So it was that, towards sundown on Friday, July 19th, the *Golden Hind* (Captain Thomas Flemyng) entered the Sound under full sail and gave her breathless message. The ship (of 80 tons, and not that in which Drake went round the world) was one of the original Western Squadron, but now one of the Lord Admiral's pinnaces. Flemyng was a professional seaman: not, probably, a west-countryman, because he was related to the London merchant-family of Gonson (and therefore by marriage to Hawkins); and not, *pace* Charles Kingsley who traduces his character in *Westward Ho!*, of the swashbuckling, near-piratical type. Yet there were no flies on Flemyng: his record was always good, and he was yet to do at least ten years' solid service in command of various royal ships. Now he had performed a very delicate piece of reconnaissance work. England owes a great debt to Thomas Flemyng for coolness and dispatch when time was of the essence. This early information gave the commanders at Plymouth just sufficient time to extricate themselves from their dangerous strategic position.

A very old story, the best-known and loved of all Armada traditions, tells how Flemyng found the English commanders relaxing after their dinner in a game of bowls on Plymouth Hoe. It is not quite contemporary, but it has been traced back to 1624, when many veterans of the great fight were still living. So it may well be true – and let us hope it is, because it is altogether consonant with the known character of Drake. 'Let them wait their turn,' runs the best-known version. 'There's time for that and to beat the Spaniard after.' And he stooped to finish the game.

How could he say such a thing? Surely every minute now counted? Of course it did. But Drake had been in many a tight place before, and knew as well as any man living the effect of even momentary panic in the leader whom men trusted. It is extremely likely, then, that the story tells the truth, and nothing but the truth. But it can hardly tell the whole truth. Obviously, one piece is missing, because it has not the same dramatic quality of survival. We may be very sure that he said something else too – sent a most urgent, forcefully worded message to all the fleet's masters, boatswains and men. 'Get to it! Warp the ships out of harbour, any way you can! Begin *now*, and do not let up until the lot of them are riding in the Sound!' Then, but only then, he stooped to finish the game.

All through the night of the 19th the laborious process went on, and by the morning of the 20th every ship had left harbour. The first, the most crucial move had been safely accomplished, by skill born of long practice and hard experience. The next move began. To beat out of the Sound on a sou'westerly breeze called for nice seamanship. But there was plenty of the nicest seamanship to hand, and this too was safely achieved. Soon after midday of the 20th most of the great ships were up with the Eddystone, beating for the open Channel. And now, through a typical west-country mizzle, the English saw the Armada for the first time, some leagues to the westward, and windward. Just then, damped off by the fret, the wind fell to nothing, and the English struck sail, to make themselves as inconspicuous as possible.

It was nearly nightfall before the Spaniards saw the English. As it fell dark, the lookout in the *San Martin* reported a fleet lying to to leeward. Sidonia had no idea what to make of it, nor who they were. Soon, however, the truth began to dawn on him. At about 1 o'clock on the morning of Sunday, July 21st, Ensign Juan Gils returned in triumph, bringing with him the Armada's first (and, as it proved, last) prize – a Falmouth fishing-smack with four terrified fishermen on board. Their moral resistance, if they made any, was soon broken down, and they told all they knew. It was hot news indeed. They had seen with their own eyes the Lord Admiral and his Vice-Admiral beating out of Plymouth Sound only a few hours before. Here was luck for the Duke, and his first reaction seems to have been one of relief. Anyway, he now knew, or thought he did, to whom those dimly glimpsed sails belonged: and, further, all that dangerous talk of the hotheads – entering a defended harbour forsooth! – was out of date. The birds had flown; it was no longer necessary to raid their nest. Now, with a clear conscience, he could fall back comfortably on his master's orders and carry on up-Channel. But could he? The thought struck him – or his accredited adviser Flores de Valdez – that, if he went on through the night, he might pass the English by, and find them in the morning to windward of him. So then and there and rather short of the entrance to the Sound, he dropped anchor, warning his squadrons to do the same, and to be prepared for an attack in the morning from the direction in which he had last seen the English.

Evidently he did not know his Drake, or even his Howard. The sou'wester got up again with the moon, and instantly the English stood out to sea, straight across the bows of the anchored Armada. The Spaniards did not see them, their attention being distracted by the movements of certain unknown sails inshore of them. It is tempting to think, as one Spanish eyewitness does,* that they were placed there by the fiendish subtlety of *El Draque* to blind the Spaniards to his main move. But the English were not quite so subtle as that. The ships in question were the last of our fleet to clear harbour and Sound. Now, finding themselves too late to follow Howard and Drake across the enemy's front, they were beating up-wind, inshore and on short tacks, with just the same motives as the rest – to gain the wind. Both forces succeeded; but Howard with the main fleet had a long start and much more sea-room. At first light on Sunday, July 21st, he had reached his bourne, to windward of the Spaniards and a little farther out to sea. Thereupon he put about, and bore down upon the enemy, making contact first with the weathermost tip of Bertendona's Levant squadron.

Sidonia was taken completely by surprise. He was keeping a good lookout, in two directions – to leeward, to the northeast, where he had last seen the English main fleet; and landward, to the northwest, where the last of the inshore ships which he

* Purser Pedro Calderon, whose *Relacion* is one of the most detailed.

had been watching all night had just got clear to the west. Unhappily for him, however, both directions were quite wrong. Howard was coming at him from sou'sou'west, seaward and to windward of him. He had been outwitted at every turn. He had missed the best chance he was ever to have – to catch the English embayed. Having lost the wind, too, he was compelled to give battle not at his own, but at the enemy's, convenience: nor could he now attack that enemy and, at the same time, advance up-Channel. Instead, he was committed to an uncomfortable rearguard action, with his covering force constantly having to put about, to ward off attacks from behind; and his main-battle, including all his really front-line ships, stationed right in the rear of the new action. Nor had he been forced to accept these conditions at the cannon's mouth; they were his lot before ever a shot was fired. By sheer quick thinking and quick moving, Drake and Howard had turned the tables on him.

9

THE ACTION OFF PLYMOUTH

Sunday, July 21st

AT FIRST SIGN of dawn Sidonia had weighed anchor and was making a tentative inshore move, towards the spot where he had last seen the English. But he was scarcely under way when he perceived a very strong force bearing down upon the extreme tip of his right, southernmost, seawardmost wing. So surprised was he that he did not believe these ships to be the ones last seen the evening before at precisely the opposite point of the compass. He supposed it a new fleet altogether, just come out of Dartmouth farther east. Instantly he stopped his inshore movement and turned to fight for his life. Nor was this the only shock in store. The speed and ease with which the attackers moved, and the rate at which they fired were things quite new to him. But here a word of caution is necessary. Factors like speed and rate of fire are relative terms. We of to-day should, of course, regard the English approach as snail-like, and their rate of fire like the discharge of minute-guns. So even would Nelson in his day. These things only struck the Spaniards as phenomenal because they were altogether brisker, in fact, than any previous sailing-ship attack in history.

They were also being done in a new way, and that too was a cause of surprise and uneasiness. For these were the new English battle tactics, their first large-scale attempt to decide a sea fight with gunfire alone: and for this purpose they were using their new broadside artillery and their new sailing-boat mobility. But all was experimental, and experiments, however promising for the future, seldom achieve full success first time. We must constantly bear this in mind because, again and again as the fighting rages, we shall find the Spaniards gasping with amazement at what we were doing; yet, when we look into the detailed results, we may well stand amazed at how little we accomplished. We must be sure, then, that we appreciate just what we were trying to do and just what was new about it.

The Spanish formation has already engaged our attention. What of ours? This is a very difficult question, which earnest experts have long been trying to answer, and with no final success. The main difficulty is obvious enough. Since the whole method was new, there was no tactical experience from other fights to draw upon. If an Elizabethan wanted to know how best to conduct a battle between galley fleets, there existed for his instruction a whole library full of textbooks, with a vast wealth of historical illustration. He would have no difficulty whatever in discovering how Themistocles won the battle of Salamis or Don Juan the battle of Lepanto; but the shelf reserved for sailing-ship tactics would be quite empty. Nor is the modern student in a much better position. Certainly those who actually invented the tactics, in fight and as they went along, will not help him much. They were not that kind of man. The idea of Drake sitting down to write a tactical textbook is merely comical. Fortunately, however, there was one man who was a clear-thinking writer as well as seaman, soldier, statesman, colonist, courtier and many other things. Sir Walter Raleigh has left on record how he proposed to fight a small fleet under his command in 1617, and there is every reason to think that he was drawing upon his knowledge of what was done in 1588. Certainly his general principle is the same: to single out for attack the weathermost ship or ships of the enemy's formation; that is, of course, the ship or ships least easily succoured by the rest, who would have to beat to windward in order to assist. This is obviously what Howard and Drake were doing in that first Sunday attack, and they continued to do so, whenever possible, on all days thereafter. This method also fitted in with that other cardinal aim already discovered, of hammering the enemy wherever he was, without running the risk of being boarded by him.

For actual sailing information, Raleigh definitely ordains a 'line-ahead'. This was in fact the only logical arrangement for a squadron of broadside-firing ships, for only so could the broadsides be discharged without risk to one's neighbours. It was accepted, in the end, as the standard formation for whole fleets, which came to form one long, evenly spaced, follow-my-leader line, usually close-hauled to the wind. But this ultimate development was not yet, certainly not in 1588. It is quite certain that at no instant in the fight was the whole English fleet in single line-ahead. Yet it is equally certain that some limited form of line-ahead was used, and used throughout. Often, no doubt, it was no more than a handful of ships, anything from three to eight, which so aligned themselves for some specific attack. Pine's engravings show, probably, one such occasion – the very first to present itself. There we see, very clearly, four English ships in a colourable representation of line-ahead, passing the starboard tip of the Armada. The rest of the fleet, however, lies beyond, in no recognizable formation at all. The corresponding Adams chart shows an even better attempt at line-formation, but clearly, even there, *fleet* line-ahead is neither attained nor attempted. Further, it is certain that the whole fleet never even tried to act as one corporate body. Again and again we glimpse groups of ships, led by the Lord Admiral or Drake or Frobisher, operating quite independently from the rest; sailing from, and to, quite different points of the compass, sometimes miles apart and not, apparently, co-ordinated by any one mind. Later in the battle we shall see the fleet divided into squadrons; but, before that, anything like *fleet* tactics simply did not exist.

One corollary of this confusion must be faced at once. It is quite impossible now (it was probably impossible in 1588) to illustrate the Armada fighting by means of a set of neat, detailed diagrams, such as can readily be drawn to illustrate Trafalgar or Jutland. Neither combatant can be so stylized. We have ventured upon a diagram of the Spanish formation (p. 117); but it must be read as representing an ideal, the order which Sidonia would have liked to maintain. He certainly failed to maintain it; though for a long time (and herein lay its strength) he contrived to regain it. As it was, every few hours, if not every few minutes, its neat symmetry received cruel jars: ships were pushed hither and thither, tacked, backed, worn. No one could possibly portray the details diagrammatically, even if he knew them; and still more certainly if he knew as little about them as we do. All this holds true with the English ships also, only more so, because there was not even an ideal formation such as Sidonia had. We can only, then, pick our way as best we can through a maze of disconnected, and sometimes almost contradictory, clues, glimpsed sometimes in the Spanish authorities, and sometimes in ours.

The first shot of the battle had a superbly medieval ring. The Lord Admiral of England sent his 'defiance' to his opposite number. From the ranks of the English there emerged, all alone, a pinnace. Straight down she sped, making for what Howard evidently thought, though quite wrongly, to be the Duke's *San Martin*. When almost upon it, and still quite alone, she hauled up, and discharged a piece – of popgun size in such a ship – into the hull of her adversary. Then, daintily, she danced back unscathed. She was an 80-ton bark, commanded by Captain James Bradbury. And her name? The *Disdain*.

But to more serious matters. Having swept past the most exposed seaward tip of the Levant squadron, the English pressed on across what they supposed to be the concave hollow of the quarter-moon, and fetched up to windward of Recalde's squadron of Biscay. Here they set to work, and, plainly, the Spaniards did not like it. Several of their captains (of private, not of flagships) gave way to panic, left their stations and plunged foward into the forest of ships ahead of them. This phenomenon was to happen several times and, almost always, a closer examination of the ships concerned reveals the significant fact that their commanding officers were not noble, and, more important, that the military officers on board were not noble either. Needless to say, however, grim old Recalde himself, immune to such a disease, came about at once, and stood his ground manfully. Of his immediate squadron, it seems, only his vice-admiral, the *Gran Grin*, turned to his support. But then she carried two grandees, one of them Pimentel, the Colonel of a *tercio*. These two ships were thus left to the mercies of the English, and that unequal contest lasted for full two hours. Then slowly, and most inconveniently for the whole Armada, relief came. It took the form of the fleet-flagship, the *San Martin* herself, closely supported by the *San*

Mateo of the same squadron. These were Spain's real sailing-warships, engaged now for the first time. They had come, of course, right round the Armada in order to support Recalde, and it may readily be imagined what an upset this caused to the enemy's 'ideal' formation. Indeed, in the course of those two long hours, the main body of the Armada, moving slowly up-Channel, had fallen to leeward of Plymouth, forfeiting all chance of attacking it. Yet it could do none other than plough on, bringing the whole fight slowly up-Channel; for otherwise it would have been not two hours, but perhaps four or five before Sidonia could reach his hard-pressed rear. The whole episode, only the first of many, pinpoints the wrong positioning of what was now the main Spanish reserve.

This episode reveals something else. Whatever strictures we may have to pass upon the unfortunate Duke, we must admit that nothing whatever was wrong with his personal courage. Only once did he seem to fail there, so long as the fighting lasted, and that, as we shall see, was probably his Chief of Staff's fault. In fact, if only he could have served in a capacity better suited to his talents, as, say, a military captain, we should very likely never have heard of him, but at least his obscurity would have been an honourable one.

It was now about noon and, seeing the other galleons of the Spanish main-battle beating up behind the Duke, the Lord Admiral decided to hold his wind and call a temporary halt. This gives us an illuminating glimpse into Howard's mind and intentions. Though afterwards condemned in some quarters for half-heartedness, he was probably right. He was evidently feeling his way like everyone else, and he had not yet his full force around him, the inshore squadron (perhaps under Hawkins) not joining him till the afternoon. Nor was he yet prepared to risk physical contact with the enemy's heaviest-armed and best-soldiered ships. The Spaniards, not unnaturally, put quite a different interpretation on his action. They thought he was afraid of them – and that, in a limited sense, was true. But they could not come within a mile of catching him, and therefore turned to resume their defensive formation and their up-Channel course.

They had done neither, however, when fighting broke out anew. The reason was this. A ship in Oquendo's squadron was suddenly seen to blow up. She was his vice-flagship, the *San Salvador*, bearing the Spanish Paymaster-General and much of such treasure as the Armada carried. Sidonia infers that the explosion was an accident, but Calderon and others tell a different story. A gunner on board, not a Spaniard but a German (or in some accounts a Fleming), had incurred the wrath of his captain who had thrashed him. In revenge, he went below in order, as he said, to discharge a gun whose powder had got wetted, fired it, threw the port-fire into an open powder barrel, and jumped overboard. The explosion wrecked the ship's poop and the two highest decks aft, blew out her stern and killed some 200 of her people. Howard decided to take advantage of the resulting confusion, and attacked. Sidonia, as before, came back to defend, and Recalde in his damaged ship came across for the same purpose from his port wing. He soon found himself in the thick of it, and in his turn, needed rescuing again. The task this time fell to the lot of Pedro de Valdez, whose Andalusian squadron (see p. 117) formed the forward half of Recalde's rearguard. He therefore came about in his flagship *Nuestra Señora del Rosario*, only to run foul of another ship of his own squadron. The collision was serious. The *Rosario* lost her bowsprit and snapped the stay of her foremast which fell on to the mainmast. He too had to call for help.

The unhappy Duke now had no less than three cripples to attend to: and again he did not dither. Here was the sort of emergency he understood. His Castilian code demanded that he should stand by his greater ships. So he reached the nearest, the blazing *San Salvador*, extinguished the flames and hustled her into the main body of the hulks, where most of her treasure was removed. Then he went back and did a similar service to Recalde's *San Juan*, which was once more extricated. There remained the *Rosario*. But she, totally incapacitated and almost motionless, had fallen dangerously behind. Yet he reached her, and so did two of the galleasses, which tried to send across a hawser to take her in tow. But the wind had risen, the sea was too rough and the attempt failed. Then Sidonia decided to abandon her, and sent two *pataches* to take off de Valdez and his men. But that officer would not come. Here was one of those troublesome clashes of honour: Valdez felt he could not leave his ship; Sidonia felt he could not leave Valdez. Then the Duke, once more out of his depth, consulted Flores de Valdez, who advised leaving both commander and ship behind. To pass a moral judgement here is unprofitable. Technically, no doubt, Flores was right, and so was Sidonia in taking his advice. But, in his own code and that of all other Spaniards concerned, both were wrong; and his action lost the Duke the last scrap of respect in which his subordinates held him. Don Pedro was furious, as well he might be. But it was Flores who had to take the principal blame. Pedro and Flores, though cousins, were known to dislike one another, and it may be imagined what angry people said. When the Chief of Staff returned to Spain and the last account was made up, it was this episode more than any other which cast him into prison; and, meanwhile, he became, and remained, the best-hated man in the fleet. The surviving squadron leaders could no longer even be civil to him. After this, leaving the flagship of the Andalusian squadron to her fate, the Armada reformed as best it could, and limped off up-Channel.

Where lay the honours of the first day? It is fairest to pronounce them even. The Spaniards had been badly shaken, especially in morale. They had lost (or were now almost certain to lose) two ships of flag-status and one outstanding officer. They had been hustled far beyond Plymouth. But they were still on the way to their goal; their formation, though twice thrown into confusion, had been restored; and they now knew, or thought they did, the worst that those unpredictable heretics could do. But, oddly enough, the English were mildly shaken too. Howard himself was practically confessing as much when he wrote that night, 'We durst not adventure to put in among them, their fleet being so strong.' Even Drake was impressed; for he wrote, 'As far as we perceive they are determined to sell their lives with blows.' The English, also, had expended the valuable weapon of tactical surprise, the dividend of their new methods: they had not thrown the Armada into such irremediable confusion as they had hoped, and they had made no lasting impression upon its tight defensive formation.

It is perhaps more important, however, to gauge the effect of those new methods; for here we begin to see the shape of things to come. Did they now begin to suspect that they were not going to be an unmixed success? Perhaps not – yet. But the omens were there. Already they ought to have done better. For what were the tangible results of this first all-out gun-duel between rival fleets? Here, unfortunately, the greatest modern authority on the Armada fighting is not of much assistance. Anyone who reads Sir Julian Corbett's pages, and nothing else, would conclude that, by nightfall on the 21st, all was as good as over, though Corbett has to admit later, of course, that this was far from the case.

> In a moment he [Recalde] was cut off and surrounded. . . . Drake, Hawkins, Frobisher and several other vessels were there pouring into him at musket-shot a murderous fire such as never before had been seen at sea. . . . It was not until Recalde had stubbornly borne his punishment for two hours, and had his vessel completely disabled, that Sidonia succeeded in getting up a sufficient force to relieve him.

Now the odd thing about these desperate wounds, this devastating treatment, is that neither Recalde nor any of the Spanish writers seem to have noticed them. That might be merely a case of concealing losses, common enough in wars of all ages. But it certainly becomes very odd indeed when we find the persons alleged to have inflicted the damage remaining so invincibly modest as not to claim any! Let us take the evidence of those immediately concerned, on both sides.

> DRAKE: The 21st we had them in chase, and so coming up unto them, there passed some cannon-shot between some of our fleet and some of them.
>
> HAWKINS: We met with this fleet somewhat to the westwards of Plymouth upon Sunday in the morning, being the 21st July, when we had some small fight with them in the afternoon.

Delightful nonchalance, we may think at first. What was 'murderous fire' to the devoted Spaniard was a mere bagatelle to the great English seamen, to be alluded to and dismissed in a single airy phrase. But let us hear some more evidence.

HOWARD: We durst not adventure to put in among them, their fleet being so strong.

HENRY WHYTE (a volunteer in the *Mary Rose*): The majesty of the enemy's fleet, the good order they held, and the private consideration of our wants did cause, in my opinion, our first onset to be more coldly done than became the value of our nation and the credit of the English Navy.

What, next, of the evidence from the other side? What actual and substantial damage was inflicted upon the ships of Spain by this concentrated 'close-range' assault?

The *Rosario* was brought to a standstill, but by bad Spanish seamanship, not by good English gunnery. The latter did her no harm – Don Pedro himself says as much. He also gives a rather disconcerting reason:

Our ordnance played a long while on both sides, without coming to handstroke. There was little harm done, because the fight was far off.

The *San Salvador* was shattered; but by a deliberate act of sabotage from within, not by gunfire from without. The English had nothing to do with it.

What, finally, of the *San Juan* herself, flagship of the devoted Recalde, assailed at musket range, according to Corbett, by the three hardest hitters in the English fleet 'and several other vessels' (Sidonia says eight in all), completely disabled in the morning, yet somehow managing to get into the thick of it, and to be further hammered in the afternoon? Surely we shall hear of some substantial and definitive damage at last, some real ship damage, hull damage, leaks, shots between wind and water from those low-down, low-firing Englishmen?

But no: there is no hint of any wounds of that sort. The ship did not escape scatheless, of course. 'I sent a pinnace,' wrote Don Pedro, 'unto Juan Martinez de Recalde, to know whether he had received any harm: his answer was that his galleon had been sore beaten, and that his foremast was hurt with a great shot.' Sidonia confirms this, with a little more detail, but he also explains it in the same disconcerting way. 'The enemy attacked him [Recalde],' he wrote in his Diary, 'so fiercely with cannon (but without coming to close quarters) that they crippled his rigging, breaking his stay and striking his foremast twice with cannon-balls.'

Clearly the plain fact of the matter is that if Drake, Hawkins and Frobisher were really engaged as closely as Corbett says, then indeed the English artillery was by no means fulfilling the purpose for which the English had designed it, to batter, even sink, the enemy without giving him the opportunity to board.

Things were not quite so bad as that, however. All the evidence makes it abundantly clear, not only that Corbett has erred, but also where he is in error. It is in his estimate of the range. He assumed that the English came to point-blank range and having done that, thought (rightly) that, *at* point-blank, our roundshots, light as they were, must have been able to penetrate the enemy's hulls, and he therefore assumes that they did. The truth clearly is that they failed to do so. Why? Because the range was not point-blank, but much greater. Indeed, every contemporary writer, on both sides, stresses its length. Nor should we be surprised, considering the English fighting policy already described: to keep the range so open that the heavy Spanish pieces would not reach, and yet not so open that the long English ones would fall short. This disappointing result of the first day's firing, in fact, indicates clearly enough that we had made a miscalculation. We had demonstrated that we could dictate the range, at culverin-shot but outside effective cannon-shot. But we were finding, to our chagrin, that such a range was also outside *effective* culverin-shot. The guns we had provided, in fine, though long enough for our purposes in range, were too light for them in shot.

As for the Spaniards, Recalde doubtless replied to his persecutors as best he could. But neither he nor any other Spaniard claims that he hit them. Yet, if really surrounded for two whole hours by English ships firing at musket range, even the Spanish

gunners could hardly have scored nothing but misses! For the
rest, we are specifically told that de Levya played at long bowls
with some English ships (the inference being that they were
too far away to be hit); and that the *San Mateo* did not even
fire, hoping thus to induce the English to come nearer. The
English, of course, did not oblige and, in their turn, do not
own to being hit at all, at any stage. All this goes to corroborate
the rest of the evidence. The English were too far away to be
hurt, but also too far away to damage anything but masts and
rigging in the enemy ships.

10

THE ACTION OFF PORTLAND

Monday, July 22nd

THERE WAS LITTLE fighting on this day. The principal reason for this was a rather mysterious incident which took place during the night of the 21st–22nd. As dusk fell Howard had called a council in the *Ark Royal* and the English commanders took stock. As practical men, they concluded that Sidonia was bound to try to seize the Isle of Wight. It was the only sensible thing for him to do since, once past it, he would have no sheltered anchorage whatever in which to wait, if Parma was not exactly on time. Indeed, the Spaniards knew this too, and, though an assault on the island was contrary to Philip's ill-conceived orders, Medina's sailor lieutenants had persuaded him that it must be made. He does not admit this in his dispatch, partly because it was against orders, but mainly because (having failed to do it) he saw no point in admitting failure both to keep orders and to achieve anything having broken them. To counter this move, the English could easily have sailed ahead, and occupied the entrance to the Solent themselves. But that would have meant giving the Spaniards the wind, and so abandoning both their defensive strategy and their fighting tactics, since both depended upon retaining the windward position. They decided, therefore, to follow the enemy, as closely as possible without actually coming to grips or losing the wind; torment and hustle him at every opportunity, and be right on his tail when he came abreast of Wight. They pressed on into the night, then, with Drake given the honour of leading the fleet, and the rest following the gleam of his great stern lantern.

All went well at first, but suddenly, the light went out. Confusion followed. No night signals existed, and no orders covered this contingency. Some held their course, some shortened sail, some stopped. Howard, as puzzled as any, pressed straight on with those near him, and, when dawn came, found himself hard up against the Armada off Berry Head. Of his own fleet, a very few were in immediate company, a few more hull down to the west, and the remainder out of sight. Things might have gone very ill with him had his opponent shown any enterprise at all. But Sidonia's orders were 'Up-Channel', and up-Channel he proceeded. None the less, he did benefit greatly from nearly a whole day's respite, and the Armada made valuable ground unchallenged.

Gradually the English fleet closed up again, and Drake re-appeared, to explain how, in the very early hours of the morning, he had seen strange sails passing him to starboard, moving down-Channel. Instantly he suspected that they were Spaniards deliberately trying to steal the wind, and, since this must be prevented at all costs, he had turned, to follow and stop them. He extinguished his stern-light because he did not think that Howard would want the whole fleet to come with him, thus losing precious distance from the enemy.

This sounded all right. Unfortunately, however, by no means everyone believed in those ghostly sails, notably the forthright Frobisher, who never lost an opportunity of suspecting the worst of Drake. Moreover the rest of his story lent some colour to the charges of his enemies. He soon discovered (he said so himself) that the westbound ships he had seen were German merchantmen pursuing their lawful occasions down-Channel; and he was just coming about to rejoin when he found himself in the presence of a large enemy ship wearing a full suit of Spanish colours. She was all alone, save for one small English craft which hovered near, ostensibly waiting to see that her big adversary did not slip away. The Spaniard was *Nuestra Señora del Rosario*, with the intrepid Pedro still on board. The English ship was the *Margaret and John*, 200 tons, Captain John Fisher, one of the London squadron and the property of John Watts, citizen (and later Lord Mayor) of London. Drake soon resolved that problem. He summoned de Valdez to surrender, and the Spaniard instantly complied. This was in the code too: a flag-officer might without dishonour surrender to a flag-officer. Indeed, if we may believe the courtly Don, it was a positive privilege to yield to so renowned a captor; and Drake, no wit behind in such courtesies, instantly had him on board the *Revenge* (along with his valuables), housed him in his own cabin and, fetching up his best plate, dined him at his own table. It was indeed an important *coup* – a fine flagship and an officer who, after Recalde, constituted the most grievous loss that Spain could suffer. The English were delighted: it was just the moral fillip they required. So pleased were they, in fact, that (save for Frobisher and his friends) they even forgot to inquire how Drake came to be there. If we do that, we shall find it full late in the day to reach a conclusion. On the whole, though, we must surely acquit him. That he deliberately decided to let down Howard, the whole fleet and the nation in deadly peril; that he invented the whole story of the mysterious sails simply in order to pick up a hypothetical prize (for he cannot have known where the *Rosario* was) are suppositions much less likely to be true than was his own story. There is simply no proof of his guilt, especially since magic mirrors have lost their potency as evidence. On the other hand, if he did see the sails, he was making the right choice between difficult alternatives.

Accompanying him was one of his own larger auxiliaries, the *Roebuck*, 300 tons, Captain Jacob Whiddon, a ship belonging to Sir Walter Raleigh. Drake now dispatched Whiddon with his prize into the nearby harbour of Dartmouth, with orders to strip her of guns, powder and shot without delay. All these commodities were in very short supply just then. In every south-coast port lay 'voluntary' ships, prevented from joining in only because they had neither powder nor shot; and Whiddon's orders were to distribute the stuff immediately. Here, for once, we are allowed a peep behind the opaque veil which shrouds so much that was picturesque in that exciting week. Whiddon had no sooner passed the lovely entrance to the port than boats innumerable put out, and the men of Dartmouth swarmed over the *Rosario*'s side. The local magistrates, Sir John Gilberte and Sir George Cary, apprised of the event, hurried to the town. But they were much too late. As far as great guns were concerned, Captain Whiddon was a fervent believer in the motto of 'first come first served'. Out of 12 or

13 which were considered worth having, he appropriated 10, and never disgorged them thereafter. Much of the smaller ordnance, the magistrates complained, was instantly 'imbeass-elled away' by some person or persons unknown who arrived before they did. For the rest, 'there are four or five pipes of wine and vinegar privily hoised over board'. In fine, concluded the harassed Cary, 'I was never mitch experienced in these causes before this time: but now I find that all these sea-goods are mixed with bird-lime: for no man can lay his hand of them, but is limed, and must bring away somewhat. Watch and look never so narrowly, they will steal and pilfer.' Then, more in sorrow than in anger, the worthy gentlemen went home – with a couple of pipes of wine apiece.

Later in the morning the English plucked another fine feather. The half-burnt *San Salvador* declined to go any farther, and the Duke ordered her to be emptied and sunk. There were, however, many badly scorched men on board, and before the task could be accomplished the leading English ships caused the Spanish demolition party to withdraw. The Lord Admiral sent Lord Thomas Howard and Hawkins to take possession, but they did not stay long. 'The stink in the ship was so unsavoury and the sight within board so ugly' that they soon departed, leaving it to Flemyng of the *Golden Hind* to take the prize into Weymouth. There, no doubt, something of the Dartmouth scene was re-enacted, but no details have survived.

It was late in the afternoon before the reunited English fleet came within extreme range of the Armada, and then the wind fell dead, with the combatants lying nearly off Portland. Sidonia, meanwhile, had used his respite for quite a consider-able reorganization. Realizing now that the main English strength lay behind him, he decided to augment his covering force. The old vanguard and rearguard were united into a single rear, and put under the command of de Leyva, the ex-van's commander. His combined squadrons were then further strengthened by four of the Portuguese galleons, the best ships in the fleet, and by two more of the galleasses. Thus 43 of Spain's true fighting ships were now concentrated in the rear. The rest of the formation was retained, in modified form. The

English noticed these changes, which are reflected both in their (still vague) descriptions of the Spanish array, and in some at any rate of the Adams Charts. Our writers now refer to the enemy's formation as a 'plump', or a 'roundel', and no longer as any form of moon; and Adams sometimes depicts the Armada as sailing in an almost circular clump. What had happened, probably, was that de Leyva, now commanding a single 'rear', saw that its outer squadrons, hitherto trailing away to the west, had been too easy a prey to our attacks, and too hard to succour when attacked, and so advanced them at least to the level of the inner squadrons. More likely, he advanced them even farther, thus causing the concave side of the quarter-moon to face, no longer west (towards the pursuing English), but east, to curl round the central body of hulks; and, by approaching nearer to the van division's galleons, to enable these key ships to turn more easily to their support. Such a formation, with its now convex curve of retreating sterns, would, when viewed from sea-level, suggest a plump (or a roundel) rather than a quarter-moon.

That afternoon, too, Sidonia performed a very necessary duty. He put police sergeant-majors and provost-marshals into a pinnace, and sent them all round the new rear division, with a plan of the exact position allotted to every ship. They were armed with halters, and definite instructions to hang every captain who left his assigned station. The panic flight of some of Recalde's ships on the Sunday was not to be repeated. It was vital to retain the Armada's defensive formation, and Sidonia knew it.

Tuesday, July 23rd

The engagement off Portland on Tuesday, July 23rd, may be best understood if the account of it is allowed to start on the Monday evening. There was a bright moon shining, but still no breeze, when the English became aware of a stir in the Spanish ranks. They thought they saw the flash of oars. Were the galleasses moving, then? Was this to be the trial of strength between the rival types? It was certainly perfect galleass weather. But it was not to be just yet. The attack never came because, the English said, the enemy's heart failed him. That was not the reason, which was at once more picturesque and, to the Spaniards, more sinister. Don Hugo de Moncada, the haughty knight of Santiago who commanded them, had approached the Duke earlier, and asked leave to launch his heavily armed craft at the English flagship; and Sidonia had refused him. It was the code again. By that strange all-binding convention 'like fights with like'. Only Sidonia could, in honour, challenge Howard. Moncada's pride was stung. Like Achilles he retired to a position remote from the scene of action, and sulked. But now the other high-ranking officers all saw that the hour of the galleasses had come, and went in a body to Sidonia, urging him to let Moncada loose. He agreed. But evidently the Commander-in-Chief himself stood in some awe of his fierce subordinate, because he took two precautions. He sent the popular Oquendo to convey the order in person and he added, by way of *douceur*, the promise of an estate in Spain worth 3,000 ducats. But Moncada would have none of it. He simply ignored the order, and the chance passed.

At about 5 am the breeze came, and it came offshore from the northeast. For the first time the Armada had the wind. Despite this handicap, however, it was the English who moved first. A number of ships worked inshore, attempting to weather the enemy. Leading them, indeed, probably lying farther to the north from the start, was Frobisher who, not for the last time, was to show more valour than discretion. It was a tempting move, but dangerous, and perhaps he should not have made it. For he was successful: with six ships he worked to windward (i.e. northeast) of the enemy, or very nearly. Moreover, being apparently almost up against Portland Bill, he had little room for manoeuvre. Nothing could have promised better for the Spaniards: here was a splinter of the English fleet to the north, inshore and all but isolated. Howard, meanwhile, had started with the same intent but, either failing or seeing the danger in time, had given up and headed northwest, hoping to work round to Frobisher that way. Here he was stoutly attacked by the rearguard leaders de Leyva, Oquendo and Bertendona, who made very determined efforts to board him and his consorts; and Sidonia soon joined in. It was the closest that the combatants had yet got to each other, and there was heavy firing. It even looked for a moment as though Howard meant to close. He steered towards the *San Martin* followed, in that rough line-ahead already described, by several of the Queen's greatest ships. Sidonia, supported by a similar number of his best galleons, stood his ground, and the rival flag-ships passed fairly close. Then, according to Sidonia, the rest of the English thought better of it, opened up the range and passed at a much greater distance, apparently with ease, even though deprived of the weather gauge. Anyway, an immense amount of ammunition was expended on both sides, with results which we shall shortly consider.

Meanwhile, Howard had not rescued Frobisher, the bulk of the Armada still lying between them; and Frobisher's position, theoretically, was precarious. For now (a Spanish eyewitness tells us) Sidonia himself ranged up to the galleasses, and sent an officer expressly to 'say aloud to Don Hugo de Moncada certain words which . . . were not to his honour'. Thereupon the proud man, still rather sulkily, launched his quartet at Frobisher, and the nearest galleons followed as best they could.

Frobisher has always been acclaimed the hero of the fight which followed; and rightly, though perhaps he should not have been there at all. The engagement showed anyone ready to learn that the hybrid galleass, as a type, had no future against our sailing galleons. Frobisher's ship, the *Triumph*, was the biggest on our side, perhaps on either side. But she was an old ship, of pre-Hawkins vintage, and as a sailer was nothing like so flexible as, say, the *Revenge*. Yet Frobisher (who at least had nothing to learn about seamanship) succeeded in keeping his distance without difficulty, hampered for sea-room though he was. At the same time he inflicted serious damage on his adversaries: not by holing them – his shots at his chosen range were not heavy enough for that – but by aiming at the rowing-decks, disabling their primary motive power by killing and wounding the rowers and smashing their oars. These huge sweeps, cumbrous at the best of times, were almost impossible to handle when they lost rhythm and fouled one another. So Moncada was constrained to reset his sails – a means of progress known to be inferior to the sailing performance of a galleon. In fine, he took a good beating, and quite failed to corner any Englishmen. None the less, this first phase of the action off Portland was an altogether harder affair than anything before it.

Now, around midday, the wind began to veer, steadily but quite quickly, to east, southeast, south and, finally, southwest. And almost at once the enemy had an unpleasant surprise. Out of the clouds of smoke, till now drifting seawards, there suddenly appeared a body of ships which the Spaniards estimated at 50 sail. It charged full tilt into the starboard wing of their rearguard, and drove the whole Armada beyond the Bill and up-Channel. To meet that attack Sidonia had to withdraw everything he had from his northward attack, and Frobisher was at once released. No one, in either camp, has ever told us what these ships were or who led them. Yet there cannot be much doubt. It was Drake in the *Revenge*. What had happened, probably, was this. Watching Howard's efforts to reach Frobisher on the shoreward flank of the battle, Drake had realized their futility, and did not follow. Instead, more weatherwise than most, he anticipated the change of wind: for morning land winds, later veering to sea winds, were common in the Channel. While awaiting the change, he worked quietly out to sea unnoticed by anyone, and was thus, when his prophecy came true, in exactly the right position to launch his attack, quickly, and with the maximum advantage of surprise. This brought on the last phase of the day's fighting, and it was perhaps the fiercest yet: for Howard, seeing the advantage Drake had gained, instantly turned and attacked the *San Martin* herself, while Drake seems to have isolated Recalde yet again ; and again he had to be extricated.

But still the Armada survived to sail away, with no further losses and with its formation re-established. Once again the rather disappointing results contrast strangely with Corbett's dramatic narrative. 'His [Sidonia's] punishment was terrible.' The English 'poured their fire into the helpless flagship. . . .'

'The *San Martin* was in a desperate plight.' Was it? But again neither side said so at the time, and again, surely, the answer was the same. The English were too lightly gunned to smash the enemy at any but point-blank, and they still did not intend to close to that range. Certainly some of the fighting was closer than any off Plymouth; both sides say so, mentioning even ranges like 100 and 120 yards. But even that – if correct – was evidently too great: for neither side, though each claims hits and human casualties (one Spaniard admits 50 killed in the flagship), claims any material ship-damage. Yet, if Sidonia is to be believed, he stood up to the fire, in succession, of the *Ark Royal* and her powerful consorts, acquitting himself so well, that the last half of the squadron opened the range, and then sailing away with no damage of fabric to report. Calderon, it is true, does own to a little, but its very triviality is revealing. 'The enemy shot at the Duke at least 500 cannon-balls, some of which struck the hull and others his rigging, carrying away his flagstaff and one of the stays of his mainmast.' Notice that word 'struck', not 'pierced'; and, at really short range, would it be physically possible for a roundshot to hit a flagstaff? The Spanish claims are even vaguer. All Sidonia can say is that the enemy's flagship *seemed* to have suffered some hurts. Calderon is a shade more definite. The *San Martin* 'fired over 80 shots from one side only, and inflicted great damage on the enemy'. On its nature he is silent, and, in the same breath, he is admitting essential failure because, during the whole fighting period, 'we were trying to come up with them', and demonstrably failing.

The whole episode, however, is an interesting one and shows, perhaps, an English range experiment. Very likely the *Ark* did come close for a short time; but the ships following her, seeing the weight of the enemy's heavy shot, perhaps for the first time, realized that the moment for closing was not yet, and wisely kept farther away. Indeed, Corbett may be right when he affirms that both sides missed golden opportunities that day – the Spanish of cutting Frobisher off for good, the English of breaking the Armada in half in the last phase. But, here as elsewhere, he seems to be ignoring the weight of the enemy shot, and forgetting the purely military odds against England. One or two lucky hits from 50-pound balls might well have done Sidonia's business for him. No English ship, not the *Ark* herself, once seriously crippled aloft, could have survived. Nor is there any evidence that Drake ventured any nearer. Certainly he obstructed neither the retreat nor the re-forming.

This Portland round, in fact, may be judged a draw, slightly in favour of Spain. The Armada was a day's sailing nearer its bourne, with no more ships lost and order still intact. The English had pricked the galleasses' bubble, but they had fulfilled none of their declared aims. They had not impeded their enemy's progress, nor broken them up, nor even plucked any more stray feathers. Nor was time on their side. The Armada was already almost halfway from its Cornish landfall to its Flemish rendezvous. Lastly, judged solely as a punching match, the round had proved distinctly tame. England's longer reach had warded off punishment, but she had inflicted very little.

The attack on the *Capitana* Galleass off Calais, July 29th

Don Miguel de Oquendo

The *Flavit Jehovah* medal, 1588.
Obverse and reverse

The track of the Spanish Armada
(*The number of Spanish ships shown between Cape Clear and the French Channel-coast is greatly exaggerated: only three or four are known to have taken this course*)

11

THE ACTION OFF THE ISLE OF WIGHT

NOW ANOTHER precious day was lost, or nearly. There was a little fighting towards evening when Recalde, once more leading the rear, was again attacked, and when the flagship of the hulks, *El Gran Griffon*, was all but cut off, escaping only after Sidonia had brought back his galleons. But, compared with either the preceding or the following action, the affair was insignificant: and all day the Armada made good progress towards the Isle of Wight. Our reluctance to close, said the Spaniards complaisantly, was due to our fear of the stern-fire of the galleasses now bringing up the rear. This, of course, was absurd. The real reason was far more serious. Howard is quite frank about it:

> There was little done, for that in the fight on Sunday and Tuesday much of our ammunition had been spent, and therefore the Lord Admiral sent divers barks and pinnaces unto the shore for a new supply of such provisions.

He obtained some, but not nearly enough. Thereafter the shortage was chronic, and grew worse and worse until we had no ammunition at all. Here, probably, we touch the root cause of England's failure to secure overwhelming victory in battle. True, she won, but, to do it, she had to summon nature and geography to help her. Who was to blame for the shortage? The Government? Yes, the Government must always be the first scapegoat when this sort of breakdown occurs. The ministers, even though watched by a Queen notoriously hawk-eyed where expenditure was concerned, certainly ought to have provided more: which, in a perennially unprepared country like ours, means that it ought to have had the foresight to establish powder-mills, foundries and shot-towers not then in existence, but ready against the day. In short, the

Government ought to have displayed a degree of foresight so remarkable as to incline us to excuse it for its failure. Moreover the prescience necessary to foretell how this particular event would go would have been the more wonderful, the more exceptional, because the event itself was unique, so far, in our history. One all-out fight in the Channel – yes; that was to be expected, and provided for. Two? Well, perhaps; and that was covered, or nearly. But four, with several minor skirmishes! That was the size of it in the event.

As for Spain, Philip, who (in his own eyes anyway) had some reputation as a planner, certainly thought that he had made ample provision when he furnished his fleet with 123,790 roundshot and 517,500 pounds of powder. He appreciated the need of a generous stock too, since replenishments would almost certainly be unprocurable in the Channel. But, like the English, he could not prophesy what vast calls would be made upon the stock. The four set battles caught him as they caught the English, though it must be recorded to his credit that his provision (never replaced at any moment of the campaign) lasted better than ours, which was frequently, if inadequately, replenished; also that his Armada, though it ran out of roundshot, at no time ran out of powder.

Yet both governments had been warned, and by people who presumably knew. Drake was telling the council as early as March 30th that he had enough powder in his squadron only for one and a half days' fighting – a pretty accurate estimate. And Bobadilla, the Spanish military commander, made an even more accurate forecast. He told the King, before he left home, that 'if the enemy did not allow us to board them, and if the artillery fight lasted four days, he might tell me what we might do on the fifth day'. Could Cassandra herself have done better?

No figures survive to show what store of ammunition the English expended first and last; none, in all probability, were ever produced. Here again the investigator suffers from the fact that, whereas the Armada was organized from the start as a unified expedition, our defence, throughout, was makeshift. Years ago the present author attempted to reach some finite conclusion, and succeeded up to a point, but to a point only; and he was more successful with powder than with shot. Thus he discovered that, in England in 1595, there existed the wherewithal to manufacture 595,285 pounds of powder. But not half this amount can have been available for the English fleet in 1588; probably not nearly half. Several formidable subtractions must be made. First, the fleet catered for in 1595 was a good deal larger; second, the unfortunate failure of supplies in 1588 must have rubbed in the lesson that more was necessary; and, third, the 1595 figure represents all the powder in England, not the Navy's share. Now in 1588 there were many other calls upon powder stores; to name but a few, the requirements of all the local land-defence forces in all the countries, provision for both the mobile armies already described, the stock for all defended towns and cities and all the forts round the coast, especially for the castle of Berwick-upon-Tweed, well-gunned and garrisoned by a substantial army designed to see that James of Scotland behaved himself. But, though there remains no exact figure of the powder carried by our fleet, such numbers as we do know are on a scale altogether smaller than the half million pounds in the enemy's holds. Thus, in February 1588, the stock in the Tower, the Queen's central depository, was only 70,000 pounds, and that not all made up, but in its primary components of charcoal, sulphur and saltpetre. This is not so helpful as it might be, because we do not know what was then in the ships; but that quantity was not probably very large since comparatively few of them were then ready for sea. Again, after the fighting started, some 60,000 to 70,000 extra pounds were scraped up, on which, presumably, the English fleet fought its last two actions. These figures, incomplete as they are, seem sufficient to show that our stocks were nowhere near the half million carried by the enemy.

Further, there is evidence that this half million was no pious hope, not even a minimum. Almost certainly the Armada carried more. Naples alone furnished 430,000 pounds, and Florence and Carthagena enough to bring the total well over the half million, which is thus reached without counting any from the rest of Spain, Portugal and the Empire. Also, it was all first-grade powder, of maximum strength and efficiency, and suitable for use in every type of firearm, even the harquebus. This required a sort known as 'fine-corn', which was one-third more efficient than 'coarse-corn'. (Our heavy pieces were still firing coarse-corn, and some of them a brand less efficient still, known as 'serpentine'.) Thus, in quality no less than quantity, the enemy was ahead of us. Nor did they ever run short. To the last they had a store of fine-corn which they could have used in their great ordnance had their roundshot lasted.

But for this fact, the roundshot story is substantially the same. Again we know the Spanish grand total – 123,790 cannon-balls, and we know what was carried in some named ships, notably the galleasses. These had the extraordinarily high average of 134 rounds per gun. This was much above the general average, which works out at only 51 throughout the fleet. But the last-named figure means little, since obviously the hulks and pinnaces, etc., would carry very few as compared with the fighters. From such figures, and other odd ones which survive, we may safely conclude that, in the ships which fought, the average per gun was at least 80, probably rather more. Again English totals are not available. But an examination of known numbers in individual ships leads to the surprising conclusion that the official shot-per-gun allowance in English ships was nearer 20 than 30; and this was for royal ships, which one would expect to be better supplied than auxiliaries. The largest-known average figure of the whole period, that in the two royal ships which Drake, the great gun-lover, took to the West Indies in 1585–6, is only 36. In fact the English average cannot have been larger than 30. This is indeed amazing. What a paradox! The Spaniards do not believe in the gun as the main weapon of sea warfare. The English do: they rely on it entirely. Surely, then, the Spanish shot-lockers will be comparatively empty, the English bulging to overflowing? Yet it is the other way about. The clue to the conundrum is, I believe, partly supplied by Drake and Bobadilla. Our ships were supplied (rather grudgingly) with a ration for one and a half days' fighting. The enemy's supply was designed to last for four days. This brings the respective averages to something like equality: but even so some radical English neglect is indicated. It lies, probably, in the Government's and above all the Queen's obstinate refusal to face the full implications of Drake's policy which they pretended to have accepted, and a short-sighted effort to cut down the cost of this vital commodity.

Howard had recognized the danger early, when he ordered a swift redistribution of the *Rosario*'s and the *San Salvador*'s stocks. After Portland the crisis was upon him. It must have been clear to him, too, that these scarce and precious commodities had been recklessly expended in the first two fights. In the excitement of those early clashes, all our ships had been blazing away irrespective of results. No doubt the chiefs themselves had been guilty of this, not unpardonably because they had to discover at what range their guns could profitably be used. Now, almost too late, they had gleaned some knowledge on that point, and they could fairly easily control the fire of their own flagships in future; and perhaps that of their near neighbours. But in a fleet which possessed no squadron organization they could exercise little if any control over most of the ships; and these, unless something was done quickly, might well continue in their fatal course until no ammunition was left. This was one reason, and perhaps the main one, why, on that quiet Wednesday – quiet because the ammunition *had* been wasted – Howard decided upon an important reorganization. He divided the fleet up into four groups and allotted to each a responsible commander. One he gave to Drake, one to Hawkins, one to Frobisher and the last he kept himself. As a measure of ammunition-economy alone it was a great advance.

There were other reasons too. The lack of all orders and system, prevailing up to this moment, had meant a serious loss of concerted effort, and, no less serious, an almost complete loss of unified control. Hitherto, save in a most general way, Howard had not been commanding his own fleet; neither had Drake, nor anyone else. How far this liberty to go-as-you-please existed among ordinary (non-flag) ships is far from clear. We dimly see this leader or that – 'with four ships', 'with eight ships', or even 'with 50 ships' – emerging from the fog of time and battle for an instant and engaging in some enterprise or other: part of a semi-unified command for a moment, but not continuing as such, and apparently not ordered to be such. Individuals seem to be going their own sweet way to a degree which would have horrified a Jellicoe, a Nelson or even a Blake. Drake is ordered to lead the fleet on Sunday night, but were any other ships formally 'attached to his flag'? Probably there were not. When he turned to seaward in the darkness, a few followed him for a while, but, by morning, only one ship, the *Roebuck*, was in company. He found the *Margaret and John* watching Don Pedro, however. How came she there? That question, as it happens, can be answered, because her captain afterwards put in a claim (which survives) for a share in the prize. No one had told him to follow the wounded Spaniard. It was entirely his own doing: he positively boasts of the initiative which he had shown. Or again, on a higher level, what was Frobisher doing off Portland Bill on the Tuesday? Who, if anyone, told him to try and steal the Spaniard's wind? Assuredly not Howard. What were the five ships with him, and who told them to be with him? Or again, on an even higher and larger scale, did Howard order Drake to make his seaward move later in the day? Did he detail 50 ships to accompany him? The answer to both questions is almost certainly 'No'. How, then, did Drake collect those 50 ships? There is no evidence that they were in any permanent way attached to him. They were certainly not all members of his original Western Squadron. Did he then just hail any passing ship with a 'Ho, you there! Follow me'? It is possible, but, more likely, the affair was more haphazard even than this. A number of private captains, with no immediate idea of how to make themselves useful, perhaps caught sight of Drake's flag, recognized it, and thought, 'There's Drake. He's the man for me. He'll lay us near a Don if anyone can!'

Conditions of such chaos are a little hard to visualize. But they must have existed, if only for one reason. Signalling from ship to ship, by flag or any other means, was virtually non-existent. The Commander-in-Chief could issue a summons for a council and an order for battle; and, probably, other ships could, by firing guns at different intervals, communicate information like 'I am aground', or 'I see strange sails', but little if anything else. Thus any subordinate outside vocal range was left entirely ignorant of his superior's wishes. There was, however, one minor exception. It would appear that those few ships which were royal (a bare 20 per cent of them all) had general instructions from their commander which sometimes governed their conduct: orders, for instance, to 'support his flag', or at least to keep his flag in view. No written instructions of this sort and of this date survive, however, and if (as is probable) they did exist, they would be only of the most general nature. They would, for instance, prevent the Lord Admiral from finding himself quite isolated in the face of a strong enemy concentration; they might enable him, at fairly short notice, to form one of those temporary 'lines' just mentioned. It was something; but not much because, in the smoke and heat of a *mêlée*, such directions would lose all potency. Then individual captains had to judge for themselves.

There was one more reason why Howard had to try to reduce the chaos when he did. His fleet was growing daily, almost hourly. All the way up-Channel, from almost every port however small, there issued new volunteers: Englishmen roused: fierce, fearless men led by their natural leaders, the local gentry; dead set upon having a go at the enemy they hated, but with little experience in such matters and, of course, with no directive whatever. It must be regretfully recorded that, in practice, these gallant and devoted people did not pull their weight. There was a time when our patriotic historians would have had us believe that it was this cloud of knights-errant, buzzing like a swarm of angry gnats about the ears of the devoted Spaniards, which fairly stung them out of the Channel. This is demonstrably absurd. If the Navy Royal and the cream of our Merchant fleet, adapted for war, could not break the Armada's tight formation, what chance had these new ships, mostly very small, not designed for fighting and unsuited to it, armed for the most part (when armed at all) with old iron pieces scrounged from heaven knows where, and furnished with a minimum of that most sought-after commodity, ammunition? Indeed, could that have been taken from them and distributed among the fighting ships which lacked it, the navy of England would have been the stronger for it, even though that meant the little ships staying in port. Still, no true Englishman will regret that they sailed. In the realm of moral values, as an indication of the spirit of the times and the English people, the bare fact of their putting out had intense importance. There was to come a day, 352 years later, when, with not identical but still very similar motives, the Little Ships put out again, to play their own unforgettable part in 'our finest hour'. The parallel between these 'voluntary ships' of 1588 and those of Dunkirk in 1940 needs no labouring.

This reorganization into squadrons, then, was very necessary, and it certainly reduced the chaos. In future every captain would at least know where his first allegiance lay. Henceforth he must watch his own leader's flag, be prepared at all times to support him, and be within reasonable distance of him and the rest of his squadron. And this wise move did in fact contribute towards making the subsequent actions a thought less chaotic; though, even so, they would still have brought on a fit of apoplexy in Blake, Nelson or Jellicoe. But somewhere a beginning must be made, and here, beyond all doubt, is the true beginning of English sailing-fleet tactics.

Thursday, July 25th

From tactics we turn to strategy. We have reached the strategic crisis of the Channel fights. At first light on the Thursday the Armada, still intact, was off Dunnose, the southern point of the Isle of Wight. It had already passed the first entrance into the Solent, but that meant nothing, because the Needles passage was not then considered safe for ships of any size. Every principle of strategy dictated that Sidonia should enter the Solent from the east and occupy the Island. It was no new idea. In our previous wars with the French, they had almost always started with this intention. Moreover on the last occasion – which, being only forty-three years before, was still in living memory – they had occupied and used the anchorage of St Helens, and even landed troops. Once they had it, Sidonia and Parma between them might well be able to dictate the timing of the remaining moves, and Sidonia spared the dangers of the shoal-strewn Flemish waters.

And the English must prevent it. They had chafed at Wednesday's delay, and they meant to lose no more time. Having received some small replenishment of ammunition, they would not wait even for daylight. The weather was quiet, the moon nearly full, and they decided upon a night-attack. They could hardly risk their big ships in so uncertain an enterprise. But they felt justified in considering as expendable 24 small ones, six from each of the new squadrons; and these were detailed to penetrate into the heart of the Armada and try whether the surprise they caused could upset that stubborn formation which had so far defied them. The scheme deserved a better fate. In the event, the wind died away altogether and the attack could not be launched.

But it was still very early morning when the fight began. It is an exasperating one for the historian because, with only reasonable luck, he would be able to record in some detail, for the first time, what really happened. Beyond doubt the movements of the English were more co-ordinated than on the earlier days. Clearly the four squadrons acted as separate entities, the ships in each remaining under the control of their commanders. But our luck is out, because, this time and on the other side, there was a definite conspiracy of silence. The Spanish commanders did not want anyone, even Philip, to know what happened. Their accounts, therefore, are deliberately disingenuous. That Sidonia intended to seize the Island we know from his previous correspondence. But, as he failed, he was not going to mention it, and in fact says nothing about the attempt. Less help is to be expected from the English side, because our main authority, Howard's narrative, is never helpful in elucidating fleet tactics. As ever, it confines itself almost entirely to what he saw; and since (as at Portland) the other squadrons operated on their own, and at times far away from him, he fails entirely to tell us what they did. Drake's name is never mentioned. Some said at the time that this omission was deliberate, either through jealousy or because he had not forgiven the *Rosario* affair. But this sounds quite unlike Howard, and is not borne out by any other evidence. More likely, he never had a full and true picture of the whole action himself. Even his narrative, called *Relation of Proceedings*, and usually regarded as an official report, was not written by him, but, immediately after the event, by a Florentine named Ubaldino. This man later approached Drake, purposing to write a longer version incorporating the Vice-Admiral's own material. But delays occurred, and his enlarged second edition, which appeared only in 1589, is disappointing. It seems too anxious to praise everyone indiscriminately. Drake receives a little more attention, it is true, but still there is no real hint of what he was doing, especially on this day. This second edition, in fact, has lost the authentic ring of the first. That, one feels, was at least based upon information received direct from Howard. This hardly sounds like a contemporary document at all. It contains little that is new, though it borrows a few personal anecdotes from other writers; and it throws little further light on the actual fighting. Thus posterity still only knows that Sidonia meant to attack the Island, but did not: did not even enter the Solent, but was somehow driven right past it. But how, and by whom? On these points all contemporary writers remain obstinately silent.

None the less, an attempt can be made to answer these vital questions. The explanation in these pages will follow, in the main, that of the modern historian whose interpretation seems at once the most imaginative and the most likely. Sir Julian Corbett may have erred on some of the more detailed points of guns and gunnery, but on the whole strategy of the campaign and on its wider tactics he remains unrivalled.

The battle off the Wight bears a marked tactical resemblance to that off Portland, though now the English had the much more specific strategic aim of denying the Island to the invader. The four English squadrons, close on the Armada's heels, were disposed in the following order. Northernmost, and therefore nearest to the Island, was Frobisher, just as, at Portland, he had been nearest to the Bill. This would be his accepted place – on the left, the position usually allotted to the junior flag-officer. Next, to his south, came Howard, then Hawkins (though possibly these two were the other way about). Howard would certainly be in the centre, but unfortunately there is no exact centre of four. This leaves Drake on the extreme right, the Vice-Admiral's natural place. All four squadrons were as near the Island as possible at the start, nearer a little than were the Spaniards. This too was natural. Our object was to stop the enemy entering the Solent, and the most obvious way to accomplish this was, if possible, to pass round the left or landward wing of the Armada, and occupy the entrance ourselves.

The first fighting began with the dawn, and it might have been Portland over again. The English spied one hulk, the *Santa Anna*, and one galleon, the Portuguese *San Luis*, which had dropped astern of station during the night. Hawkins was sent (or, more likely, went) to attack them in the usual way. A morning breeze, however, must have been blowing off shore, light, probably, but again just as at Portland; for his ships had to be towed to the attack. Thereupon three of the galleasses, at their best in a light breeze, came forth with de Leyva's *Rata Coronada* to challenge him. The Lord Admiral came up to support Hawkins, and partial action was joined. According to Howard, much execution was done upon the galleasses, though, when he condescends to details, they are by no means impressive. One 'lost her lantern which came swimming by, and another her nose'; but the third, he claims, was 'carried away upon the careen', which, for once, implies that she was holed. Still, the Spaniards seem to have had the last word in this round too, because they brought their lame ducks back to the Armada in safety. But, before that was accomplished, the *San Martin*, which had come back to help, had a close call, the Spaniards admitting more fatal casualties and the loss of her mizen-yard halyard. This time she was rescued, not by the royal galleons which usually supported her but by some of the rearguard who chanced to witness her distress.

All this, however, was but a prelude. Thereafter the parallel with Portland is for a while closer than ever. The eager Frobisher had, as before, pressed on under the Island so firmly (if not so rashly) that he was much too far east, and in momentary danger of being cut off again; especially since (as at Portland) the wind now began to veer, slowly and clockwise, until at length it settled at SSW, or even at SW. He was almost if not quite alone too. At this point the Spanish accounts are most unhelpful; not deliberately – as yet – but because of their persistent habit of calling any English flag-bearing ship 'the enemy *Capitana*', which, of course, should mean Howard's *Ark Royal*. Now Sidonia, his own danger passed, reports 'the enemy *Capitana* to leeward of him, alone and cut off'. It cannot have been the *Ark* which, though very likely to leeward of him early in the morning, was now, as the wind veered, lying more and more to his windward. It almost certainly was not Hawkins's *Victory*, which was much farther south, still less Drake's *Revenge*, farther south still. It was obviously Frobisher's *Triumph* which, as we have seen, was not only isolated but also, now that the wind had come round, to leeward of most of the enemy fleet. In that body there was great excitement. They thought they had him for certain: the English C.-in-C.! According to Purser Calderon, the ship's helm was injured and she could not steer, but this seems to have been wishful thinking. They admitted, however, that she was game. In no time she had dropped 11 boats, which tried to tow her. The Spaniards leapt to the kill, but then, suddenly, the wind freshened, and the situation changed in a flash. Even as Sidonia, Recalde and every other Spaniard within reach crowded on all sail, 'certain that we would this day succeed in boarding them, which was the only way to victory', she instantly left them all standing. 'She began to slip away from us,' moans Sidonia, 'and to leave the boats which were towing her.' Meanwhile Calderon was watching with growing amazement, and envy. 'She got out so swiftly,' he wrote, 'that the galleon *San Juan* and another quick-sailing ship – the speediest vessel in the Armada – although they gave chase, seemed in comparison with her to be standing still.' In the whole fight there is perhaps no better illustration of the vast sailing superiority which the English enjoyed.

It is just here that Sidonia and Calderon begin their calculated deception. The impression they wish to give is that, after such an uncanny exhibition of mobility, Sidonia concluded that he could not catch those swift though cowardly heretics. So (in his own words) 'he discharged a piece and proceeded on his course, the rest of the Armada following in very good order, the enemy remaining a long way astern'. Calderon loyally backs him. 'This being seen by the Duke, and the weather being fair, he proceeded on his voyage.'

This begs the whole question. So far, according to them, they were winning all along the line: the enemy was on the run. But, if so, the Solent lay open before them: that ripe plum, the Island, was waiting to drop into their mouths, and yet, in a fit of pique because they could not catch the English ships, they sailed off, leaving the plum on the tree. Why?

Sir Julian Corbett's answer to this question is his most brilliant contribution to an understanding of this crucial phase. Where, he asks, was Drake all day? And where, after his minor brush early in the morning, was Hawkins? Is it reasonable to suppose that the two greatest English sea-captains were just looking on? Of course not. So he searched for evidence of their activities. The big, well-known records would probably not help him, because they did not mention Drake at all. Yet he did re-examine them and, in the English *Relation*, he found, right at the end, a brief and cryptic reference to the *Nonpareil* and the *Mary Rose*, which 'struck their topsails and lay awhile by the whole fleet of Spain very bravely'. That was all. But it suggested something more when he realized that the *Nonpareil* was the ship of Thomas Fenner, Drake's Vice-Admiral at Plymouth and still in Drake's squadron; and that the *Mary Rose* was commanded by Edward Fenton, Hawkins's brother-in-law and in Hawkins's squadron, probably indeed second-in-command of it. Moreover, Howard's somewhat offhand reference to these two ships (of the missing squadrons) sounds as though they were the last to be engaged with the enemy, and in a locality remote from Howard and his own action.

Then among the documents printed in Captain Duro's *La Armada Invencible*, Corbett found the answer, not in the big authorities, but in the *relacion* of the private captain of a Seville ship, so obscure that his very name is unknown. This man had one advantage over Sidonia and Calderon, and, for that matter, over Howard. His ship was on the right (the seaward) wing of the Armada; and the battle which he describes might almost be a different action altogether: at least, his emphasis is entirely different. He has nothing to say of any of the episodes so far described here. 'We had them broken,' he writes,

> and the victory all but won, when the enemy *Capitana* turned upon our *Armada*; and the galleon *San Mateo* which occupied the point of the upper [i.e. weather] wing, gave ground and retreated into the body of the Armada. Seeing that, the enemy . . . charged upon the said wing in such wise that we who were there were cornered, so that, if the Duke had not gone about with his flagship, instead of the conquerors that we were, we should have come out vanquished that day. Seeing that, those of his armada that had been cut off, bore up to rejoin.

Like the rest of them, the nameless captain mistakes the English *Capitana*. This one cannot possibly have been Howard's or Frobisher's. But otherwise the fresh angle which he presents really elucidates everything, including the mystery of what Drake and Hawkins were doing. They were repeating Drake's move off Portland, working out to sea when the wind blew wrong, charging full upon the enemy's weather flank when it came right. They timed it to perfection. We need not believe with the Seville captain that Howard and Frobisher were on the run, but it does look as if they were in no position to impede Sidonia's entry into the Solent. With Drake (and probably Hawkins) breaking the Armada's weather flank, however, crowding it in confusion to leeward (i.e. in a north-easterly direction) the whole situation changed at once. Just there, beyond the Solent entrance towards Selsey Bill, lie the dangerous Ower Banks, and Drake was thrusting the whole right wing, with the bulks, straight on to them. To prevent that Sidonia, who may well have been in the act of entering the undefended Solent, had now to make all sail eastwards, to rally the fugitives before they went aground by driving Drake off. He succeeded. This was because Drake, who had pursued the right wing northwards, nearly to the Banks, now saw the Spanish main-battle bearing down on him from the west, with the wind (now at southwest) almost behind it. It was no part of Drake's programme to accept action under those conditions. He therefore broke off the chase and swiftly stood out to sea on a southeasterly course, then tacking back safely to his own people. This took time, though, and no doubt accounts for a statement in Sidonia's account, not otherwise explained yet probably true enough, that the English had fallen a long way astern.

Yet, before he went, Drake must have seen that his move had succeeded gloriously. Sidonia could not turn back now. The only way out of an ugly situation was to hold straight on to the east, until the Banks were astern of them all. And the result? Well – 'the weather being fair, he proceeded on his course' (Calderon). So he did, every moment leaving farther and farther behind him not only the Isle of Wight, but also his last chance.

Once more it is not easy to say who gained the tactical victory in this, the last Channel fight. We hear nothing of ship damage on either side, and no details of any kind about Drake's masterly intervention. Certainly, however, no ship in either fleet was lost or totally disabled: and again the Armada was off up-Channel, its obstinate order quite unbroken. Yet of one thing there is no doubt. The battle was a resounding strategic victory for England and a fatal strategic setback for Spain.

Part Four:

THE DECISION

12

CALAIS AND THE FIRESHIPS

Friday, July 26th

DURING THIS AND the following day not a shot was fired by either fleet. On our side the reason was stark enough. Howard knew that he must husband the ammunition he had against the crisis which would arise when Sidonia gained touch with Parma. The Spaniards, on the other hand, were only too glad of the respite. It is tempting, now, to endow them with a feeling of triumph. Indubitably they had performed a very notable feat: they had forced the passage of the Channel against all that we could do. But such a view ignores elementary psychology. They must have been tired out, and morale on board must have been falling rapidly. True, their tale of lost ships was small. Of all which left Corunna, only seven were no longer in company, three of the big auxiliaries (but good ones, all of flagship status) and the four galleys (which were no real loss, though some may still have thought them so). But where was the glory: where the sweet fruits of victory to which these proud Castilian gentlemen were accustomed? Rather, they must have felt all too like a flock of silly sheep, prodded up a long lane by impertinent shepherd-boys, helpless even to turn upon their nimble persecutors.

Sidonia had other reasons for relief. For one thing, he had fought three actions, involving a much larger expenditure of ammunition than anyone had expected, and he was running dangerously low. His only conceivable source of replenishment was Parma, and already, as long ago as the Monday, he had been dispatching daily pinnaces up-Channel, asking ever more urgently for supplies of powder and shot, and for small craft in which to convey them. It is clear that Sidonia never in the least grasped Parma's problems. That great man held all the embarkation-ports he needed east of Calais (which was French). But he had at his disposal nothing but the smallest of craft, themselves barely sea-going; and closely watched, as we have seen, by English flyboats, and relentless Sea Beggars. It is clear enough that he did not want to send anything to Sidonia, but it is even clearer that, in fact, he could not; nor by any conceivable means could he embark his army, un-protected, in his miserably inadequate flotilla, and wait about for Sidonia at sea. Yet this, apparently, is just what that good man expected.

Lord Howard spent the morning of the 26th in the congenial task of using his Lord Admiral's prerogative, and knighting some of his chief captains. Hawkins was one who received the honour, long overdue, one would have thought. Frobisher was another, for the intrepidity he had shown, presumably, rather than for his tactical skill. The other recipients were three gentlemen captains (Lord Thomas Howard, Lord Sheffield, Roger Townshend), and George Beeston, an old officer who had been serving Elizabeth throughout her reign. Was it chance or policy, it may be wondered, which induced him to preserve the careful balance: three seamen, three non-seamen? Another of his activities on that quiet day was to turn away musketeers shipped off to him by the Queen's express orders. So much for the grasp which the Queen had, even now, of her officers' new sea policy. But other reinforcements shipped off from the Sussex coast were emphatically not rejected: a dribble of shot and powder snatched by the Earl of Sussex from forts and castles along the shore: even, it is said, some ploughshares hurriedly broken up to take the place of cannon-balls. There was also some small store of welcome victuals, to stock holds which must have contained as little food as they did munitions.

Later that day, as the fleets moved up-Channel, scarcely perceptibly on the lightest of winds, the veteran seamen of England received news which must have made them chuckle in their beards. The first of many reports reached them that the Armada had won a resounding victory over the heretics, and was chasing the survivors hither and thither at will. Such rumours spread like wildfire over Europe, and continued long after the Spanish threat was dissipated for ever. Who circulated them, and why, has never been fully explained. Some of them, possibly, were officially inspired, to induce a reluctant Pope to fork out that million ducats which he had promised, but would pay only when the Spaniards had actually landed. More likely, however, they emanated from the many fanatical persons in Catholic Europe who were so sure of the Almighty's predilections that no other result could be contemplated.

Saturday, July 27th

This day saw the silent procession advance, the Armada still leading in its compact, unbroken 'plump' or 'roundel', and separated from the English fleet by the inexorable gap of 'one culverin-shot'. The northward trend of the continental shore brought Sidonia over to the French side as he drew nearer, and then rounded, Cape Grisnez; and at 4 o'clock he was off French-held Calais. Time was running out. What now? His spate of messages to Parma was still flowing, but the responses he received were slow in coming and, he thought, disturbingly vacillating when they came. Again, as by now we should expect of him, he called a council. There, he tells us, opinions varied (as well they might), leaving the cruel decision to him. This time, he probably did the right thing: he made the best of a bad job and, at 5 pm, anchored. Indeed he could hardly do otherwise in face of his pilots' unanimous opinion that, if he proceeded farther up-coast, the turbulent off-shore currents would, at worst, drive him on to the banks of Flanders, or (at best) carry him right out into the North Sea and away from Parma for ever. He was far from happy; and, very soon, two English moves made him unhappier still. The first was the behaviour of Howard's fleet. One English authority, describing how the Armada came to rest off Calais, even ascribes to Sidonia a subtlety to which he lays no claim himself. He anchored so suddenly and 'so politicly . . . purporting that our ships with the flood should be drawn to leeward of them'. But, if this was so, the English were too wide-awake. They too dropped anchor, one culverin-shot short of the Armada and dead in the eye of the wind: unpleasant bedfellows, not con-ducive to pleasant dreams! And then, just as night was falling, a very considerable fleet detached itself from the northern haze and joined hands with Howard. The Spaniards thought it was '*Achines*' – Hawkins, their eldest enemy, to be feared only less than *El Draque* himself. But we, of course, know that it was Lord Henry Seymour with the 'Narrows' contingent of the English fleet.

He was there on Howard's orders, but against Elizabeth's: who had just ordered him, characteristically enough, to go and lie off Dunkirk, well to leeward of the Armada. But Seymour, though a courtier and no seaman, was a brave, intelligent and patriotic man. He would probably have taken the not inconsiderable risk of disobeying the Queen anyway; but, as it was, hastened to obey Howard, though (again characteristically) he had only three days' victuals on board. So he found himself, in late evening, on the port or seaward wing of the combined English fleet. He was panting to begin and, like Howard before him, led off with a 'defiance', one of his greater ships deliberately ranging along the Spanish rear and loosing off a single broadside before rejoining. So at length the full Navy of England was united. Howard himself says that he now had 140 ships in company, ships, moreover (according to the honest Seville captain who helped us to unravel the fighting off the Island), of which 'the worst, without their main-course or topsails, can beat the best sailers we have'.

Sunday, July 28th

In the morning two more pieces of news shattered Sidonia's Sunday calm. First, one of his emissaries to Parma returned with the news that, as late as yesterday, the Prince had not appeared at his place of embarkation – Dunkirk – but was still at Bruges, some miles inland; and that neither men nor munitions were being embarked. Sidonia had scarcely digested these unpalatable tidings, when a messenger from the very friendly French Governor of Calais arrived on board to warn him that his chosen anchorage was an excessively dangerous one. Later in the day, the news grew, if possible, even gloomier. His own secretary, Arceo, dispatched to hurry Parma on, reported from Dunkirk not only that there was no sign whatever of Parma, but that, in his opinion, Sidonia could not expect to see him for a fortnight!

But we must be wary. All this was Sidonia's story. Parma's, told after the event when he found he had to defend himself, was very different. His zeal for the enterprise, he protested, had been throughout as keen as anyone's; and, though he had constantly warned the King that there were certain things which he could not do, he had pressed on with his preparations to the verge of the impossible, and was indeed fully set for the attempt when, on Monday, July 29th, he heard that the Armada was gone! His account differs so radically from Sidonia's that it must be quoted *verbatim*:

> On the 7th August [N.S.: to us, Sunday 28th], when Secretary Arceo came, and I left Bruges, I saw already embarked at Nieuport 16,000 foot soldiers; and when I arrived at Dunkirk on the 8th [i.e. Monday July 29th, the day of the Battle of Gravelines]* before dawn, the men who were to be shipped there had arrived, and their embarkation was commenced. They would all have been on board with the stores and the rest, as everything was ready and the shipping was going on very rapidly, if the embarkation had not been suspended in consequence of the intelligence received of the Armada [i.e. of the Battle of Gravelines]. But for this they might well have begun to get out of port that night [Monday July 29th], and have joined those from Nieuport during the next day.

Parma must be entitled to our sympathy. He was being asked to perform the impossible. In fact, he could never have left either Nieuport or Dunkirk, until his Dutch and English watchers were driven off, without courting certain massacre. But we cannot so easily acquit him of disingenuousness. He is inferring here that he could, and would, have come out on the night of Monday, July 29th, or, at latest, on Tuesday, July 30th. But could he? Of course not: the blockaders were still

* Parma actually wrote 'Tuesday, the 8th'. But the 8th was a Monday, and the rest of his defence makes it clear that he meant Monday the 8th, and not Tuesday the 9th.

there. And would he? Again, of course not: he was too good a soldier to take so insane a risk. Surely what he was saying in effect, though very diplomatically, since even a potent prince must be careful how he criticizes a despotic monarch, was something like this: 'Because you are King and can ill afford to be exposed, I'll stretch a point in order to cover you. I'll say that I was about to start on the Monday or Tuesday. This will perhaps help to conceal from the world the fact that your scheme was thoroughly impracticable from the start. But I am not going to take all the blame. It was your folly, not mine, and I warned you. So I must also tell you that, as your general and vicegerent, I should never have deliberately thrown my forces into the bottomless pit which engulfed Sidonia's.' It is reasonably clear too that Philip read the letter in some such sense, and was glad enough to acquiesce: for, though others said hard things of Parma (how he had spoilt it all because he wanted it spoilt) Philip did not. He left it at that.

We return to Sunday, July 28th, when, all day, the Spaniards lay at anchor, growing more and more apprehensive: all of them, from Sidonia who was receiving almost hourly ill-tidings down to the common people who, before evening, were thought to be in such need of encouragement that the commanders themselves spread a rumour which they knew to be false: that Parma would join next morning. One culverin-shot to windward, however, the atmosphere was markedly clearer. The time was obviously ripe for yet another attempt to break down that stubborn formation of the enemy and, as everything else had failed, a last resort must be tried: fireships! Here was no sudden flash of inspiration on somebody's part. The launching of such vessels was already a well-known stratagem of war, particularly suitable against ships with no way on. That it had been mooted some days before, probably by someone in Howard's fleet, is certain, because Walsingham had already sent to Dover for a number of fishing smacks and a store of faggots and pitch. But on that Sunday morning, the English commanders, assembled in council, knew that no delay could be allowed, not even time necessary to bring the proper fireships from England. Drake set the ball rolling by offering one of his own ships, the *Thomas*, a well-found vessel of 200 tons, and Hawkins followed with one of his, the *Bark Bond* of 150. Six others were selected, of burdens ranging from 200 to 90 tons, and all hands instantly set about preparing them from material in the fleet itself. There was not time even to remove guns and stores, for the ships were to be used that very night. To lead such an attack needed courage, skill and, above all, nerve. It is a little surprising, therefore, that more notice was not taken of the men who did it. Not even their names are recorded in any official account; but Camden, not always an impeccable authority, says that they were Captains Young and Prowse. The first-named (John) was an old west-country skipper who had served the Crown even in the days when Mary wore it, and he sailed to the hazardous assault in his own ship, the *Bear Yonge*. Of Captain Prowse there is no other mention.

Monday, July 29th

The flames spurting from the Calais fireships have never been extinguished in England. To this day they are perpetuated in the pages of the smallest history-books. And Monday, July 29th should be ringed about in red in the calendar of English warlike achievement. For on that day was fought one of the decisive battles of the world.

Action began betimes. Even before midnight the tide had turned, and, pushed by a rising wind behind it, was setting up-Channel in all that dangerous strength of which the Calais governor had just warned Sidonia. On it, a minute or two after midnight, came the fireships, sailing large and aimed straight at the dark mass of the Armada, kindling, one by one, as they approached. Sidonia himself, seeking once more to condone his errors and advertise his vigilance, asserts that he was not taken by surprise: that he had actually sent out in advance a very trustworthy captain in a pinnace, to grapple any fireship that came his way, and tow it ashore. But (said he) his people fell into panic when the ships appeared, seeing in them not ordinary fireships, but *maquinas de minas*, mine-machines: weapons which had inspired peculiar horror in the Spaniards

ever since 1585, when they had been used by the rebel Dutch
at the siege of Antwerp, with appalling effect.* The second of
these assertions is certainly true. The first is probably false: at
any rate, every other authority on either side says that the
surprise was complete.

In the narrowest, most literal sense these famous fireships all
failed. They made no contact with any Spanish ship; all finally
drifted ashore a little east of Calais and burned themselves
out. None the less, they were a brilliant success: they did for
England what, hitherto, all her captains had failed to do – they
broke the Armada's formation; and, once broken, it was never
regained. That the Spaniards, one and all, gave way to panic
is quite clear, in spite of Sidonia's face-saving denial:

> The Duke . . . gave order to weigh and also for the rest of
> the Armada to do the same, intending when the fires had
> passed to return and recover the same position.

This is at once untrue, and nonsense. It was untrue because the
Spanish ships did *not* weigh anchor upon their Commander-
in-Chief's studied order. They waited for no order, but
weighed anchor if they could, and, if they could not (which
was the case with most of them), they just cut their cables and
fell away down-wind in any, or rather in no, order. And it was

---

* The 'devil-ships of Antwerp', designed by the Italian Giambelli,
were vessels of 80 and 70 tons respectively, cleverly converted into
floating mines which would not be despicable even by modern standards. They contained over 3 tons of powder compressed in stout
brick-built chambers. Parma, in his siege of Antwerp, had built a
heavy wooden bridge across the Schelt, to keep out relief from the sea.
Mingling with a cloud of small but normal fireships, these infernal
machines were floated on the tide up to the bridge. The larger one,
the *Fortune*, was boarded by an intrepid Englishman in Parma's
service. He stumbled upon the slow-matches leading below, severed
them, and towed the ship away. Then the smaller, the *Hope*, approached, and became entangled with the bridge. She too was
boarded, but she was more subtly constructed than the *Fortune*,
having a clockwork fuse buried in the heart of the charge. Before the
Spaniards could spot her secret, she exploded, carrying away 200
yards of the bridge, killing 800 men and wounding an unknown
number more, including Parma himself who was knocked out by a
heavy baulk of timber.

nonsense because no ship, least of all a Spanish ship, having slipped anchor and fallen to leeward on that wind and tide, had any chance whatever of returning to her original anchorage, especially as the English fleet had reached and passed it long before any Spaniard even tried to come about. Indeed, Purser Calderon, usually so jealous of the Duke's reputation, lets the cat out of the bag this time, and baldly states that 'the Duke ordered our cables to be cut'. Here he puts his finger on the second great catastrophe which the fireships inflicted upon the Armada. They deprived it not only of its formation, hitherto its most valuable tactical asset, but also of over 150 anchors and as many cables: for in the strong tide-rip every ship had two anchors out. This loss, so irreplaceable, it was to feel henceforward, and to the very end of its bitter journey.

Here, now, is a strange fact. Explain it as we will, a fact it remains. The very first ship to come to her senses was not seaman Recalde's or seaman Oquendo's; not the dashing de Leyva's or the pertinacious Bertendona's. It was the *San Martin*, flagship of that egregious Duke whose haverings have earned the world's scorn for so long. In fact, the panic on board of her was of the briefest. As soon as the Duke realized that the fireships were safely passed, he brought up short and re-anchored (though not, of course, in his original position). It may have been the doing of the detested Flores de Valdez, but one has the feeling that it was Sidonia himself who did it. Such a theory is not so wild as it seems at first sight. Planning and deciding were the Duke's weak suits, not action: and the subsequent events of this nightmarish day were to prove it again and again. If only he could have fallen that day on his own quarter-deck and in the thick of the fight, people, and especially his own people, might even have awarded him a posthumous halo, paler than, yet not altogether unlike, that of a Richard Grenville. At least it becomes somehow churlish to abuse a man who dies gloriously facing impossible odds. Yet Sidonia did all this – except, that he failed to die but survived to be markedly less glorious! But that was not yet. He began very well. As one of the fireships passed close astern, many of his agonized officers, momently expecting another 'devil of

Antwerp' to blow them all to heaven, crowded round him and besought him to seek safety in a pinnace, which could land him on the coast. He not only refused indignantly; he even contrived to bring the officers to their senses.

He had lost ground, but not much: and now he fired a signal gun to call the rest to anchor. Few heard it, or, if they did, would or could obey. The *San Marcos*, a fine Portuguese royal galleon which was probably his 'second', brought up and anchored astern of him; so did two or three other ships, mostly galleons. But the rest were scattered, still running east in complete confusion: all, that is, but one, and she was lost indeed.

In the chaotic darkness, lit only by the angry glow of the fireships, and confused by the crash of their loaded guns going off as the flames reached them, the *San Lorenzo*, *capitana* and pride of the treasured galleasses, fouled the cable of the large auxiliary *San Juan de Sicilia*, and lost her rudder. The fiery Hugo de Moncada could only force his way out of the press and, with oar and foresail, make for the shore, coasting it until he could come under the guns of Calais castle. He succeeded, but at a fatal loss. Ignorant of the channels, he drove her practically on to the beach, so hard that she was irremovable, and so tilted landwards that none of her very powerful armament could be brought to action. It chanced that the first object which the dawn revealed to Howard was this grotesquely tilted galleass; without hesitation, he turned the *Ark* landward towards her, and he was followed by his whole division. It was much the worst blunder the Lord Admiral ever made. Nothing could show more clearly the basic difference of outlook between the noble and the seamen commanders. Here was the opportunity for which he had striven throughout the week's fighting. The enemy was really scattered, really (for the moment) on the run. Now if ever pursuit must be swift, concentrated, with every ship, man and weapon pressed into the service. Fortunately Drake, Hawkins and Frobisher made no such mistake. They ran straight in to get among the fugitives before they could rally. So, it is only fair to add, did the noble Seymour, but then, on the extreme left, he was probably too far away to see what was happening off Calais. We should not be too severe on Howard. His upbringing and background were against him here. Clearly he never quite grasped all the implications of the new sea warfare. To the last he could write, with evident complaisance, that 'we pluck their feathers by little and little'. To him, as to almost everyone else in the world outside Drake and his small coterie, war was still that formal, stately thing which it had been throughout the Middle Ages, and it had its Code of Procedure for him, as it had for Sidonia. Only, it would seem, when he was under the immediate spell of his Vice-Admiral could he realize what Drake was getting at; it never came naturally to him. Hence the minor episode of his defiance off Plymouth (and Seymour's off Calais) before getting down to business; and hence, now, the much more serious urge to 'pluck another feather', especially such a large and bright one as the Flag of an enemy squadron. For that, in his code, was a foe which he was entitled, and expected, to engage.

He must have discovered very soon that he himself could not have the pleasure of the actual capture. The sharply shoaling water stopped the *Ark* when still some distance off. So (still in accordance with his code) he told off several of his favourite officers to take the long-boat, board the galleass, and 'have their pillage of her'. Other boats from the other ships of his squadron dutifully (and no doubt eagerly) followed the Admiral's example and raced for the prize. Foremost among them was our former acquaintance Master John Watts, citizen, now actually on board his own *Margaret and John* – even, it would seem, in her long-boat hurrying landwards. So, fortunately for us, was the ship's Lieutenant, one Richard Tomson, a youngish man, probably from Norfolk, who possessed certain qualities unusual among contemporary lieutenants. He could speak French and German – and he could write English. It is his long, lively report to Walsingham which gives us another welcome peep behind the scenes. But for him we should know nothing of what happened on the only occasion throughout the campaign when one of the combatants boarded an enemy ship and took her.

Tomson's pinnace and the *Ark*'s long-boat arrived first, and together. They drove

> hard under the galleass's side, being aground: where we continued a pretty skirmish with our small shot against theirs, they being ensconced within their ship and very high over us, we in our open pinnaces and far under them, having nothing to shroud us and cover us; they being 300 soldiers, besides 450 slaves, and we not, at the instant, 100 persons.

Tomson's modest claim to gallantry is justified. Here was no picnic. The galleass was designed, among other things, to repel boarders: the soldiers were, for once, in their element in an exchange of musket fire. Yet the English prevailed, and that quickly. One reason is plain. The enemy, veterans as they were, and for all the natural strength of their position, were in poor moral shape. For half an hour the forceful personality of de Moncada kept them at it. But then a lucky English musket-ball penetrated his head from the side, destroying both his eyes. He fell, and died almost immediately. This was the end. Most of the soldiers, almost all the sailors and gunners (who were Italians), and (of course) all the rowing-slaves who could manage it leapt over the landward side and waded ashore. The staunch few who remained, seeing a whole flotilla of small craft racing in for the kill, 'put up two handkerchers upon two rapiers signifying that they desired truce'. Thereupon an ever-growing horde of Englishmen tumbled aboard, and eagerly began the principal course in the repast, the pillage.

Meanwhile, the honest burghers of Calais stood watching on the beach. But soon a party was seen shouldering its way between them, and on the *San Lorenzo*'s deck appeared a kinsman of Monsieur Gourdan the Governor. He, in courtly tones (which Tomson translated), praised the boarders for their courage, and told them that his master had graciously consented to let them have their lawful pillage of the galleass; but they were on no account to remove either the guns or the ship herself. Tomson gratefully accepted these terms, which he evidently thought generous enough, and both sides parted with mutual compliments. Unfortunately, however, even while these civilities were in progress, 'some of our rude men, who make no account of friend or foe, fell to spoiling the Frenchmen, taking away their rings and jewels as from enemies'. The victims, when at length they regained the land, rushed instantly to the Governor to complain, and he, not unnaturally outraged at such unpardonable, and to him ungrateful, conduct, ordered the castle's batteries to open fire. This quickly brought the revels to an end, since the ship lay within a furlong of the fortress's wall-pieces, guns of the very largest size. The English departed without more ado and with what they could carry. In this skirmish, which was after all only a sideshow that ought never to have happened, the English casualties were fairly heavy. One Spanish source assessed them at 50 killed. An English narrative (Ubaldino's second), while admitting only 'a few' killed in the action, adds a further 20, drowned in the hasty evacuation.

13

THE BATTLE OF GRAVELINES

Monday, July 29th (continued)

WE LEAVE THE SIDESHOW and the misguided Lord Admiral, and follow his Vice-Admiral into the great battle of Gravelines. Once again, the reader will have to rest content with a most confused picture of the general action, though a number of individual episodes and exploits have escaped oblivion. For, this time, there was a real mix-up. The Spaniards were in no tactical formation at any time: the English, if they ever had one, soon lost it. Each individual commander, as he saw his opportunity, went close in with the enemy and hit as hard as he could. But still, for the most part, the English kept the wind, hammering the gasping foe to leeward of them; forcing them ever eastward along the seaward fringe of the shoals towards the spot where the water off the Flemish shore shoaled away to nothing. But the English did approach in squadrons, Drake arriving first, then Hawkins, then Frobisher, then Seymour, and finally Howard who, to his credit, recovered his sense of proportion as soon as he saw the galleass in English hands.

On the Spanish side, all the credit goes to three of the Armada's components, the fleet flagship carrying Sidonia the Fighter, the other flagships with their fighting squadron commanders, and the regular navy ships, the galleons of Portugal and Castile. We have seen how the *San Martin* made the first stand, deliberately placing herself in the path of four English squadrons. But the Duke soon saw that Drake and company were not after plucking single feathers, even the finest feather of them all, his flagship. Obviously, while some of the enemy attacked him the rest would merely by-pass him. He would therefore be sacrificing himself in vain if he stood his ground too far to windward of his fugitives. So he fell back, fighting all the time, acting as cover for the rest, the while trying to induce any ship which could see or hear him to rejoin him if possible, but at least to haul up and try to beat away from the fatal coast. Certainly the Duke had no cause for shame that day. We even catch a glimpse of him (if his own words may be taken literally) climbing to the tops of the flagship to get a better view over the smoke of battle: no place for a Commander-in-Chief in action, no doubt, but none the less the station of a gallant man.

His retreat, slow as it was, helped all those who could – or would – rally to his flag; and gradually a number did so. These were, mostly, his royal galleons and his chief lieutenants in their auxiliaries. Among the latter especially there was no hanging back. In all the Spanish accounts the faces of Recalde, Oquendo, de Leyva, and the *tercio*-leaders Toledo and Pimentel keep emerging for an instant through the murk of battle, grim but game, and even bright. Always they are 'surrounded by 17 ships of the enemy', or 'defending themselves against three flagships, a vice-flagship and 10 or 12 other vessels'; or 'skirmishing with 10 of the enemy ships and making them retire'. There is doubtless exaggeration here – the hard-pressed Spaniards had other things to do besides counting ships. But it is less gross than it sounds. Their ships, limited in mobility at the best of times, were becoming ever less mobile as a result of the hammering they were receiving, while the English, with mobility scarcely impaired, and as ever using it to the utmost, could weave almost at will through a nearly stationary enemy; striking when and where they pleased, here one moment, and gone the next. If the Spaniards liked to call this 'beating us off', they are welcome. Besides, only a fraction of the whole Armada (though of course the cream of it) was really engaged. All day many of the ships were drifting too far to leeward to take any serious part.

To add to their discomfiture, quite early in the fight their stock of roundshot began to give out; and, naturally, that happened in the good ships which were doing all the work. Gradually their heavy guns fell silent, and, as they did so, the English kept closing the range. Of course they did. At last the only cause which had kept them at a distance was ceasing to operate.

It is this fact which makes the battle of Gravelines so very different from the three earlier ones. Once more it is a question of range, as it must always be when the subject on hand is a gun-duel at sea. Hitherto, as we have seen more than once, our light-shotted long guns were not really hurting the Spanish hulls at all. Indeed we had scarcely claimed any ship damage, and the enemy had admitted none. One galleass, we had once said with glee, 'was fain to be carried away on a careen', but that is all. Up to now the enemy had lost eight ships. But among the causes of their loss the English guns still did not figure. Those causes were: by weather, five, by collision, one, by internal sabotage, one, by boarding, one: by gunfire – none. A surprising testimony of how ineffective our fire had been comes from an 'advice from England; telling of the damage found (by Englishmen) in the *San Lorenzo* when they took her. Though she had gone through most of the heaviest Channel fighting, and had lain on Calais beach, her guns pointing sky-wards, her bottom half exposed, while some 15 or 20 English ships bombarded her at leisure, our informant can say that 'not one of the English cannon-shots had pierced the hull of the ship, but only her upper planks above the oars'. And Meteren, Hakluyt's Flemish correspondent, says that it was the same with the galleons. True, he consistently overstates the might of the Spaniards and, even here, attributes our poor results rather to the strength of their ships than to the weakness of our guns. But here are his own words.

The lower worke [of the said galleons] and the timbers thereof were out of measure strong, being framed of plankes and ribs foure or five foote in thicknesse, insomuch that no bullets could pierce them *but such as were discharged hard at hand*:* which afterwards proved true, for a great number of bullets were founde to sticke fast within the massie sub-stance of those thicke plankes.

We may not believe implicitly in those 'five-foote plankes'. But that, in a sense, is immaterial. Both the above pieces of evidence show that the English roundshot was, so far, not

* Author's italics.

achieving the purpose for which it was designed. If, nowadays, we gave our troops an anti-tank gun which failed completely to penetrate the enemy's armour at the range required, we should unhesitatingly vote it a failure; nor would it really matter whether the failure lay in the gun's weakness or in the tank's strength. So in 1588, up to the moment of Gravelines, we must admit the failure of the long English culverin-types.

Fortunately for their reputation and ours, however, Gravelines was yet to come, and to be fought at a different range altogether. Of this there is plenty of evidence, impossible to ignore. The English did close the range and, having done so, began to secure very different results, and with those same long guns. That evidence now pours in, from both sides indifferently, both of the new shortness of range and of the effects of our fire. That the Spaniards said so carries more weight, perhaps, than testimony from our side, because hitherto they had admitted to no damage at all. So we will confine English testimony to one particularly striking passage, from the pen of the Queen's veteran officer, Sir William Wynter. Then we may take rather fuller evidence from the other camp. Sir William wrote:

> I deliver it unto your Honour upon the credit of a poor gentleman that out of my ship the *Vanguard*, [not hitherto engaged, whence no doubt the wealth of ammunition] there was shot 500 of demi-cannon, culverin and demi-culverin: and when I was farthest off in discharging any of the pieces, I was not out of shot of the harquebus, and most time within speech of one another.

This propinquity, even the last graphic illustration of it, is borne out fully by the other side. Purser Calderon (in words which make crystal-clear the ordinary Spaniard's attitude to our new methods) gives this version of the story:

> The enemy inflicted great damage on the galleons *San Mateo* and *San Felipe*, the latter having five of her starboard guns dismounted. . . . In view of this, and that his upper deck was destroyed, both his pumps broken, his rigging in

shreds and his ship almost a wreck, Don Francisco de
Toledo in the *San Felipe* ordered the grappling hooks to be
got out, and shouted to the enemy to come to close quarters.
They replied, summoning him to surrender in fair fight;
and one Englishman, standing in the maintop with his sword
and buckler, called out, 'Good soldiers that ye are, surrender to the fair terms that we offer ye.' But the only
answer he got was a gunshot which brought him down in the
sight of everyone, and the Maestro de Campo then ordered
the muskets and harquebusses to be brought into action.
The enemy thereupon retired, whilst our men shouted out
to them that they were cowards, and with opprobrious
words reproached them for their want of spirit, calling them
Lutheran hens and daring them to return to the fight.

Could anything reveal more starkly the gulf yawning between
the old and the new, between the school which thought the
gun ignoble and the one which proposed to win the battle
with it and nothing else?

More, and even more conclusive, Spanish evidence survives.
In one of these short, furious duels, an English ship ranged
right alongside the *San Mateo*, which was actually boarded –
though only by one lone Englishman whom 'our men cut to
bits instantly'. In the *San Martin* 'the holes made in the hull
between wind and water caused so great a leakage that two
divers had as much as they could do to stop them up with
tow and lead plates, working all day'. And, in the *San Mateo*
again, 'her hull was so riddled that she was in a sinking condition, the pumps being powerless to diminish the water'.
All this reporting of ship-damage is conclusive: it is new, and
it is confined to the last action.

From 9 am to 6 pm this very one-sided affair went on. Towards evening the *San Felipe* was thought to be sinking, and
Sidonia, watchful as ever, sent a hulk to take off her people.
It did so, but word then went round that the hulk itself was
going down. At that, de Toledo remarked nonchalantly that
it would look better to be drowned in a galleon than in a hulk,
and promptly returned to the *San Felipe*. Fortunately, he was

not called upon to make the supreme sacrifice. His ship, completely waterlogged, drifted at last on to the beach between Spanish-held Nieuport and Ostend. The Zealanders made a dash for her but, just before they arrived, some pinnaces from Nieuport reached her, in time to remove the gallant Maestro de Campo and his survivors. The Dutch secured the ship, however, floated her off, and got her into Flushing.

The *San Mateo* was less fortunate. She too was sinking, and, struggling to the *San Martin*, begged for a diver to stop the worst of her leaks: and Sidonia sent one, though he could ill spare him. But the task was beyond the man, and the ship dropped astern. Finally, she too took the ground, but farther east, between Ostend and Sluys. Three Dutch ships attacked her as she lay helpless, and many more were coming up. But Maestro de Campo Pimentel would not surrender, and fought for two hours more before accepting the inevitable. He himself was taken prisoner: he represented good ransom money. But so fierce was the rancour between Dutchmen and Spaniards that the poorer sort had little hope of mercy, and found none. Almost to a man they 'were cast overboard and slain at the entry'. Like the *San Felipe* the wreck was safely towed to Flushing.

The last certain victim of the fight was the *Maria Juan*, Captain Pedro de Ugarte, one of the Great Ships of Recalde's squadron. At sunset she signalled that she was sinking. The faithful Sidonia hastened to her instantly; but rescue work was slow, because his boats were leaking and the wind was rising. Only one boatload had been removed when she went down with 275 men still in her. It was notoriously rare, throughout the days of wood and sail, for ships to be sunk outright by gunfire alone. That such a fate undoubtedly befell the *Maria Juan*, is certain proof that the English guns were not inefficient, when fired at their correct range.

Contemporary Englishmen claimed that they saw other ships go down. This may well be so. Two at least of these reports come from trustworthy people, and various modern writers have accepted them. But it is no use trying to discover the truth by taking a final count, because many Spanish ships remained untraced to the end. They did not reach home, but where, when and how they sank no man knows to this day. To be on the safe side, then, we will follow the Spanish accounts, which are usually quite objective in dealing with their own losses. They mention no more in the battle itself. So we will assume that, by nightfall of July 29th, 11 in all had gone: the eight already accounted for as lost from other causes, and now, at last, a certain three lost by English gunfire, two of which were units of the enemy's crack squadron, the royal galleons of Portugal.

So much for ships totally lost to Spain. But this is by no means the tally of ships shockingly mauled, some half dismasted, some leaking dangerously, some with half their people dead or incapacitated. We do not know the Spanish losses in men, on this or any other day. But we do know that they admitted to 600 killed and 800 wounded on this one day, and the figures were certainly much bigger than these, especially when the drowned and those caught and slaughtered by the Dutch are added. Moreover the great preponderance both of material damage and of human casualties had occurred in the best ships, the best-found, the best-officered, the best-manned. The Armada never recovered from the hammering of the English guns on Monday, July 29th.

What now of the Spaniards, their guns and gunnery? What execution did they do upon the English fleet? Briefly, the verdict must be this. The English had hit, but (till the last battle) had not hurt: the Spaniards had hardly hit at all, and, therefore, not hurt either. This alone is proof of a long range before Gravelines: for, however poor their guns and bad their gunnery, they could not have done so badly at really short range. On the other hand, once the distance rose above point-blank, all hitting was largely a matter of chance, because none of the pieces, on either side, possessed any sights: and the 'windage' of them (that is, the difference between diameter of shot and diameter of gun-bore – at least half an inch) meant that the direction which the shot took on leaving the barrel depended upon whereabouts in the bore it made its last contact. The resulting inaccuracy, vast as it was, did not matter so much when the target was the bulk of a ship a few yards away; a clean miss was hardly possible. But, obviously, the margin of error increased rapidly with every yard of range added, even when guns were laid for point-blank fire, i.e. at a range where elevation did not have to be guessed. We can also see more clearly now why the English guns, though they did fail in the earlier fights, yet failed less conspicuously than the Spanish guns. The point-blank range of the English culverin-types was greater than that of the Spanish cannon- and perier-types; and the range at which we were trying to fight the actions was within culverin-point-blank but outside cannon-point-blank. So long as we had our way, then, our culverin-shots would carry to the target without the wild uncertainties introduced by elevation; but the Spanish cannon-shots, if fired at point-blank, would plunge into the sea short of our ships, or, if elevated, would almost certainly miss, whistling over us and finding the sea beyond. Clearly this is what was happening on the Spanish side. But we, trying (perhaps wisely) to avoid being hit by their heavy missiles, had kept, if anything, too far away, not realizing, it seems, that extreme culverin-point-blank was not going to be good enough: that it was too long a range to allow our lightweight shot to penetrate the 'massie plankes' of their hulls. This in fact was our major miscalculation. This is why, though our shot had often struck their hulls, it had not penetrated them. At Gravelines, however, things were very different, on both sides. The range was now to the Spaniards' liking, but they had little left to fire; while we, seeing this, lost no time in closing to a range which would correct our miscalculation, and allow our guns to do the business for which they were intended.

The utter failure of Spanish guns and gunnery is no matter of surmise. It is revealed in every scrap of surviving evidence. The English, quite certainly, lost no ship; nor did any ship receive serious hull-damage (even the alleged hurt to the *Triumph*'s helm and the *Ark*'s mainyard finds no mention in English circles). This can only mean that the hurts, if inflicted, were reparable on the spot; for, after the fighting was over, the whole Navy Royal was submitted to a searching survey, which survives. A number of objects, some vital, are 'worn', 'half-worn', 'decayed'; there are a few 'cracked' beams; several ships' boats have been lost; several ensigns have been 'spoyled by shot'. But of real damage by gunfire there is no mention at all.

As for casualties, no list survives, not even an unofficial one. But contemporary opinion is unanimous in agreeing that our losses were 'little more than 100', 'hardly 100', 'less than 100'; and this steady figure covers the whole fighting. Indeed, the few surviving details almost make one wonder whether the figure is not an exaggeration! Sir George Cary, reporting the Isle of Wight battle (which he watched), gives us a vivid view of what was really happening:

> It continued from 5 of the clock until 10, with so great expense of powder and bullet that during the said time the shot continued so thick together that it might rather have been judged a skirmish with small shot on land than a fight with great shot on sea . . .

Heavens! The mountains have laboured! What horrid monster will they bear? . . . A mouse!

> . . . in which conflict, thanks be to God, *there hath not been two of our men hurt.*

Indeed, the figure of 100 is certainly an exaggeration if understood to refer to roundshot casualties. Even if as many as 50 Englishmen lost their lives in boarding the *San Lorenzo*, not one, presumably, was killed by a great-shot, because her artillery could not fire at all. Again, in the close-fighting at Gravelines, some more ('barely three-score', says one eye-witness) were killed or wounded, but, even here, mostly by the Spanish muskets and harquebuses. So we may safely reduce our roundshot casualties by half at least. Moreover, of that near-50, it seems certain that no single officer of note lost his life. Of the lesser fry, the man in Calderon's story, rather unsportingly picked off as he called for surrender, may be one; but he may not have been an officer, and he may not have been killed. Otherwise, the known total of officer casualties slain is *one*.

The man to earn this unique if melancholy distinction was no gentleman officer, but a certain William Coxe of Limehouse. Not all his previous life was quite so heroic as its end. Some twelve years before he had been the Master of the bark *Bear*, part of a small expedition to the Spanish Main. Why, or with what justification, we do not know, but he seems to have marooned his commanding officer in the bay of Honduras, where the unfortunate man was presently slain by the Spaniards. Coxe's ship was lost soon afterwards but, after the greatest of hardships, he escaped to England where he was promptly tried for murder, and imprisoned for several years. He was probably, however, too experienced a seaman to be left pining in gaol and, some years later, he was master of yet another *Golden Hind* in Sir Humphrey Gilbert's famous expedition to Newfoundland. In 1588 he commanded the 'Pinnace called *Delight*', belonging to Sir William Wynter, and was twice mentioned favourably in dispatches: first, in March, for bringing tidings from Spain of the Armada's preparations, then for his gallantry in the wild rush for the *San Lorenzo*. He survived this, but later that same day he was hit in the head by a Spanish shot: and, this time, it would seem to have been a cannon-shot, perhaps one of the last random balls fired by the despairing enemy. On England's great day, he certainly wiped out the blot which stained his distant past. Fate has done its best to rob him of his place on the Roll of Honour. Chroniclers and historians alike have conspired to conceal his identity. Lediard called him 'Cope'; Fuller, 'Cock'. Southey followed Fuller, while Motley could get no nearer than 'Wilton, Coxswain of the *Delight*'.

There are, it is true, some rather light-hearted stories, emanating from Drake's flagship, if not from Drake himself. But they only show us – if we believe them – that some Spanish shots did penetrate, not that anyone was killed by them. There was in the *Revenge* one particularly ill-fated bed – it was Drake's own in most of the versions. A gentleman was reclining upon it when a saker-ball penetrated the side of the cabin, and smashed the bed to pieces without even scratching the gentleman. And, very soon afterwards, the same bed (having meantime been somehow miraculously restored to its former perfection) was again supporting the weary bodies of two other gentlemen – one positively a nobleman, the Earl of Northumberland – when another shot, this time from a demi-culverin, passed clean through the cabin, not daring, we suppose, to touch such very important people, but only 'scraping the foot' of a person in attendance, and removing a toe. We may feel the less disposed to credit these merry yarns when we learn that both incidents happened 'after the battle was over'.

Thus, throughout all the fighting the sum of the Spanish artillery's achievement was: no ship lost, no ship damaged appreciably, one humble officer and some two-score English seamen killed: and to effect this, they loosed off 123,790 rounds of great shot. It was not exactly impressive.

Tuesday, July 30th

The fighting was over, but not the battle: nor the drama, for the climax was still to come.

After dark on the Monday night, the rising sea rose higher, until it assumed something of the proportions of a gale. The wind shifted too, gradually, from southwest to northwest: and that began to look like the end of the Armada. For now, coasting with shortened sail, as close-hauled as it could, the fleet could not avoid making dangerous leeway towards that gleaming line of broken water to starboard which marked the fatal shoals. Well before day broke, the wind died down somewhat, though it was still blowing fresh from the northwest, and the white streak to leeward seemed from the Spanish decks to be creeping ever nearer.

Dawn broke at last. The *San Martin* was still in the post of honour, some distance astern of the main body, still scattered and still clawing out from the breakers. She had in company seven ships, which included the three remaining galleasses, the faithful *San Marcos* and the flagships of Recalde and de Leyva. A notable absentee was Miguel Oquendo. Sidonia does not mention him, perhaps for a reason which Calderon hints at and other Spanish accounts enlarge upon. Clearly nerves were stretched almost to breaking-point that morning. Oquendo was hot-blooded, excitable at the best of times. He despised the Duke; he loathed his Chief of Staff. According to the duke-loving Calderon, he had, very early in the day, come within hail of the flagship; and Sidonia, in his deep depression, called out to him, 'Señor Oquendo, what shall we do? We are lost!' Undoubtedly this was unseemly, and, with all the crew listening, it must have sounded criminally defeatist to Oquendo. Infuriated at so total an abdication of leadership, he replied with bitter sarcasm, 'Ask Diego Flores!' Then, adding 'As for me, *I* am going to fight, and die like a man', he flung away: though where he went to, and what else he could do that Sidonia had not done, is not recorded. Other and less official Spanish chroniclers make the angry man say things a great deal more outrageous, and more personally insulting to the Duke. Thereafter Sidonia does not once mention him again.

Dead in the wind's eye was the English fleet, compact, sailing trim and easy, and well clear of the banks; but, this time, rather more than a culverin-shot away. The Duke concluded that the Armada's end was at hand, and his own. The enemy would at any minute bear down in irresistible force upon his forlorn little group, the only cover left, and drive it and the whole fleet to destruction. Moreover, what made it all the more unpleasant to contemplate was the knowledge that Justinus of Nassau, with 30 fresh ships belonging to the Sea Beggars, was waiting for him just over the horizon at the mouth of the Scheldt; waiting, not to attack him yet, but to pounce upon him and his flock as soon as they took ground. A horrid thought indeed, for Sea Beggars and Spaniards regarded each other as rats to be exterminated on sight rather than as honourable foes. There would be no quarter. We have seen what happened to the *San Mateo*, and no Spaniard could hope for anything better.

But the English held back. To the demoralized Spaniards this could be accounted for only in one way. A member of Sidonia's

own bodyguard, Luis de Miranda, has left a picture of the
gloom prevailing in the flagship:

> We saw ourselves lost or taken by the enemy, or the whole
> Armada drowned upon the banks. It was the most fearful
> day in the world, for the whole company had lost all hope of
> success and looked only for death. But it pleased God to
> blind the enemy so that he did not fall upon us, and to
> work a miracle in preserving us from such a disaster.

Here, however, was no miracle. It was not the English eyes that
were at fault, but their guns, which were all but empty. The
very last shots in their lockers, the scrapings of their powder-
casks they felt they must husband against the moment when
the Armada struck the shoals. In fact, they were bluffing.
On this wind, they knew, there was no way out for their
enemy: so why not let the elements do their work for them?
Not one shot was fired in anger all day.

The hours crawled on. The *San Martin* took soundings: six
fathoms. The *Patrona* galleass, farther inshore, made five
fathoms. Now the Duke's officers crowded round him again,
and besought him, with tears in their eyes, to take a pinnace
while yet there was time and go ashore with the Holy Banner:
only so, they urged, could the heretics be denied their unholy
triumph of capturing both. But, though he was dazed, the
habits of a lifetime prevailed. He refused. He did take the
opportunity of the unexpected lull, however, to be confessed
and shriven.

Maybe this helped; certainly the Duke thought so. '*Solo
Dios lo podia remediar*', he recorded afterwards. 'God alone
could rescue them.'

Suddenly, almost without warning, the brisk breeze deserted
the northwest, and, 'by God's Mercy', blew from the southwest, fresh, but not too violent for the battered ships. This
made all the difference. Instantly the whole fleet came round,
and steered northwest without difficulty: right away from the
waiting shoals and the deadlier Zealanders, right out into
the North Sea.

And the English let them go: they had no means of stopping them. The Armada was saved – for the moment.

The rest of the day was, by comparison, bathos: on the English side a council and a spate of letter-writing, on the Spanish, a council and a sharp bout of face-saving. The English concluded that the immediate crisis was over: that the Armada might try to re-enter the Channel, but not on that wind. Howard's main fleet, therefore, was to shadow it, while Seymour's division was to return to its watch on Parma. Seymour was furious, suspecting the hand of Drake in thus depriving him of honour. But he was wrong. It would have been folly, until the Armada's next move was known, to leave the invasion ports unmarked. Incidentally, the decision was inevitable too: the Straits squadron was found to possess only one day's victuals!

The Spanish problem was harder. Providence had saved them from the lion, but would it perhaps be tempting Providence just a little too far if they deliberately replaced their heads in the lion's mouth? Who was going to be the first to say so, though? Philip certainly would not approve of their giving up like this, and Philip's shadow was long. Would he not, for instance, inquire when they returned who first suggested it? Sidonia thought they should return forthwith to the Channel; at least, so he said. But then, ever since the launching of the fireships he had been ordering his pilots to take him back there, and with all the obstinacy of ignorance only half believed their plea of impossibility. Diego Flores now joined him. He felt, no doubt, that he had plenty of leeway to make up, and would have yet more when his cousin Pedro, de Leyva the favourite and that offensive Oquendo sent in their reports. Then all the rest temporized, including Recalde and de Leyva (Oquendo had not been invited) and the council finally decided, *nem. con.*, to return to the Channel when circumstances permitted; but that, at present, they did not permit. In fact, it is just about as clear as such compromises can be that not one of them intended to return if he could possibly avoid it. Indeed every military reason supported that view. The Armada, strong in its unassailable formation, with ships largely unhurt, and with adequate stocks of ammunition, had failed completely in its main purpose. How, lame, shot through and through and with no punch left, how should it succeed now? So northward they limped, and never turned back nor, as a body, ever seriously thought of doing so. Let us make no mistake. Let us not be distracted by Spanish tales of fearsome tempests and treacherous rock-bound coasts, uncharted and unknown. Such things underlined and exacerbated the disaster to come; but the initial disaster from which all others stemmed befell them in the running fight off Gravelines on Monday, July 29th, and nowhere else. For there the Invincible Armada was thrashed beyond redemption, in body and in spirit alike.

Part Five:

AFTERMATH

14

THE VICTORS

So NORTHWARD, propelled by brisk sou'westerlies, sailed the
Spaniards, like a gang of disgruntled poachers, flushed from
rich game-preserves by angry keepers. Yet both parties were
understandably nervous: the poachers of the keepers' shot-
guns, the keepers lest the poachers should discover them to be
unloaded. Then, in an age when news travelled but slowly and
uncertainly, pursued and pursuers alike vanished into the
void, and rumour took over once more. Thus, in the faded
sheets of a score of 'authentic advices', there occurred a major
action on August 2nd off Harwich – or was it off Hull? Or
Newcastle? Drake, imprudent for once, had, it seems, overrun
the Armada, which at last got him where it wanted him, to leeward. The earlier accounts were comparatively sober. The first
was from Harwich on August 3rd. The *San Martin* and the
Revenge had had a fight to the death which brought on a general
engagement. Drake was taken with many ships, and 16 more
had made Harwich much damaged. On August 8th Philip
himself wrote to say that advices had come, from Rouen of all
front-line places, confirming the news, with embellishments.
The Armada, gaining the wind, had sunk the English flagship
and 14 other ships. Next day (also from Rouen) Drake was
wounded in the legs. On the 14th 'advices from Antwerp' had
better news still. There had been another fight off Newcastle
in which 'about 30 English ships' were taken. By the 20th
(says Dunkirk *via* Lille) it is 'a positive fact that the English
have lost 4 ships'. The flagship has been sunk (again?), the
vice-flagship too, and 'the great sailor John Hawkins has also
gone to the bottom'. But *El Draque*, it now appears, must have
exercised his well-known occult powers: he has escaped in a
boat, wounded, but only in the cheek. On the 21st and 22nd
Rouen is busy again. The Armada has now sunk 20 and captured 26 more 'in perfectly good condition'. It has also occupied

Newcastle (alternatively Edinburgh), where it reposes well and comfortable while 27 desperately wounded English ships have limped up the Thames. And so on. These stories gained little credence in England, but raced like beacon fires across the Continent. Philip himself was more sensible. He hoped they were genuine, but he was not giving the signal for universal rejoicing before he was quite sure. The impression he managed to convey was that he feared them too good to be true: which indeed was the case, neither fleet having fired a single shot at the other, having still no shot to fire.

The reality, then, was much tamer. The English followed (out of range) until Friday, August 2nd, with the wind behind them all the way. Then, seeing that the enemy had not once altered course towards the English coast and were now 60 miles offshore, opposite Newcastle, they began to think about their return journey; the more seriously because it would involve a long beat to windward, with very little food left and practically no water. There was still the Forth, it is true; and no one even yet could foretell what the King of Scots might do. But it was no good arriving there destitute: for, if by any chance James were to favour the enemy, he was hardly likely to allow the English to replenish their supplies. A change of wind on the 2nd decided them. It shifted to northwest, which made it impossible for the Armada to reach any part of the Scottish coast. So, leaving behind only two small, swift ships to continue the shadowing, they turned for home. It was as well they did because, when off Norfolk, they met a westerly gale which made them run for shelter into various roads from Harwich to the Downs; hence, no doubt, the rumour of the action off Harwich.

Thus the fleets separated, finally. Neither side was very happy, the Spaniards for obvious reasons which will be examined later. But the English too, both seamen and people, were far from elated. They were uncertain of the future. They did not know the completeness of their victory. They did not realize the damage they had inflicted, either material or moral. They only knew, at least the seamen did, that the material results had been disappointing. For long they had tried in vain to break that stubborn formation, and had succeeded only at the eleventh hour when, with their ammunition all but spent, it was almost too late. Further, they had to do, mainly, with the intrepid few of the enemy, and they had no real evidence of the extent to which Spanish spirit was quenched. Many letters survive from this period. Some of them are distinctly captious. Many cannot understand the breakdown in munitions and victuals; and, though they one and all spare the Crown, they clearly (and rightly) feel that 'something is wrong somewhere'. Individuals are disappointed: Seymour sulking with Howard and Drake, Frobisher purple with rage about the latter. Hawkins consoles himself with the reflection that the Armada was much more formidable than we had expected, wants to get his beloved ships into dock before deficiencies get out of hand, yet is too wise to suggest demobilization until much more of the Armada's movements is known. Drake is oddly cheerful, confident yet not boastful. Howard is greatly concerned with the welfare of his men: they are without water or provisions, and disease is spreading daily through the fleet. A master-gunner writes to point out how bad our gunnery has been, owing, of course, to our perennial shortage of gunners. And through it all quivers a note of real nervousness. Where is the Armada, and what is it up to? Had we given it lesson enough, or would it return to begin all over again?

But the person who was causing the chief trouble just then was the Queen herself. So long as the danger had been at its height, she had been magnificent, showing herself at Tilbury Camp, vowing that she would lead her loving subjects, if necessary, in the last ditch, and uttering those ringing words which neither her people nor their descendants have ever quite forgotten:

I know I have the body of a weak and feeble woman, but I have the heart and stomach of a King, and of a King of England too; and think foul scorn that Parma or Spain or any Prince of Europe should dare invade the borders of my Realm: to which, rather than any dishonour shall grow by me, I myself will take up arms. I myself will be your General, Judge and Rewarder.

Yet, as soon as the peril was past – or rather, in her advisers' eyes, well before it was past – the set of her mind reverted to its habitual economy. Her expenses must be instantly reduced, her armies disbanded and sent home; the hired ships discharged, most of her own laid up, and their crews demobilized. So Howard was sent for, to leave the fleet and advise how best, and how quickly, these things could be done. Papers of all kinds were sent for too, and closely scrutinized. Where was the account of the ammunition which Lord Sussex had collected and sent to Howard in the Channel? Who had authorized it? Were Hawkins's latest accounts to the Navy Board in, and, if in, checked? Where was Darell's list of men victualled? Were the dates right? Had he taken every precaution to see that he was not cheated by the contractors? For that matter let him straightly show that he has not been cheating himself. What a mistress! Daily she harried Walsingham and Burghley who, in their turn, had to harry Darell and Howard and Hawkins. No one was spared, from minor dockyard officials to major executive officers: all were subjected to a ruthless, nagging inquisition, until at last old John Hawkins, most faithful and hard-worked of her servants, worn to a shadow by most ex-acting duties both executive and administrative, could only bow his weary head and say, 'God, I trust, will deliver me of it ere it be long, for there is no other hell!' Yet he turned upon the Lord Treasurer when that much-tried minister so far forgot himself as to hint that the men who had died or been discharged sick constituted a good and legitimate saving to the Government, as wages due to them could now go towards pay-ing others. Hawkins reminded him with dignity and patience, but with unbending firmness, that these poor people had de-pendants, to whom the deceaseds' wages already belonged in both justice and equity.

The demobilization caused many difficulties and much heartburning: for custom, and the men themselves, demanded that payment and discharge should go together; and there was no money for payment. The generous Lord Admiral grew more and more desperate as the vicious circle developed. If the men could not be paid, they must remain; but if they remained the wage bill continued to grow. They must also eat, and there was little food, and no money to buy it. Howard is here shown at his very best. He was a humane man, honestly attached to his seamen, knowing how well they had acquitted themselves. He refused absolutely to discharge them unpaid and starving. Having been ordered to collect from Drake the money and plate taken in the *Rosario*, he kept it, without warrant of course, but informing Walsingham, of what he had done. With it, he paid as many of the seamen as he could, and then spent as much again out of his own pocket, yet promising to repay the *Rosario* money when he could collect more of his own. It was, he wrote, too pitiful to have men starve after such service. He was sure, he said, that her Majesty would not want it so. He seems, however, to have been somewhat dubious about the efficacy of any appeal to her sense of justice and fair play, because he followed it up with the argument of pure expediency:

> Therefore I had rather open the Queen's Majesty's purse something to relieve them, than they should be in that extremity; for we are to look to have more of these services; and if men should not be cared for better than to let them starve and die miserably, we should very hardly get men to serve.

At this point the good Admiral's emotion gets the better of his grammar. But, paraphrased, his next sentence can only mean this: 'All I ask is that the Crown will put down as much as I have. God knows I am not rich, but I would rather have never a penny in the world than that they should lack.' History is silent on whether he was ever repaid; the odds are certainly against it. Ultimately the bulk of the men departed, though some certainly starved. Here at least was something like, if not true greatness, at least true goodness and real altruism. No one can pretend that it is one of the duties of C.-in-C. Grand Fleet to pay half his men's wages and victualling bills.

Unfortunately, shortage of food and cash was not the worst evil which struck the luckless men who had just saved England. Far worse, in mortality anyway, was the pestilence which invaded the fleet. Sickness in ships, even when they had been at sea only a little while, was in that day the rule rather than the exception. Already, during Howard's forlorn trip to Corunna in early July, we read of mounting sick-lists. But here, it would seem, was something graver than the normal outbreaks. It was a major epidemic. It is never easy to discover the nature of a disease in days when contemporary physicians failed to identify it. In this case, almost all historians have assumed that it was an exceptionally fierce outbreak of what was then the commonest of sea-diseases: the 'gaol fever' or typhus, a malady which thrives in environments where over-crowded and underwashed humanity congregates, be they gaols or slums or ships: a disease that, for the next three centuries or nearly, was to take more lives at sea than the hottest action or the wildest weather. In 1588 the Spaniards were its victims too. There is evidence of it in the Armada quite early on, and well before the end it was raging all but unchecked. On August 11th Sidonia is reporting 3,000 cases of sickness, mostly typhus. In the English fleet too there were unques-tionably many cases. But the deadly disorder now under examination was, according to the latest medical authority,* not typhus at all. It was 'food poisoning in its most virulent form with rapid death from toxaemia'.

Anyone who has groped among the exiguous records of hygiene in Tudor ships will not be at all surprised at such an epidemic; rather, he may be surprised to find that it was not endemic. Dr Keevil records how victuals were normally pre-pared for consumption afloat. The ovens, or hearths, were built of loosely spaced bricks, lying open in the hold on top of the foul, bilge-soaked gravel of the ballast (this to minimize the danger of fire, arch-enemy of wooden ships). The atmosphere was putrid and constantly humid: every article of food capable of growing whiskers grew them. Through the deck above, and into the hearths, and the uten-sils upon them, seeped the contaminated filth of the decks above them, as well as the accumulated horrors in the gravel itself, never moved and never purified. Any washing of these

* J. J. Keevil, *Medicine in the Navy*, Vol. I, Livingstone, 1957.

utensils was done with 'bad' water, drawn normally from crowded harbours into which whole fleets were constantly discharging their own filth, even their corpses, and of course their excrement. 'Good' water was collected from the shore, and used (though usually after it had gone bad in wooden casks) for drinking only, being far too precious a commodity for any other purpose.

So much for the cooking. What of the food cooked? It was often putrescent from the start, and putrid when its turn came to be consumed. Here our nip-cheese method of victualling greatly contributed. Normally, when the stuff became too disgusting to swallow, the men would refuse it, or look so ugly that it had to be thrown overboard. But when, as was happening throughout this campaign, only a day or two's ration remained, even the most pestilential barrelful had to be husbanded, and scraped to its last loathsome dregs, its taste disguised where possible by lavish use of salt or strong-tanged spices. The beer, as we saw, was actually admitted to be bad: and that must have been bad indeed.

The men themselves could never undress completely, and were never allowed ashore. No water was ever issued for washing; soap of course was unknown. So were privies. Though (probably) the officers had primitive 'conveniences' within-board, the common people had none. They used the 'heads' of the ship, the external curving timbers right forward on each side of the stem. At least, those were the orders; but thereby hangs a tale highly relevant to this epidemic. Men trained to the sea can hardly have failed to appreciate the advantages of a certain elementary hygiene, and would tend to obey the rules not only through fear of punishment but also for their own safety. In the earlier days of this campaign most of the people were seamen, or, if not quite that, at least country-bred folk, relatively well-nourished and comparatively cleanly. But, from the start, a few were not. They came from the towns, mainly London, where undernourishment and personal squalor were far more common; and such men had neither sense nor will to adapt themselves to the peculiar conditions of sea life. As the campaign progressed, and the various diseases germinated, swift replenishment became necessary: those immediately available came mostly from London and, for that matter, from its lowest slums. Thus the standards both of resistance to disease and of personal cleanliness constantly deteriorated, with the proven result that the epidemic grew progressively worse, both in numbers and in deadliness.

Once more, nothing like exact mortality figures can be given. All we dare say is that they were immense. The few relevant documents which survive do not help much, but they contain hints. Thus Hawkins reported to Burghley on September 4th that there was a shortage of about 1,000 men in the Queen's five Great Ships, *Ark*, *Triumph*, *Victory*, *Bear* and *Elizabeth Jonas*. Here, strictly speaking, we are only summarizing his report. He shows the shortages in the first four-named ships, while opposite the fifth, the *Elizabeth Jonas*, he leaves a blank: for which reason at least one English authority has assumed that all her crew were casualties. This, however, is a little too grim: Howard himself informs us that he had cleared her survivors out in order to fumigate the ship with fires of wet broom. But she was the worst hit of all; and as we have reached our absentee figure of 1,000 by giving her only the same shortage as the *Bear*, the next-worst hit, we certainly have not exaggerated. But we cannot say, of course, that 1,000 were dead of (or down with) the food-poisoning epidemic. On the one hand, there were innumerable other ills (typhus, say, or even starvation) to lay the poor sailor low; while, on the other, we have no idea how often the complements of these ships had been renewed since the campaign began. The *Bear*, for instance (in which Hawkins shows a shortage of 240 out of 500 – almost 50 per cent), had certainly housed far more than 500 in the last six weeks. Very likely 1,000 had been in her, first and last; in which case her wastage was not 240 out of 500, but 740 out of 1,000; not 50 per cent, but 75 per cent.

It is a sobering thought. The Spaniards themselves, it may be recalled, accounted, at the very most, for 100 of our people. It is thus perfectly possible that, in this one ship alone, there were lost, by food-poisoning, typhus, starvation, etc., seven times as many Englishmen as fell to the Spanish weapons in the whole fleet of some 150 fighting ships. We can go no farther, but, evidently, it would be quite safe to assume that for every man who fell to the violence of the enemy, not far off a hundred succumbed to the filthiness of their own diet and way of life.

Where lies the blame? Reason recoils at the task of apportioning it. Surely the realist answer can only be 'Everyone – and everything', but most of all, that factor which is least possible and profitable to blame: the general attitude and the general state of knowledge of Elizabeth's England. We will spend no time on scapegoats, only pausing to note the one that found most favour at the time. At least it reveals how very far contemporary Englishmen, even the best of them, were from spotting the real causes of their sufferings. On August 26th, Howard wrote:

> But, Sir, the mariners have a conceit (and I think it is true, and so do all the Captains here) that sour drink hath been a great cause of this infection among us; and, Sir, for my own part I know not which way to deal with the mariners to make them rest contented with sour beer.

He must have our sympathy again. Has anyone, even in this enlightened age, solved that particular problem?

The English people awoke slowly to the realization of victory. When they did, Londoners were given several of those spectacles which, though far from lavish, delighted the simple tastes of the day. On August 20th 'the Lord Mayor, Aldermen, and the Companies in their best liveries went to hear the Dean of St Paul's preach at the Cross'. On September 8th there 'were set upon the lower Battlements of the Church eleven Ensigns or Banners taken from the Spanish Fleet', whence they were carried in state to the Cross in Cheapside and, next day, 'hanged on London Bridge towards Southwark'. But it was not till Sunday, November 24th, that the greatest day came. Then

> the Queen, attended by her Privy Council, by the Nobility and other honourable Persons as well spiritual as temporal,

in great number, the French Ambassador [who, however, thought he was only attending the 30th anniversary of the Queen's accession], the Judges, the Heralds and Trumpeters all on horseback, came in a chariot supported by four pillars and drawn by two white horses to St Paul's Church, where, alighting at the West Door, she fell on her knees, and audibly praised God for her own and the Nation's signal deliverance; and after a sermon suitable to the occasion, preached by Dr Pierce, Bishop of Sarum, she exhorted the People in a most Royal and Christian manner, to a due Performance of the religious Duty of Thanksgiving, then going to the Bishop of London's Palace, where she dined, she returned in the same order as before, by Torchlight, to Somerset-House.

What a woman! Everyone was happy, and it had not cost much. Nor had the awards she meted out afterwards:

Upon all occasions she distinguished the rest of the Officers, Soldiers and Sailors with particular marks of her Regard and Esteem: but their rewards consisted generally more in words than in deeds.

What a woman! Yes, but what a Queen! Have these pages dealt over-harshly with her? Perhaps; for we need reminding, every time we hint at her dislike of opening her purse, that, in a responsible ruler, there may be a worse, or at least a more dangerous, quality than parsimony. There is such a thing as recklessness, especially in a person whose means are straitly limited: for anyone who spends money which he does not possess is set fair upon a rake's progress towards one of two things, bankruptcy or plain swindling. Elizabeth, as Queen, commanded very little money; not nearly enough, anyway, to pay for what she must do, let alone for what she wanted to do. She was doomed, always, to a never-ending series of difficult and distasteful choices. Can we therefore really blame her, if, having decided that such-and-such a course of action was essential for the safety of herself and England, she accepted the action, but economized, in every possible way, on the means? Hardly. Yet this is what often makes her look so mean, meaner than she really was.

But Elizabeth had assets other than monetary ones, and surely we see one of them here. She had made her servants and her people so love, honour and obey her that, in their eyes, service to her had become a thing worthwhile in itself, and its reward was not to be measured in money. This was a great, a truly queenly gift of hers, and she was using it now. She had been forced into opposing Philip's all-out effort to destroy her, and she had succeeded. But it had cost her all she could afford, if not more. There was nothing left in her purse for such comparatively minor calls upon it as the gratifying of her servants with material rewards, or her people with costly spectacles, much as she knew that they deserved them. She could still reward them, however. She still had that precious gift of making their hearts brim over with pride, loyalty and love; and this, though it put nothing into their pockets, yet had the inestimable advantage of taking nothing out of hers. The deal was fair enough, always provided that the bare fact of being thanked and smiled upon by the Queen's Grace did seem to them a pearl of great price. And beyond all doubt it did. What mattered it to her loyal Londoners if the two-horse chariot was quite an inexpensive turn-out for so momentous an occasion, even when eked out with colourful liveries (which the Companies paid for) or banners (supplied by Philip), or by the sermon laid on by the bishop and the dinner by another (both of whom had their stipends anyway)? Far more important to them was the presence, in their very midst, of Her Majesty in person, kneeling – yes, positively kneeling, there at the West Door where everybody could see her – smiling upon them, commending them in clear firm tones worthy of the great Lady she was. Who can doubt that they went home that night with full hearts, regretful only, perhaps, that husband or lover, brother, father or son, was not there to share their happiness? What a Queen!

15

THE VANQUISHED

DURING THIS MONTH of August the Spaniards too had their problems, not the same as ours but certainly no less acute. One of the first in point of time was the problem of discipline. Panic and discipline are ill bed-fellows. The first symptoms appeared on the very first day's fighting, when some of the captains sought shelter among the hulks. There are guarded hints of others in the passage up-Channel – there was, for instance, the *San Mateo*'s lapse off the Isle of Wight – while, as they lay off Calais, there were two more. One was perhaps only a hint still; the other was an unpleasant certainty. On the night of the fireships, the bluest-blooded man in the Armada, Philip's natural son the Prince of Ascoli, was sent to carry instructions to other ships. He failed to return: in fact, he landed at Dunkirk and took no further part in the adventure. He said that circumstance, not choice, dictated his action; that he wanted to, but could not, return. This may or may not be true. When he explained his conduct to his father he omitted to mention that he had taken with him on his trivial errand a full-blown captain, three servants and his private chaplain. Of the other case, however, there could be no doubt. On the previous night the master and the pilot of the *San Pedro El Menor* deserted to the English. True they may have been Flemings, bound to the Spaniards by religion and not by patriotism; but, to faltering morale, their example was distressing. No one wanted to be reminded just then of rats and sinking ships.

At Gravelines itself the panic had been widespread; at first perhaps universal. Moreover it is clear that many of the minor captains (though none of the major ones) did not recover all day. The first fleet order after they had been extricated by the providential change of wind shows that disciplinary trouble was brewing, and that someone was not prepared to wink at it. Nor was that 'someone' Sidonia who, as soon as the fighting was over, seems to have given way to the lethargy of despair. Thereafter he handed over the day-to-day conduct of the fleet, not to Diego Flores, whom, very likely, no one would have obeyed, but to the military officer commanding all the *tercios*, Francisco de Bobadilla. Here at least was a man who would stand no nonsense. In Sidonia's name he gave orders that no captain, upon pain of ignominious death, should ever get ahead of the flagship. There was to be no *sauve qui peut*. Nothing untoward happened until the next evening (or possibly that of Thursday, August 1st), when two ships were seen some two miles ahead. Bobadilla instantly sent over an officer who arrested the captains and brought them to the flagship, where they were sentenced to immediate death by hanging. One of them, Cristobal de Avila, though a Don, was summarily hoisted at the yardarm. The other, Francisco de Cuellar, was luckier. He had many friends, one of whom was Martin de Aranda, the Auditor of the Fleet. This magnate allowed him to state his case, which sounds quite a good one. Many of the more damaged ships, he said, finding difficulty in keeping up, had made a practice of going ahead whenever sail was shortened in the flagship. They then lay to, repairing their worst defects: and this is all that he was doing. Very likely de Avila was only doing the same, but, evidently, not knowing the right people, he was never allowed to say so. Aranda took it upon himself to reprieve Cuellar, unless the full rigour of the sentence was insisted upon. As it was not, Cuellar was spared, to suffer (and survive) the incredible hardships of which we shall hear more later. Calderon says that other captains, and some military officers, were condemned to the galleys, for this and for unsoldierly conduct at Gravelines. But the Duke is silent upon the point.

The Armada ploughed on into northern waters. Various writers, both contemporary Spaniards and subsequent commentators from other countries, seem to think that this uninterrupted retreat, which finally brought the survivors northabout and home by the open Atlantic, was forced upon them by the winds that blew, and they infer that Sidonia never definitely gave up the idea of returning by the Channel. This is quite wrong. It is obvious that, as far as the winds were concerned, he could easily have come south again, certainly as from August 2nd. For this is what the English (then in sight of him) actually did, and without undue difficulty. And he did not come to his decision to return north-about in ignorance of what that involved. He knew the immense distance to be covered and the dangers of the navigation; and he knew the shortness of his provisions – indeed, on Saturday, August 3rd (the day after the English left him) he put everyone on the strictest daily ration of half a pound of bread, half a pint of wine and one pint of water. Then the fleet proceeded north, for the next five days, on a wind which would have been a good deal more favourable to it had it been running south. Beyond question, every responsible Spaniard was tacitly agreed upon how they should return, even if none of them said so out loud: and the decision, all things considered, was probably the right one.

This fact has an important bearing upon that oldest of misconceptions which has, ever since, clung about the ill-fated Armada: that the winds of Heaven and not the arms of Man were responsible for its disasters. This theory has been assiduously advanced, by both sides, for a reason which is neither military nor political. The whole Anglo-Spanish war, though economic and national, was, nominally at least, religious, and both parties were concerned to show that the Almighty favoured his Own: that the Catholic Cause – or alternatively the Protestant Cause – was the one He favoured, and therefore the one He helped. Hence the Englishmen's almost childish glee at a story, broadcast by every means at their disposal, of certain wretched Spanish captives, their morale quite gone (and probably their bellies quite empty), who had made – or were alleged to have made – a great admission; to all Catholics (and, let us hope, to all decent Protestants too) a horrid blasphemy, 'that in all these fights Christ showed Himself a Lutheran'. Hence also, on a more respectable plane, Sidonia's fervent 'God alone could save us' – which of course He did. Hence too the Protestant medal with its well-known inscription *Flavit Jehovah et dissipati sunt*, a most unequivocal affirmation of the very Protestant proclivities of God's winds. What is less well known, perhaps, is that this medal was first struck in Holland, not England. The islanders who, after all, had actually thrashed the Armada in full flight, were perhaps not quite so ready to let all the credit go elsewhere, though they were perfectly prepared to admit (indeed, wanted the fact established) that God had guided their arms. There is nothing in the least irreligious, or boastful, in this. It is merely anticipating by some two generations the saying attributed (probably wrongly) to Cromwell, 'Trust in the Lord and keep your powder dry': it is only an illustration in life of that far older proverb 'God helps him who helps himself'. Of course Atlantic winds will howl, even in summer. The present writer, who has spent some ten August holidays on the western shores of the Outer Hebrides, and three or four on the wild headlands of Connemara, can testify to their strength, their sudden rise and their yet more sudden, uncanny fall. Of course the grey-green rollers generated by these far-travelling winds are large and fearsome, especially to mariners whose experience lies in sunnier seas; especially to ships leaking from shotholes and only hastily botched up. Of course the iron-bound coasts of western Scotland and Ireland can be exceedingly perilous to sailing-ships, especially if they are short of sails, spars, anchors and cables; and more perilous still if their owners are venturing that way without charts, or with inaccurate ones, and with few if any pilots who have sailed those seas before. But, it is only fair to ask, why were the Spaniards there now? Not assuredly because they wanted to be, nor because they had expected to be when they started. Had that been so, they would have deserved all they got for not equipping themselves better for the ordeal. No. The thing is perfectly plain. They had a straight choice: to face the winds, the waves, the rocky shores of the Atlantic, or to face the ships of England in the Narrow Seas. Of their own free will they chose the former.

Accompanying the Armada, probably in the flagship, was an absolutely first-rate navigator. We do not know his name – indeed, there may have been more than one. But he has left a

memorial of his ability. From the flagship, sailing-orders were
issued to the whole fleet, laying down in considerable detail
'the course that shall be held in the return of this Army into
Spain'. Its exact date of issue is unknown, unfortunately, because that would indicate beyond all dispute when the 'north-
about' decision was finally made. But it must have been earlier
than August 10th, almost certainly earlier than August 8th,
when the Armada was off the Moray Firth, most probably
very soon after the English left them on August 2nd, and possibly on that very day. This order could hardly be improved
upon. The fleet was to keep together, and steer nor'nor'east
up to the latitude of 61½°, which would bring it well north of
the Shetlands, but also well to the east of them – not very far,
in fact, from the Norwegian coast. The Armada was then to
run due west until it was back on the meridian of the Shetlands; then to steer west-sou'west, holding that course until it
was in latitude 58 north. This would allow it to miss the
northernmost point of the Shetlands by a good 30 miles, clear
Cape Wrath and the outer isles of Scotland by at least 100
miles, and even pass to the north and west of the Rockall
Bank. Only when clear of these dangers, and right out in the
open Atlantic, was it to steer to the southwest, holding this
new course until it reached 53 N. At that moment it would
be nearly in the latitude of the Shannon, though some 400
miles to the west. Thereafter it could make a straight run to
any port of Spain, on any course between southeast and
sou'sou'east. The man responsible for this certainly knew his
job. Ill-found, overstrained shot-wracked ships might not survive the ordinary Atlantic weather, but at least the risks of
rocks, and shore-currents on coasts but indifferently charted
could be eliminated altogether.

The results prove the man's skill. The *San Martin* herself, as
far as we can see, held closely to this course, with one marked
exception,* as did a number of other ships which were sound
or lucky enough to keep company with her. The flagship

---

* This was that the whole fleet seems to have cut its first corner,
and passed into the Atlantic through the sound between Orkney and
Fair Island, an unnecessary risk, which, however, led to no disaster.

reached Spain in safety and, navigationally speaking, without difficulty, making indeed a tolerable passage as things went in those days; 1,500 miles in 30 days through an area where the prevalent winds could hardly be expected to be really favourable. Moreover, her log shows no exceptionally bad weather. The worst was a two-day gale on September 2nd and 3rd, severe, but having nothing in it to daunt well-found and well-handled ships, in the open ocean where there was room to run. That it cannot have been too dangerous a *tormenta* is clear from the fact that the *San Martin* (which, disease-ridden as she was, could hardly be described as well-handled, and certainly not well-found) yet survived it, if by no great margin. She sighted Corunna on September 11th but, just failing to make it, had to run east to Santander, arriving on September 13th. Of the ships in company with her we cannot speak with equal certainty, because we do not know the names of all of them. So many Armada ships, however, have remained quite unaccounted for to this day, simply disappearing without trace, that, in all probability, some of this group could not take the Atlantic's buffeting, and foundered. But it is morally certain that no ship which stuck to the flagship was *wrecked*.

Those whose ill fate is known were the ones which, for one reason or another, lost touch with Sidonia. The Spanish pilots' ignorance of the west coast of Ireland may seem astonishing, for not a few of them must have been there before. But there it was, abysmal, and revealed again and again. Most of them, and those not the least responsible ones, really seem to have been unconscious of the great westerly bulge of Connaught while there is hardly a headland anywhere between north Donegal and Cork which someone or other does not call 'Cape Clear'. But all this only serves to underline the excellence of Sidonia's master-navigator, who contrived to avoid all the perils of geographical ignorance by avoiding the coast altogether. Sidonia never saw any land at all, probably, from the moment he passed the Orkneys to his first landfall off the Spanish coast.

Faulty navigation alone, however, cannot account for all the calamities which befell the rest of the ships. Hardly any of them, probably, lost touch with the flagship on purpose, and nearly all the ships then surviving seem to have been in company as late as August 15th, being then some 70 miles northwest of Rockall, and well on the prescribed course. Then a heavy sou'westerly blew up and dispersed them. One ship at least, the galleass *Zuñiga*, even found herself in latitude 63 N., a long way west of the Faeroes, and not very far from Iceland. Many, but not all, reassembled, and, about the 17th, which must have been the last day when the bulk of them were together, there was an anguished council meeting. The crux here was not so much navigation as starvation and lack of fresh water. Diego Flores de Valdez advocated making for the Spanish coast, on the grounds that death from want was more certain than death from shipwreck. But Sidonia seems to have been persuaded by Purser Calderon and others to stick to his own sailing orders and so, as we have seen, to escape. A considerable splinter group evidently decided that Ireland was the lesser evil. But Recalde himself led this party; and his known record should convince us that here was no insubordination, but downright necessity. Though already a very sick man, he was the least likely of them all to give way to panic or despair. It may well be, too, that he had not been able to rejoin after the gale of the 15th, and was not, therefore, at the council table on the 17th. Certainly, throughout, his flagship, the Portuguese galleon *San Juan*, had been more knocked about than most.

Yet, for whatever reason it was taken, the decision was desperate and it proved fatal to at least half those who took it; also to many who did not, because, as Recalde approached Ireland from the northwest, he sighted a number of other ships which had been driven ashore by the weather and had lost the Duke. Now they joined up with him. Probably, in the end, about half the fleet sighted that ill-omened coast; at any rate, the English Lord Deputy was able to report home that no less than 59 Spanish ships had been seen from the shore. This figure is probably an exaggeration; doubtless some ships were counted more than once. But 50 is not too high an estimate. Of these a certain number (of which Calderon's hulk the *San Salvador* was one) evidently disliked what they saw of the coast upon their first view of it, and favoured by a fortunate though temporary wind, tacked northwest, gained an offing, and escaped. The rest bore down on Ireland, and made land all the way along the west coast. Those who started most to windward would come in on to the Munster coast, Kerry or Clare. Others, with less offing, would hit Galway or Mayo, while yet others, without searoom enough to clear the northwest promontory of County Mayo, would run into Donegal Bay; but not out of it.

DISPERSAL AND DISASTER

Ireland

Of these three groups the fate of about half was quite lamentable. They seemed to have hoped for succour from the native Irish who, they knew, were Catholics like themselves. But they seldom received it. In the more accessible parts there were English garrisons, whose commanders had stringent orders not only to take (and later to execute) all the Spaniards caught, but also to punish with the utmost severity any Irishmen who succoured them; and the peasants were already so cowed and poverty-stricken by years of strife that they usually would not, and often could not, help them. On the other hand, in the less accessible places where there were no garrisons, the natives were so wild and uncivilized, as well as so poor, that property of any kind was an irresistible temptation to them. Besides, like so many primitive shore-dwellers, they regarded anything which came to them from the sea as lawful perquisite, theirs by right and immemorial custom. And the Spaniards unwittingly played into their hands. Those who escaped drowning when their ships struck tried, perhaps naturally, to save such valuables as they possessed; the officers their personal jewellery and some of their rich table-plate, the men their wages, which had been paid to them at Corunna. They had far better have left them behind. In the very act of scrambling ashore, half-drowned and weak through hunger and thirst, they were set upon, knocked on the head and stripped to the skin. The few who escaped this initial fate and managed to get off the beaches occasionally found a better fate. Sometimes they fell in with slightly more sophisticated natives, or the odd friar who still ministered here and there to their spiritual needs. A very few made contact with Catholic gentlemen who loathed the English. Such men seldom gave up the wretched fugitives, but they would not face any English troops in their neighbourhood, and fled, leaving the Spaniards behind. All these, once caught, were instantly shot or hanged, save for such officers as were considered worth ransoming, and even these (who, in contemporary warfare, could usually reckon at least to escape slaughter) were much fewer than usual.

For the English authorities, both at home and on the spot, were frightened. Ireland had long been smouldering with rebellion, and once or twice the English had barely prevailed. On several occasions, too, Spanish forces had actually been landed, to form dangerous nuclei for the rebels to rally round. These facts cannot, of course, excuse such revolting barbarity to shipwrecked men. Yet two reasons for it should be mentioned. First, in that rough age, and in that atmosphere of hate which is so often engendered by religious animosities, conduct of this kind, on both sides, was distressingly common. And second, though the bedraggled wretches who crawled from the waves looked innocuous enough and deserving only of pity, they might easily, when collected, rested, refreshed and reorganized by determined leaders, become once again very formidable rallying points, capable of turning the still nicely balanced scales. Yet no palliation can remove the blot from the names of those who ordered and executed the massacre.

There is no room here for a detailed account of all this suffering. A few typical instances must suffice.

The biggest fish that swam into this deadly net was Recalde himself. But the meshes were not quite strong enough to hold such a man, and he swam out of them, though not all his consorts were so fortunate. On September 5th he brought his ship, the much-battered galleon *San Juan*, under the lee of Great Blasket Island at the mouth of Dingle Bay. He had been ill in bed, it seems, ever since Gravelines, but now he rose from it in the dire emergency, and chose his anchorage with masterly skill: for the island gave him shelter from every wind but one, and that the fair one for Spain. He remained here for 13 days. His case was by no means desperate. He was not shipwrecked. His men, and those of the ships with him, could still put up quite a formidable show when landed; he was able to take what he wanted in the way of fresh water, and even, if he could find it, food. Then, when the wind came fair, he sailed out and home, still alive, though barely. Some of his companions, however, did not follow him. The *Nuestra Señora de la Rosa* had hit a hidden rock on entering the sound and, though she succeeded in anchoring near Recalde, suddenly went down with the loss of every man but one. Another ship, probably another of the many *San-Juans*, did much the same, though many of her people and some of her guns were saved; while yet a third *San Juan* (this time *Bautista*) perished hereabouts, though whether she was actually of Recalde's party is uncertain. A little to the north another large ship, name unknown but probably of the Biscayan squadron, went aground between the Blaskets and Kerry Head with every soul on board lost. Another, a small one, was wrecked in Tralee Bay; her crew was captured, and hanged to a man.

At much the same time four large ships and three small ones got safely into the Shannon and anchored in Scattery Roads. Perhaps they were part of Recalde's original company; and, like him, they did not fare too badly. They were well-handled and navigated, and were powerful enough to be able to look after themselves. Their only casualty was the Portuguese galleon *San Marcos*, a true warship and Sidonia's ever-faithful second. As she showed signs of refusing to float any longer, the Spaniards themselves burned her; a very gallant foe, deserving a happier end. The rest ran out on a northeast wind on September 11th, and probably reached home safely.

A little to the north of Shannon-mouth is Mal Bay, on the promontory of County Clare. Here two ships were cast away. A large one, perhaps another Biscayan, was wrecked off Doonbeg, and another under Tromra Castle. The graves of their men, drowned in the wrecks or executed by the Sheriff of

Clare, were still shown at Spanish Point near Miltown Malbay until recently, and maybe still are. Here too the galleass *Zuñiga* had a very narrow escape, finding herself almost landlocked and, apparently, without a rudder at all. She escaped only by reason of her oars and managed to anchor off Liscanor castle, whence she sailed on that same northeaster which helped the ships in the Shannon. But her troubles were far from over. As she passed the mouth of the English Channel, still rudderless and by now quite foodless, she made the best of a bad job and ran before a brisk westerly wind for Havre, arriving in a sinking condition to join the *Santa Ana*. Here she was patched up with material brought from the wrecked galleass at Calais, whence, too, she obtained stores and 56 men. She also received 20 wretches who had somehow escaped from Ireland, 'naked', we are told. After endless delays and much diplomatic correspondence, she at last cleared Havre in mid-April, 1589, only to be blown back, almost miraculously, to the same port, *minus* most of her guns, anchors and stores, and badly battered in masts and hull. All was to do again. Then her crew mutinied and, to add to her trials, she got silted up at her moorings. In mid-July, 1589, she was still there. Yet – an almost entirely different ship, so much had her timbers been patched and re-renewed – she probably did reach home at last, though few if any of her original company came with her. This was well over a year after she started, which is doubtless the reason why her name has usually gone to swell the tally of lost Armada ships.

Connemara comes next. Information here is rather scarce, the country being quite outside English control. Only one ship is known for certain to have perished hereabouts, the *Falco Blanco*. Most of her people reached the shore and were for a while protected by the local chieftains, the O'Flaherties. But here, for once, they were given up as a result of threats, and sent as prisoners to Galway town. The Governor of Connaught was Sir Richard Bingham, a name to which much infamy clings. He knew his Spaniards, and their language. Fate ordained that he should know them both in the trough of their despair, here in Ireland, and at the crest of their naval triumph: he had served with them at Lepanto. Yet if he was a monster,

KEY TO SHIPS LOST

1. Gerona (galleass)
2. Trinidad Valencera
3. Juliana
4. Duquesa Santa Ana
5. San Juan (galleon, Castile)
6. Lavia
7. Rata Encoronada
8. Gran Grin
9. Falco Blanco (mediano)
10. San Marcos (galleon, Portugal)
11. San Juan (of Fernando Horra)
12. Nuestra Señora de la Rosa

A. A Flemish Ship
B. Ship of San Sebastian
C. A Zabra
D. A Biscayan Ship
X. Name unknown

what, one may ask, was his superior, Sir William Fitzwilliam, the Lord Deputy of Ireland? Let us see.

The principal prisoner in the *Falco Blanco* was Don Luis de Cordova, brother of a Marquis and evidently good for a substantial ransom. But with him, taken in his own ship or others wrecked off Connaught, were nearly 50 lesser Spanish noblemen and gentry who had escaped drowning. These Bingham spared at first (having boasted 'putting to the sword' upwards of 1,000 lesser fry). Though this does not necessarily indicate lenity on his part (it may well have been love of money) he did draw up a list of his gentle captives, which he sent to Fitzwilliam, asking for instructions. The Lord Deputy replied, by return, 'Execute them all except de Cordova and his nephew!' In a surviving letter Bingham contrives to make it appear that he was unwilling to do it, not indeed because he was shocked, but because it seemed such a waste of easy money. Still, he did it. (Among the victims, by the way, was Ensign Juan Gils whom we last met capturing Falmouth fishermen off the Lizard.) But when the prisoners were all safely worked off, seven or eight more unfortunates were caught – two gentlemen and five or six seamen-boys. For a time Bingham concealed their capture, possibly, this time, stirred by some lingering shred of natural pity; for (he says) they only came in 'after the fury and heat of justice was past'; but also, perhaps, because his brother George had the keeping of them, and would, if anyone did, draw their ransom one day. Yet the charitable will be disposed to give him the benefit of the doubt, especially where the boys were concerned: they were not Spaniards, very likely not even Catholics, being Dutch lads 'pressed into the fleet against their will', and most unlikely to be worth their keep, let alone a ransom. But in Fitzwilliam there was no glimmer of mercy. Having occasion soon afterwards to make a 'progress' of Connaught, he discovered their existence, and had them all, men and boys, executed out of hand. So only the Marquis's brother and nephew survived; and, says local report, two men who were never caught because they were concealed by charitable townsmen. Another galleon, at her last gasp, is said to have sailed almost up to Galway. She landed 70 men to

try and obtain supplies. They were instantly taken and executed. The rest stayed in the ship, which was lost with all
hands.

One honourable exception must be named. Christopher
Carleill, who had been Drake's military commander in 1585,
took 14 Spaniards in Ulster, where he was Governor. Being
an old soldier who knew the accepted rules of war, he promised
them the usual mercy extended on such occasions. But he too,
apparently, did not know his Fitzwilliam, for he sent his
prisoners to him, saying what he had done, and adding that he
would pay for their keep himself. Fitzwilliam returned them at
once, with peremptory orders to hang them all. But Carleill
would not do it, and was even prepared to risk the conse-
quences of disobedience. He hired a boat from some Scottish
fishermen, and shipped his captives off to Scotland at his own
expense.

Still moving northwards, we now reach what may be called
the principal graveyard of the Armada. The geographical key
to the disasters was the great northwesterly promontory of
County Mayo, of whose very existence, it would seem, many
of the Spaniards were ignorant. All the ships which, approaching from the northwest, had insufficient offing sighted the
land hereabouts. Any ship, failing to weather Erris Head and
Benwee Head at the angle of the bulge, would be forced into
Sligo Bay or Donegal Bay, with no prospect of getting any
farther. So we must presume, all tried desperately to do so.
Some succeeded, but barely, and found themselves in what can
only be described as a navigator's nightmare, where sea and
mountain, island and mainland, must have seemed to the be-
wildered mariners inextricably tangled: from south to north,
Clew Bay, Blacksod Bay and (between Erris and Benwee)
Broad Haven; Clare Island, Achill Island and the Mullet
Peninsula. Hereabouts four, if not five, large ships were lost.
One was *El Gran Grin*, with Don Pedro de Mendoza on board.
Running for Clew Bay, she struck Clare Island at its mouth,
and sank. Many of her people struggled ashore, but the local
chieftain, seduced by the double chance of plunder and of
currying favour with the English, destroyed the lot, including

even Don Pedro. Another ship succeeded in penetrating farther into the bay, but went no farther: there was no farther to go. Only 16 of her men scrambled ashore.

On the other side of Achill Island is Blacksod Bay, and here began what was, to the Spaniards, the most grievous tragedy of all. On September 6th (or perhaps 7th) the great ship *La Rata Encoronada* limped in, carrying Don Alonso de Leyva and his precious freight of young noblemen. She was followed by the *Duquesa Santa Ana* and another ship. After a time however, *La Rata* dragged her anchor and, having no spare one, went aground and was wrecked. De Leyva brought all safely ashore, and they fortified themselves in an old castle (probably Doona), but then, seeing the *Duquesa* still at fairly safe moorings, they crossed the bay and joined her. The wind now falling favourable, the ship weighed and stood out to sea with some 800 souls on board, the residue of the two ships' companies. But once more she could make no southward progress, and, owing no doubt to acute food shortage, Don Alonso decided to give it up and make for Scotland. She passed the entrance to Donegal Bay in safety, but was blown inshore and wrecked soon afterwards in Loughros More Bay. Once more the undaunted De Leyva led his people ashore, where once more they dug themselves in. Here they stayed for nine days. They still had all their arms, and their valuables; and evidently they were too formidable for any local force to dare attack them. Then they heard a rumour that a Spanish ship lay at Killybegs, back in Donegal Bay and a mere dozen miles to the south. They packed up, therefore, and marched thither overland. The rumour was true. The galleass *Gerona* was there, weather-beaten and rudderless. Nothing daunted, the Spanish Bayard, though crippled by an accident and unable to walk, set all hands to work, repairing her with the wood from another wreck near by. His case was not even yet quite desperate. The local magnate was the O'Neil, and not only was he disposed to help, he even invited him to stay. But de Leyva, learning that his whereabouts was known in Dublin, is said to have refused, on the grounds that the O'Neil's hospitality to Spaniards would be fatal to the host. The story accords so well with the known chivalry of the man that it is most likely true. In mid-October, therefore, he put to sea again in the refitted *Gerona*. He would leave no one behind, so that the galleass was now carrying the survivors of three large ships, some 1,300 men. Round the north coast of Ireland she crept, past Lough Swilly, past Lough Foyle, past, it must have seemed, the worst of the dangers. But then, when almost opposite the Giant's Cause-way, the patched-up rudder suddenly gave way and, on a very dark night, the *Gerona* hit the Rock of Bunbois. Third time unlucky! Nine common seamen and soldiers somehow reached the shore to bear the tidings which were to plunge all Spain into mourning: the incomparable de Leyva, with all the flower and hope of young Spain – drowned, every one of them! *

Meanwhile, into the wide bays of Sligo and Donegal drifted the unfortunates who had been unable to weather Erris Head. Here, substantially, the same scenes were enacted, differing only in details, not in ultimate results. From Broad Haven at the angle, eastwards into the depths of the bay not less than eight, and probably nine or ten, ships met their doom. We can-not follow them all. One, wrecked on the Tirawley coast, con-tained a good proportion of the church dignitaries. They fell into the hands of brother George Bingham, and their fate was a foregone conclusion. Farther east, probably between Sligo and Ballyshannon, three more ships perished, one the *San Juan* galleon of the Castilian squadron. This stretch of beach was encumbered with immense piles of wreckage, and on it were counted over 1,200 corpses, drowned, mangled, naked, and gradually covered by the natural action of waves on sandy shores. From time to time their bones are still thrown up, and still there are rocks known locally as Carrig na Spagna.

One other of this group must have a word. The *Lavia* carried that same Martin de Aranda, the Auditor-General who had shielded the unlucky Cuellar from Bobadilla's wrath. The

* In the above account, as in many other details of the Irish wrecks, I follow the invaluable work of W. Spotswood Green, Chief Inspector of Irish Fisheries in the early years of this century. His findings were published in the *Geographical Journal*, Vol. XXVII, No. 5, May 1906.

delinquent himself was still in her, under open arrest. He has left a long account of his adventures which equal in excitement and incident any escape story of the present century.* From it we obtain not only an eyewitness account of what must have befallen so many ships' companies, but also a remarkable picture of contemporary Ireland as seen through the eyes of an intelligent stranger. His ship drove ashore and went rapidly to pieces. The Captain and his officers were destroyed by a most unseamanlike attempt to save their own lives. Cuellar was left on the poop, alone but for the Auditor-General himself who, in his turn, lost his life by his foolish cupidity in cramming his pockets with ducats. But Cuellar was washed ashore three parts drowned, and so bedraggled that the natives who found him did not realize his rank. They merely stripped him stark naked and threw him aside. His land adventures then started, and lasted seven months, during which time his general direction of wandering took him right across Ireland to the Giant's Causeway. When nearly there, and for the last time at the end of his tether, he chanced upon what he took to be a wild Irish peasant, no better clad than himself. But he was wrong. The ruffian turned out to be a bishop: indeed, possibly, the Archbishop of Tuam. This good man befriended him and finally shipped him off to Scotland. There he fared better, though not exactly well, and, reaching Edinburgh, was shipped with other fugitive Spaniards to Antwerp, Parma having at length arranged for transport at five ducats a head. Even then, however, the last lap was fraught with peril. The ship was seized by the Beggars, and only three (of whom Cuellar was one) escaped death. His narrative reveals a shrewd, personable (if slightly plausible) gentleman, attractive especially to the ladies, who were thus only too pleased to help him.

The last Irish wreck to be described here was that of the Levantine *La Trinidad-Valencera*, commanded by Don Alonso de Luzon, one of the *tercio*-colonels. Though we name her last,

* Printed in full in Spanish, in Duro's *Armada Invencible* (Madrid, 1884), and both Froude (in his *Spanish Story of the Armada*) and J. R. Hale (in his *The Great Armada*) give many of the more outstanding details. Unfortunately there is not room for many here.

however, she was probably one of the first to reap disaster. She sprang a serious leak while still north of any part of Ireland, and could only run down upon its northernmost point, hoping to reach it in time. In that ambition she succeeded. But it availed her little. Having stopped to pick up some survivors from the *Bark of Hamburg* which, leaking even more than she was, was actually foundering, she was brought up all standing by a reef near the entrance to Lough Foyle on September 2nd. De Luzon, with considerable difficulty and some loss, landed the combined crews. Like de Leyva, he was by no means defenceless; but, unlike him, he was more accessible to attack. Sure enough, he had marched only a few miles inland when a strong English force appeared. A much better soldier than sailor, he was now in his own element, and resisted bravely for some time, but with heavy losses. Then he tried to make terms, but all he got was an undertaking that he and his men should be brought unharmed into the presence of the Lord Deputy. It sounds like a cruel jest of the English captains; for though de Luzon did not know Fitzwilliam, they did. On such terms he laid down his arms, and the captives were marched off to Drogheda. On the way many of the soldiers and seamen were plundered and slain by the English rank and file, while no less than four of the gentlemen, who had been segregated from the rest, dropped dead from weakness and fatigue. All the common people were soon shot or hanged. The fate of most of the officers is not known: a great majority certainly suffered death, though de Luzon himself was spared, sent to London and probably ransomed. He was lucky. It would seem that a bare half-dozen of the officers taken in Ireland ever saw their homes again.

At least 25 ships of the Armada were lost off the Irish coast, and perhaps several more.* The names of the larger ones and

* A modern author, Professor Garrett Mattingly in his *Defeat of the Spanish Armada*, seeks to minimize these Irish losses which have for so long been accepted. He reduces the figure from 25 to the surprisingly low one of 10, but does not reveal his grounds for so drastic a cut. Indeed, if, as he records, he was 'finding W. S. Green a useful guide' (as I did), he certainly shows no sign of being guided by him. For Green lists 24 as 'certainties' and three or four more as 'probables'.

the localities where they perished are mostly known, but it was perfectly possible for a *patache* or a *zabra* to perish on the wilder stretches of the west coast and to disappear, ship and people, without any news coming to the English authorities, or even to anyone capable of recording its loss on paper.

Scotland and England

The sad tale is nearly told. Two other wreck areas, however, remain to be explored. Around Scotland there were three wrecks for certain, probably more. One, or two, too shadowy to follow here, almost certainly perished in the Outer Hebrides. But of the other two much more is known: and it is more than a little interesting. The first was the *Gran Grifon*, the Admiral of the hulks.

She has usually been dismissed as having failed to get through into the Atlantic at all, and as running aground on Fair Island, midway between the Orkneys and the Shetlands on August 10th. The reality was more dramatic, and much more terrible. She kept with, or near, the main body right round the islands and out into the Atlantic. She separated only on August 23rd, unwillingly, and struggled on alone, due south, hoping to pick up the flagship again. Evidently she had not enough offing because, on September 1st, she sighted the Irish coast. But she succeeded in hauling off, and stood south until the 7th, by which time she was probably in the latitude of Galway Bay; and, being well to seaward, she then stood a good chance of clearing Ireland altogether and having a fair run home. But, though in no imminent danger of shipwreck, she was in grave danger of foundering, some of her leaks, we are told, measuring 'a hand's breadth'. They were in fact so bad that she could no longer face the wind: to survive, she must keep her stern to it. Indeed (though it is obviously impossible to prove it) it may be suspected that such a predicament was common to many of that band whose fate has never been established. They must have been wafted back and forth by every wind that blew, until their leaks opened still farther

or their companies died of thirst. The *Gran Grifon* very nearly
suffered this fate, but not quite. A few of her people lived to tell
what happened. On September 7th a sou'wester sprang up and,
helpless, she ran before it to the northeast until that particular
wind spent itself. She was then back in the latitude of North
Uist, and had a glimpse of its outlying westerly islets. Then
came a northeaster, which returned her to approximately the
position she had occupied on September 7th, once more off
Galway Bay, but still well to the west. A northwesterly or even
northerly wind would now have let her head for home. But her
luck was out: it veered again to the southwest and the whole
performance was repeated: nearly but not quite. This time she
made the Outer Hebrides again, but a little more to the east,
and so passed inside them, actually navigating the whole length
of the turbulent, treacherous Minch, between the outer and
the inner islands. That was fortunate, and more fortune was to
follow. This time the southwesterly held for some days longer
than before, and, apparently in ignorance of her whereabouts,
she cleared Cape Wrath and ran on until she hit Fair Island
at night. She was lucky again. It is but a small target, and she
was not aiming for it. Had she missed it, her crew would never
have survived to make the coast of Norway, the next land to the
east. On the island her starving people found a few miserable
fishermen from whom they received, or took, a little food.
They suffered greatly, too, from thirst, cold and exposure.
Yet their luck held. A passing fishing boat took them off
and at length brought them to the mainland, where they
were not ill treated, and whence, next year, a handful reached
Flanders.

The other Scottish wreck whose fate is definitely established
is that most mysterious and most debated of all Armada craft,
the 'Tobermory Galleon'. She was missing from the main
body earlier than the *Gran Grifon*, but her general movements
must have been essentially the same, for, like her, she appeared
on the inner side of the Outer Hebrides, turning up at Islay
on September 13th. She ran up the outside of this island to
Mull, where she came safely to anchor in Tobermory Bay.
Much ink, much time, much money (and, if possible, even

more wishful thinking) have been lavished on her, the explanation for all of which may be summed up in one word, 'treasure'. This is no place for the full story. Its literature is too large, its age too hoary. As early as 1641, a bare half-century after the event, the contagious word was on men's lips. By 1677 'the Armada treasure-ship' had been given a name and a history. It was the *Florida*; it was the *almirante* (vice-flagship) of the fleet; it had on board a vast treasure – '30,000,000 of money' was the figure. By 1683 busy 'ingeniers' were finding things. *En passant*, we may note certain inconvenient facts. First, the *almirante* of the Armada is a ship about which a great deal is known. It was Recalde's *San Juan*, the Portuguese royal galleon whose course we have followed safely home, carrying her dying commander with her. Second, no extant Armada list – and there are many – contains a *Florida* at all. Well, what matter? Ingenious scholars soon amended the old Scottish tradition which called her *Florida*, and turned her into *Florencia*. This was better: there was a galleon sometimes so called belonging to the Duke of Florence. But it was not much better, because the *Florencia* is easily proved to have been one of the lucky ones which reached home. There is a third point, too, which seems to have occurred to none of the anxious seekers. Why should the Armada saddle itself at all with such a thing as a special treasure-ship? There would be some money, of course: wages (though we know that all the men had been paid in advance at Corunna): *douceurs* to hypothetical English Catholics, perhaps a small bribe for James VI, and so forth. But thirty million!

Such considerations, however, appeal but little to the 'get-rich-quick' school, and, from that day to this, the lure has held. Their appetite, of course, has been fed from time to time: for a ship is certainly there, and it is beyond question a unit of the Armada. All sorts of things that one would expect to find in an Armada ship have been fished up – guns, anchors, pewter platters, etc.; also a number of articles of more intrinsic value, small personal ornaments, medals and the like. But specie – still less thirty million!

Around the turn of the present century, serious antiquaries

began to exercise their minds with the problem,* and, to the satisfaction of most, if not all, scholars, solved the riddle of her identity. She was the ship called in the Spanish lists *San Juan de Sicilia*, hailing from Ragusa, one of the Levantine squadron and commanded by Don Diego Tellez Henriquez, son of the Commandant of Alcantara.† He was a man with a distinguished record throughout the fighting, but most unlikely to be entrusted with treasure, even if anyone was. For he was not a flag-officer, and there is plenty of evidence that such specie as there was, was borne, where one would expect it, in the fleet flagship or one of the vice-flagships of the various squadrons. Thus distributed, the real amount carried in the Armada seems to have been about 600,000 ducats – around £90,000 – which, divided between, say nine ships of flag status, gives an average of £10,000 each. But 30,000,000! This could only be even near the truth if, by chance, the original version read 'maravedis', that proverbially valueless coin used in Spain as we use brass farthing in England.

The historian, however, is much more interested in the way

* Among them may be mentioned Andrew Lang, *The Mystery of the Tobermory Galleon Revealed* (*Blackwood's*, CXCI, pp. 422–36); and R. P. Hardie, *The Tobermory Argosy* (Oliver and Boyd, Edinburgh, 1912).

† Regretfully, we must skirt the difficulties of a pretty problem. *San Juan* was a popular Spanish ship-name – there were at least nine of them in the expedition. Some were plain *San Juan* (after the Apostle John); others added *Bautista* (after John the Baptist). Lang calls his choice, '*San Juan de Sicilia*'. But this is perhaps immaterial, since they evidently mean the same ship. But there are three other complications: (1) There were two Diego Henriquezes in the fleet; but one can be distinguished by his second name 'Tellez'. (2) Each sailed in a ship called *San Juan*: but Lang and Hardie both agree that their man was Tellez. ('Non-Tellez', a very important personage, son of the Governor of Peru, is well accounted for. He had succeeded Pedro de Valdez in command of the Andalusian squadron when that worthy was captured.) (3) Some early accounts call the captain of the Tobermory wreck 'Diego Manrique': and no officer bearing this name figures in any Armada list, though there are seven Manriques with other christian names, as well as six Henriquezes! Fortunately, however, both authorities agree that Diego Henriquez – and Diego *Tellez* Henriquez at that – was our man.

in which the ship came by her end. Here again is an element of mystery. Henriquez was clearly a man of character and resource. He soon contrived to make himself useful to the local chieftain, a certain M'Lean of Dowart. This man had a lurid record of rapine and indiscriminate murder, and he would have dearly loved to secure the ship, loot it and massacre the crew. But they were too strong for him; and, perhaps, too useful, because Henriquez, in return for provisions, hired out his men to M'Lean, who used them in his local feuds to admirable effect. After all, as members of the famous Sicilian *tercio*, they were reputed the best soldiers on earth.

In England, however, there lived a man who was a match for them all. Mr Secretary Walsingham had a long arm: his Secret Service was ubiquitous. News of the goings-on in far-off Mull quickly reached him in London, and, remarkably soon afterwards, one John Smollett arrived at Tobermory, somehow penetrated the security arrangements of Henriquez and 'cast in the powder-room a piece of lint, and so departed. Within a short time after, the lint took fire. . . .' Everyone on board perished, including Henriquez, except a few men on the upper deck, who were blown bodily ashore. The wreck sank to the bottom, and, though much silted over, lies there still. Whether M'Lean was privy to this successful piece of sabotage is far from clear. Some of his kinsmen were hostages on board, but this proves nothing. In those wild days and districts this was a well-tried device for getting rid of unwanted relatives. In *Humphrey Clinker*, Tobias claims this Smollett as an ancestor. There is little doubt, anyhow, that he was Walsingham's agent.

The fate of one more ship calls for attention. From this vessel landed the only Spanish invaders to set foot in England as free men. But they arrived half drowned, and remained free for only a few minutes. She was one of the two Armada hospital-ships, *San Pedro el Mayor*, and, for some reason never satisfactorily explained, she ran full tilt on to the rocks under Bolt Tail in South Devon. Possibly she mistook the Channel for the way home, but this could only have happened if her compasses were shattered beyond repair. More likely her case was that of the galleass *Zuñiga*, only worse; or else she was one of the leaky ones who had no say in their course. Most of her people waded ashore, and the ship was thoroughly pillaged before the local magistrate reached the scene. He, poor man, seems fated to go down to history as 'the man who came too late': he was none other than our old friend of *Rosario* days, George Cary of Cockington. Yet his second appearance is not altogether discreditable. At least he was no Bingham or Fitzwilliam. No shipwrecked wretch was slain though, in a ship so lowly as a hospital hulk, there was no quality to pay fat ransoms. He locked the captives up and wrote for orders, meanwhile spending three-half-pence a day per head on their victuals. This meant virtual starvation, the standard rate being fourpence. But before blaming him we must recall that he was spending his own money. Indeed when last heard of, he was trying, none too hopefully, to extract a refund from the Lord Treasurer.

This solitary wreck on English coasts surely disproves certain old and persistent traditions – that Armada Spaniards survived in some numbers and, settling down in the west country, intermarried with the natives, leaving behind a recognizable strain of dark-skinned folk which survives to this day. It cannot be. The hulk's survivors were few, starving and dying off daily on their penny-ha'penny ration. Assuredly they produced no children to speak of. Another somewhat similar legend insists that many an old manor and farmhouse has (or till recently had) handsome old chests of obvious Spanish design; and all of them, by family tradition which the stranger denies at his peril, picked up from Armada wrecks. The same tales occur in Ireland, with more chance of truth because there were many more wrecks there; yet, even here, seldom authenticated. But there is a much more likely explanation of both chest and dark-skinned native. Considerable and fairly regular commercial intercourse had long existed between Spain and the western parts of both Ireland and England (especially Cornwall); and during all that period the importation of both Spanish chests and Spanish fathers was by no means unlikely, or surprising.

THE COST

What forfeit did Spain have to pay in ships and men? Of ships a reasonable though by no means perfect answer can be given. Captain Fernandez Duro, most painstaking of Spanish Armada historians, found at Simancas two contemporary *relacions* which, if they do not reveal exact figures, yet provide a fair starting-point for inquiries. The first (document 180) lists the ships which returned to Spain; the second (181) records those missing. This sounds good, yet it bristles with difficulties. One such is the fact that the Spaniards had so many ships of the same names; another is their exasperating habit of using more than one name for the same ship. Further, the two lists have demonstrable faults, in three principal respects: (*a*) Three ships (of which the *Zuñiga* was one) are down as missing, though we now know that they did return, too late to be recorded as having done so. (*b*) Six more figure, apparently, in both lists, as returning *and* as missing. (*c*) Some dozen others are not mentioned in either list.

To find the true number of ships lost, then, we must edit Duro 181. The three ships in category (*a*) above must obviously be deducted, as, with somewhat less certainty, must the six ships in category (*b*). This seems sensible; for any testimony which avers that a ship has returned is more positive, and therefore more credible, than that which asserts it has not – negative evidence only, very likely due merely to lack of information. So here are nine ships, in categories (*a*) and (*b*), which must be removed from Duro's list of ships lost. They are, so far as we can calculate, three auxiliary warships, four hulks, one small craft and one galleass.

But this is not all. Certain ships must be added to the tale of losses in document 181. These will come from category (*c*) above – the 12 vessels named in neither list. They can be further analysed: (*c*. 1) Several ships (say four) probably never started and so, naturally, found no place in either list. (*c*. 2) Of the remaining eight, two must certainly be added, being first-line ships, galleons both, whose fate is well known. The omission of these, the *San Mateo* captured by the Dutch, and the

San Marcos, known to have been burnt in the Shannon, is so glaring as to make one suspect the lists' compilers of deliberate disingenuity. Is this perhaps an early example of a practice well-known in modern war, the calculated concealment of important losses, not so much from the enemy (who at least knew all about the *San Mateo*, having captured her) as from the Spanish people? (*c.* 3) There remain six, whose fate is neither revealed in Duro's lists nor otherwise known to us. Here with nothing to go upon, we must be arbitrary: but this matters the less since they are mostly insignificant ships. Let us suppose, then, three saved and three lost – an auxiliary warship and two small ships. So our addition to list 181 will be five all told – two galleons, one auxiliary and two small ships. The losses will then look like this:

	Duro, Document 181	Minus (*a*) and (*b*)	Plus (*c.* 2 and 3)	Revised losses
Galleons	2		+2	4
Auxiliary warships	20	−3	+1	18
Hulks	15	−4		11
Small Craft	22	−1	+2	23
Galleasses	3	−1		2
Galley	1			1
TOTAL	63	−9	+5	59

One more adjustment must be made. The loss of 23 small craft, shown in the last column, seems altogether excessive. Though the Spanish lists differ somewhat as to the number of *pataches*, *zabras*, etc., which set out from Spain, there appear to have been few if any more than 30; and it is hard to believe that only seven returned. Their risks were not very considerable. The enemy seldom fired upon them; indeed, they scarcely fought at all. They were used chiefly for carrying dispatches back to Spain, messages to Parma or from one ship to another. They were constantly being detached altogether from the fleet, and often, no doubt, failed to rejoin it in the heat of rapidly moving events. But this is not to say that they were lost. Many of them, even, did not make the dangerous north-about journey at all, and this may well be one reason why, of the 25 Irish wrecks, only one is recorded for certain as a small craft, though probably a few more of them were. The rest, no doubt, sought shelter in the French Channel ports, or with Parma (as Ascoli did). Possibly, though safe enough, they did not even return to Spain; or, returning so unobtrusively or so late, they were never recorded as having arrived. We shall surely not exaggerate if we assume that half of the original 30 did escape destruction: that is, that 15, not 23, were really lost.

We may come, then, to a final estimate, noting two things about it. First, it breaks up the auxiliaries' losses into flag- and vice-flag auxiliaries, and 'other auxiliaries'. Second, it includes (as Document 181 does) two ships which did arrive home, only to perish almost at once. These were the hulk *Doncella*, wrecked at Santander immediately upon arrival, and the Guipuscoan flagship, another *Santa Ana*, accidentally burnt within a few days of entering San Sebastian, a fit funeral-pyre for her brave, hasty, lovable Admiral; for Miguel de Oquendo died of shame that very day.

AN ESTIMATE OF LOST ARMADA SHIPS

Class	Number	
Galleons	4	
Flag- & vice-flagships of auxiliary warships	8	*Naves*, 33
Other auxiliary warships	10	
Hulks	11	
Small craft	15	
Galleasses	2	
Galley	1	
TOTAL	51	

It is noteworthy how small were the losses of Philip's own Navy Royal: seven only, of which two were galleasses and one a galley. Of his true front-line sailing warships he lost only four. It is not really strange. The principal victims were the temporary warships which had started life as merchantmen, and the hulks which were still largely merchantmen. Much the heaviest relative losses were sustained by the flagships and vice-flagships of the auxiliaries. These, carrying the squadron leaders, were the objects of our fiercest attack. No wonder they suffered the most; for these brave men never flinched, but bore from first to last the brunt of four fierce naval battles in ships not originally meant for battle at all.

We can only guess at the human casualties. A pamphlet written in London that autumn makes definite claims as to Spanish losses, both of ships and men. In no age, of course, are contemporary estimates of enemy losses very trustworthy as evidence. But this author, though doubtless he was making the most of what he had heard, was certainly not exaggerating his total figures, if only because he did not know the full tale of Spanish woe. His figures go only to the end of September and up till then, he says, the English had heard of 32 ships lost and 10,185 men. Of these, 17 ships and 5,394 men had perished in or off Ireland during the month of September, and 15 ships and 4,791 men earlier than that. He makes mistakes easy for us to correct now: for instance, he thought that all four galleys had sunk. But he concludes: '. . . besides a great multitude of men not here accounted for that were slain in the fight and that have died by famine . . . and many ships not yet heard of, thought to be lost'. He was right. The news of eight more ships lost in Ireland and two or three in Scottish waters was still to come; and he naturally had no tidings of that forlorn band whose end is even yet unknown, nor of the men in the 'lucky' half of the Armada who reached home and died when they got there – a very large number – or who had died before they reached home – probably larger still. In fact, even allowing for his having exaggerated the losses known to him when he wrote, we can hardly assess the final total at less than 20,000 souls. It is a grim thought that barely one out of every three who started in May was alive by the end of the year.

The Duke was among the living. For a long time it was believed in England that he and his flagship had perished on Fair Island, the origin of the story being that the *Gran Grifon*'s commander was Juan Gomez de Medina. But it was not true. He reached home among the first, in his own flagship. But he did not trumpet his arrival. Quite broken, he was instantly carried ashore and, as soon as he could travel, slunk back to his Seville home, avoiding all towns and pursued (when recognized) by the silent, half-pitying scorn of his countrymen.

Of all his countrymen, that is, but one. King Philip rose above the ruin of his hopes with uncanny calm and fortitude. He wrote soothingly to the wretched man, blaming him not at all; rather, commiserating with him and tenderly enquiring after his health. Indeed he had no word of blame for anyone, save only for Diego Flores de Valdez who, by universal consent, was cast into prison for a while. It really does seem that, for the moment, this most enigmatical of monarchs was able to look inwards, and to see where most of the blame lay. He did everything he could to relieve the sufferings of the survivors who, arriving mostly at ports deep in the Bay of Biscay when expected on the west coast, found nothing whatever ready for them: no hospital accommodation, no medical attention and precious little food. There was chaos. Men died in their bunks, on deck as they were moved, in the boats which at length brought them ashore, on the open beach when they were landed. The King took complete charge of the now leaderless fleet: ordered everything possible for those who still clung to life – food, clothing, medicines. He even commanded lists to be made of the lost, and lists of their dependants. But whether the stores materialized, or whether those sad records were ever actually made, no one knows. None survives. Perhaps the machinery for so vast an undertaking did not exist. Perhaps everyone else in the kingdom was too stunned.

16

REAPPRAISALS

BUT THE ASTONISHING Spider of the Escorial was not stunned. Outwardly he carried on just as before. On scratched the never-pausing pen, out flowed the stream of directives, meticulous, all-embracing as ever. He was reweaving his shattered web. But, beyond question, he was thinking too. What had gone wrong? Assuredly not God. The Almighty *must* mean him to win. Since, then, the Divine partner could not err, the human one must have been at fault. He, Philip, had failed. Yet he was realist enough to know that God helps him who helps himself. He must start again then. What had defeated him? He saw it at once. The English had found something which he had overlooked. With their ships they were twisting the life out of the Spanish economy, and, when he had sought to punish them, they had brushed him aside with impudent ease. They had chased his best ships away from their shores: they had drowned his crack troops, the best soldiers in the world. They had made him look a fool. And they would do it again! They would carry the war to his own shores, as they had done in 1587; they would prey upon his seaborne revenues, the precious products of Mexico and Peru. They would throttle him, unless. . . . Very well. He knew the answer now. What they had he would have too: Sea Power.

The pen scratched: out went the orders, and a new Spanish fleet began to take shape, more numerous, more powerful than the old, and as much like the fleet which had humbled him as he could make it.

So his Most Happy Armada had not died quite in vain.

Philip profited from defeat; Elizabeth learned nothing from victory. In fact she never quite understood how she had come by it. At the promptings of Drake, now at the peak of his fortunes, she decided upon a counterstroke for 1589, nothing less than an English Armada to invade Portugal and snatch it from

Philip. Perhaps it was not the best move to make anyway. The experience of 1588, in reverse, might have taught her that invasions were difficult things to bring off. The transportation of an army, stores, guns, ammunition, reserves? Surely she might have seen that neither she nor her enemy had shone in any of these things? Then, on top of this, she doomed Drake's expedition to failure, even before it started, by assigning to it a bewildering, self-contradictory and indeed impossible set of tasks. It duly failed, and she was duly angry, venting her wrath on those whom she had doomed to fail, and especially on Drake. So the greatest of English seamen went into disgrace, only to emerge once more, to undertake with Hawkins their last forlorn voyage to the west from which neither of them returned. Meanwhile, she fell back, disastrously, upon the easy way. The crux was still money; money with which to wage war, money which simply was not there unless the war itself could be made to provide it.

Unfortunately, for her and for England, such money *was* there, in the annual *Flota*, the Plate Fleet which brought Philip's revenues from the New World; and, gradually, the whole sea war degenerated into attempts to capture it. But surely this is a supreme example of taking in one's own washing: one's fleet spends all its time in securing the wherewithal to pay itself. The idea was, of course, that the enemy should do all the paying, and, if he could have been made to pay heavily enough, the thing might have worked. But the scheme depended altogether too much upon the collaboration of the enemy: and Philip was no collaborator. He saw what was happening more clearly than Elizabeth did, and his answer had been preparing ever since 1588. As year followed wasted year his new navy grew, and the English found it ever harder to accomplish even their moderate aim. Odd treasure-ships came their way, and great prizes they were. But there were far too few of them; to be exact, after 1588, only two. Never once could they come up with the real prize, the haul which might make the whole strange policy worthwhile – the annual *Flota* itself.

So the play moves to its crisis, and it is perhaps the flattest anticlimax in the history of England. At long last, in 1602, an

English squadron came up with the whole Plate Fleet in the open sea. Sir Richard Leveson, in command of a Queen's squadron of four, swooped to the attack. At last! Wealth beyond dreams! Immortal honour! Death-blow to the hated enemy!

By no means. The placidly sailing prey was guarded by 30 powerful warships of Philip's new navy. Leveson (like Lord Thomas Howard facing comparable odds) was no coward. He even attacked. But he was no Richard Grenville either, and, wisely extricating himself before it was too late, sailed sadly for home.

By now the enigmatical King had been dead for some years. The Great Queen followed him in 1603 and, one year later, James VI (now the First of England) made peace. England had not won the war which she had begun so well. Spain yielded not an inch of her trade monopoly. Yet assuredly England had not lost the war. Never again need she fear that she would be spaniardized or catholicized against her will. Moreover, though the generation which broke the threat of Spain in 1588 perhaps never realized it, the Armada fight was indeed a turning-point in our history. At first neither Government, sailors nor people appreciated the extent and meaning of their achievement. But, as the news of the Armada's tragedy slowly filtered through, and as the worst of the epidemic spent itself, it gradually began to dawn upon them, seamen and people alike, that they had astonished the world. From this sprang something altogether new – an abiding, almost intuitive trust of the people in their Navy which, though not always justified, has never faded, and seldom faltered. There grew, too, out of common perils triumphantly faced together, a new kind of collective emotion, which was patriotism; and, though it was slow in coming, a new kind of awareness of themselves and of their future. They perceived, gradually, that the sea which had been their salvation in 1588 was now to be their destiny.

INDEX

British Battles Series

These and other PAN Books are obtainable
from all booksellers and newsagents. If you
have any difficulty please send purchase price
plus 7p postage to PO Box 11, Falmouth,
Cornwall.
While every effort is made to keep prices low, it
is sometimes necessary to increase prices at
short notice. PAN Books reserve the right to
show new retail prices on covers which may
differ from those advertised in the text or
elsewhere.